"A clear and wise description of meditation practice which will be helpful to many, especially to those who have dedicated themselves to a deep exploration of the Buddha's path."

—Jack Kornfield

"I was pleased to find the Buddha's original teachings in the pages of this book. Doug Kraft narrates his personal encounter with these practices and the transformative effects they had on him. Experienced meditators will find ways to help their practices soar. New meditators will find clear instructions and ways to use their life experiences to deepen their spirituality."

—Bhante Vimalaramsi, Abbot of Dhamma Sukha Meditation Center

"Buddha's Map is filled with psychological and spiritual insights from one who has traveled far. It is an easy read, guiding the way through the mysteries of the Buddha's teachings about meditation, wisdom, and well-being."

—John Travis, Senior Dharma teacher at Spirit Rock Meditation Center

"Doug Kraft is one the most insightful Buddhist practitioners I have encountered. He brings Buddha's practical teachings and techniques of meditation to life with his vivid and accessible writing. Beginners and advanced students alike will find this volume a valuable companion on the Buddha way."

—Rev. Wayne Arnason, co-author *Buddhist Voices in Unitarian Universalism*

"Doug Kraft's book, Buddha's Map, has been a meditative life-saver for me. As a long-time meditator, I have never found such clear, authentic, intimate explanation of the meditative process and the various meditative states. Kraft's personal experiences also created a significant encouragement for me. This book provides the direct path experience of the spacious but quiet, alive, unchanging awareness that we all seek."

—Patt Lind-Kyle, M.A., author of *Heal Your Mind, Rewire Your Brain*

Buddha's Map

His Original Teachings on Awakening, Ease, and Insight in the Heart of Meditation

Doug Kraft

Blue Dolphin Publishing

Published by Blue Dolphin Publishing, Inc.
P.O. Box 8, Nevada City, CA 95959
Orders: 1-800-643-0765
Web: www.bluedolphinpublishing.com

ISBN: 978-1-57733-276-3 paperback
ISBN: 978-1-57733-449-1 e-book

Library of Congress Control Number: 2013949637

Chapter 5, Thriving in Difficult Times previously appeared in *Buddhist Voices in Unitarian Universalism,* an anthology of essays edited by Wayne Arnason and Sam Trumbore, Skinner House Books, 2013.

Printed in the United States of America

5 4 3 2 1

Table of Contents

Foreword

We all want happiness. We all want peace, well-being, and vitality. And we have different strategies for finding them. Some turn to material comfort: nice homes, good food, pleasant experiences. Some turn to relationships: loving families, caring friends, supportive communities. Yet everything in the world changes. Material comforts and relationships do not last forever. There is nothing wrong with enjoying good food and good friends. But if our well-being requires them, it is fragile.

Lasting happiness cannot be found "out there." It can only be found "in here," under our noses, as it were. Skillful meditation develops our mind's and heart's capacities for joy and ease no matter what our circumstances.

The Buddha was probably the most skillful meditation teacher the world has known. Many people woke up by simply listening to him. Others applied his instructions and awakened. But he knew that his teachings would not last. In one discourse called "The Peg," he used a simile to describe what would happen.

In this talk he spoke of a clan of people called the Dasārahas. They had a large drum called "the Summoner" which they used to call people to special festivals. The drum had a deep resonant sound that could be heard in far-off villages. In time, the drumhead developed a crack. So the Dasārahas inserted a wooden peg to keep the head taut and lively. More cracks developed. They inserted more pegs. Over the years, the original drumhead was completely replaced by wooden pegs. When someone hit the drum, it produced only a dull thud barely heard a few paces away.

The Buddha explained that his original teachings were deep and resonant with meaning. His practices were efficient and effective. In the future, rather than studying them directly, he anticipated that people would study the writings of poets and commentators. In this way, the resonance and power of his practices would be dulled and lost.

He encouraged his students to study and practice his original teachings.

The Buddha's prediction came true. He was an amazingly gifted teacher. Many memorized his words and eventually wrote them down. Others commented on what he had said. As the years went by, still others wrote commentaries on the commentaries. These later writings bore some semblance to his original teachings. But as he had foretold, they lost much of their resonance and power.

Today we see this change by comparing the earliest recorded texts of the Buddha's talks to later commentaries. There are meditation practices in the earlier texts that are ignored in later texts. And there are practices in the later texts that do not appear in the earlier ones. The later commentaries have much value. But they have lost that deep resonance. They are not as efficient as the Buddha's original instructions.

I have taught thousands of students. When I teach only the practices found in the early texts, most meditators progress very quickly.

I was pleased to find the Buddha's original teachings in the pages of this book. Doug Kraft narrates his personal encounter with these practices and the transformative effects they had on him. In this book you will find a rare view of their inner workings. You will see how serenity and insight are not separate qualities. And that they arise rapidly when cultivated together. You'll see the importance of relaxation, smiling, and a sense of humor. You will learn the Buddha's eight stages of meditation and how they unfold from joy through equanimity, spaciousness, peace, and the gradual fading of perception and consciousness. You will find these and more, interwoven with stories, experiences, and guidance that bring immediacy to the Buddha's teachings.

Experienced meditators will find ways to help their practices soar. New meditators will find clear instructions and ways to use their life experiences to deepen their spirituality. Those disinclined to meditate may find the book less useful. After all, liberation cannot be found in a book. It is only found by skillfully exploring our own experiences.

But if you are drawn to deepening your spirituality, you will find a clear path up the mountain. The path is simple, though not always easy.

Yet by following the heart of the Buddha's path of awakening, the summit may be closer than you imagine.

The book in your hands will help you learn what the Buddha really taught. May it bring you great happiness. May you inspire great happiness in others. May all beings be free from suffering. May we long protect the Buddha's dispensation.

Bhante Vimalaramsi, Maha Thera
The American Buddhist Forest Tradition
Abbot, Dhamma Sukha Meditation Center
United International Buddha Dhamma Society

Introduction

I laugh when I hear that the fish in the sea are thirsty.

—Kabir

A sweet, wise, and quivering aliveness imbues every moment. It's so clear, quiet, and unchanging that it draws no attention. We can go for weeks, months, years, and indeed entire lifetimes without noticing it. Yet, like the invisible air we breathe, it flows through us. Without it, we would not be alive.

The Buddha said little about it. Language cannot express it. Words make it sound metaphysical or abstract rather than immediate. So he referred to it as "awakening" or "the end of suffering" and left it at that.

Rather than talk about this well-being, he taught a way to cultivate the direct experience of it. This is what counts. His path has many side benefits. He said it is "good in the beginning, good in the middle, and good in the end." Even at the beginning it may give rise to calm, peace, joy, insight, wisdom, pleasant sleep, better health, closer relationships, and more. Many people are drawn to his practice because of these by-products. That is fine. However, the better we grasp the totality of this path, the better we're able to walk it, whether we intend to go a few hundred yards or the whole distance.

There are many books that talk about the beginning or the middle of the path. But few talk about the end. This book is about walking the whole distance.

In brief, the road map looks like this:

The Buddha's meditation begins by becoming more keenly aware of our immediate surroundings. To do this, we relax the tension of distracting thoughts and feelings so we can see with greater clarity. As our ease deepens, the mind-heart unhooks from the world. We see the mind itself and how its attention moves impersonally from one object to another. As serenity becomes even more pervasive, the processes of memory and perception relax so much that they cease for short periods. Subjectively we black out. We emerge from these cessations with a consciousness that is luminous, precise, selfless, and pervaded with joy. This happiness is not dependent on anything in the world. It is unconditional and lasting.

This description may sound strange. But despite the limitations of language, if we follow the Buddha's instructions, the actual experience is more accessible than we might imagine. In this book we'll explore in detail the practical steps along the way.

The path unfolds in stages that the Buddha called *"jhānas."* A jhāna is a depth of knowing based on direct experience. Jhānas are markers along the route.

Some schools of Buddhism teach that jhānas are about absorption, where the mind is so concentrated on a single object that everything else is blotted out. Such one-pointed absorption can be blissful. But it's temporary. It's a dead end. It doesn't lead to wisdom or to a deepening understanding of how the mind works. How could it? In one-pointed concentration, the mind is not allowed to move.

The Buddha tried, mastered, and rejected one-pointed concentration in favor of a mind and body that are deeply relaxed and at ease. In the earliest suttas (discourses), he encourages a consciousness that is open, receptive, and mindful rather than single-focused.

Along this path, a common mistake is to try too hard—to try to force the mind-heart into stillness rather than allow it to settle into natural ease and joy. To be sure, this path requires effort. But it does not require strain or rudely shoving attention back to the breath or some other object of meditation. When the mind's essential peace is disrupted, it may require some effort to remember to notice and relax the tensions in the body, mind, or emotions. When the mind replays the same fantasy for the hundredth time, it may require some effort not to take it personally, to let go of frustration and self-criticism, and to laugh good-naturedly at ourselves. The Buddha's path requires effort, but it is a kind and gentle effort.

For meditation practice to progress quickly, ease must play a central role.

This book explores jhānas, ease, and other insights and techniques central to following the Buddha's path. It uses stories and metaphors to convey the feel and texture of this path. It describes ways to recognize where we are and how to adjust our practice so that we can move ahead more quickly as we follow the Buddha's path from joy, serenity, and insight to lasting happiness.

The book is divided into three sections. They can be read in any order.

In the first section, "Easing Awake," I introduce myself as a case study of someone whose meditation had plateaued, despite stubborn determination. I got off that plateau when I met a jhāna meditation master who showed me how the Buddha really taught meditation. Suddenly my practice filled with joy and ease. The narrative introduces key themes that run through the book, provides an overview of the practice and gives beginning meditation instructions.

In the following section, "Insights," we'll look at some of the Buddha's key insights from the perspective of spiritual practice, which is how he intended them to be used. Many of these have been disregarded because people think they are too complex (e.g. *paticcasamuppāda* or Dependent Origination), too esoteric (e.g. *nibbāna* or *nirvana*) or too far out (e.g. *anattā* or selflessness). Others are just misunderstood—for instance, the Buddha never said that life is suffering (*dukkha*), only that life involves dissatisfaction. All these insights become instructions for training the mind-heart's wisdom.

In the final section, "Path," we'll look at the Buddha's actual path up the mountain and the eight jhānas along the way. The Buddha describes these in many talks, but some translations are misleading. And even if these misunderstandings are cleared up, the text is sparse—as the path might look from an airplane window. To actually walk the path, we need practical guidance and an on-the-ground feel for it, not just a broad overview.

However far you travel on the Buddha's path, may it bring you joy, clarity, and peace.

Doug Kraft

Section I

Easing Awake

Waking up is not easy. But without ease, it is impossible.

I didn't come to this insight easily. I used to see personal development and spiritual growth as serious business requiring determination, hard work, and perseverance. And doggedness served me well—up to a point. I still think spirituality is a serious business, but it's becoming more obvious that lightness of spirit comes more easily if approached with lightness and ease.

More than 2,500 years ago, a young man in his thirties named Siddhārtha Gautama of the Sakya clan described the peak of spiritual maturity as "waking up." *"Budh"* means "awake" and *"dha"* means "one who." Hence *"Buddha"* means "one who awoke." But he was less interested in what we call it than in describing an efficient path to get there.

There are many paths up the mountain. These paths are easier to find in the foothills where many feet have worn the ground and people have left signs—even advertisements.

But as the paths rise higher, they get simpler and plainer. Some paths go no further than a particular outlook or panoramic view. Walking these paths, we may not even realize that still higher elevations are possible. Other paths rise out of the forest of language: at higher elevations there are no words or signposts—just hints of direction.

But no matter where the paths begin, there is only one peak. In the forest of words, we find many names for it: awakening, enlightenment, the divine, realization, *nibbāna,* Buddha nature, Christ consciousness, and more. But at the top, it makes no difference what we call it or how we got there. The perspective, sky, and space that envelop it make no distinction of language or path.

This book is about the path described by Siddhārtha Gautama. And it's about my encounter with this path, since the only way I know how to talk about it is through my own seeking. More precisely, this book is about where we might look inside ourselves to find signs that show us the direction at various altitudes.

Thousands of people have followed this path to the top. Hundreds of thousands have described it. And thousands upon thousands have written various directions to follow.

Buddhism today is a complex maze of interweaving paths strewn with books, practices, and teachers. Some of these paths wander in circles in the wilderness. Some climb to a plateau and peter out. Others rise to the very top.

The colorful variety of teachings within Buddhism suggests the power and depth of Siddhārtha Gautama's inspiration. Still, it can be difficult to sort through them to find what is useful.

Buddhism has a rich corpus of texts to sort through. They include tens of thousands of talks—or suttas—ascribed to the Buddha. And they include libraries filled with interpretations—or "commentaries"—on these talks.

Bhante Vimalaramsi is a Buddhist monk who became discouraged because he wasn't progressing in his practice. He followed the instructions of his teachers and of the great commentaries but saw no personality shift in himself. So he set aside all he'd learned from the commentaries and began searching the earliest *suttas* for what the Buddha actually said about meditation in his own words. And he searched through various translations to find what those words meant in the Buddha's original tongue.

There are many practices attributed to the Buddha that can't be found in the suttas. And there are a few simple practices he spoke of frequently that are often overlooked.

By sifting through the suttas, Bhante found a simple, subtle, nuanced, and incredibly efficient practice. It had a profound effect on him and his students.

One of the surprising aspects of this practice was the importance of relaxation and ease to waking up. At least it was a surprise to me. Another aspect was how serenity *(passaddhi)* and insight *(vipassanā)* were not separate factors but different ways of describing a unified consciousness. In the early suttas, serenity and insight are cultivated at the same time. Serenity deepens insight, and insight gives rise to serenity.

Five years ago I began training with Bhante. My practice rose to heights I hadn't expected. I had been on a plateau without realizing that higher elevations were not only possible but relatively accessible.

When he isn't teaching, Bhante devotes most of his energy to creating helpful translations of the Buddha's suttas. Many translations carry too much influence from the commentaries or from scholars without deep experience in actual meditation practice.

I hope some day Bhante will write an overview of the Buddha's practice as he has discovered it. But for now his writing attention is properly focused on the core texts themselves.

So with his encouragement and occasional editorial glances over my shoulder, I'm offering this overview.

Many times while walking this path, I have come to a beautiful mountain meadow. I might have been content to stay there for a long time. Bhante would say, "Why don't you take a look behind that tree over there?" When I did, I discovered a little trail leading up to an even higher view. Perhaps I would have found that path myself in time. Perhaps not.

When I asked Bhante where he learned these nuances, he smiled and said, "The Buddha taught me." Behind that statement were many, many hours of studying the text and trying them out in many, many hours of meditation.

It is this on-the-ground feel and practical guidance that I've found so helpful. So when we come to describing the path, I'll pass on as much of that feel and guidance as I can. In other words, we'll look at the jhānas and the path from the perspective of meditative practice and experience.

One of the themes we'll find again and again in this book is how ease and taking ourselves lightly help the mind-heart become as clear and open as an alpine meadow. Lightness, clarity, serenity and insight are deeply intertwined. Ease doesn't make waking up easy—we still have to climb the mountain step-by-step. But with ease and a light spirit, it's not only possible, but a shorter climb than we might have imagined.

1

From Stubbornness to Ease

A drop of sweat slid out of the hair on my head and tickled the back of my neck. Dave, the shuttle bus driver, smiled as he said, "Yep. Ninety-six degrees and ninety-seven percent humidity." It was a little past three o'clock in the afternoon of July 2, 2007: my first visit to the Missouri Ozarks.

I sat in a torn-vinyl and fake-chrome chair in front of the Ozark Shuttle office in Farmington, Missouri. The waiting room was air-conditioned, but the walls were stained from tobacco and the air was gray with smoke. I waited outside.

I pulled the chair close to the building to take advantage of the bit of shade it offered. Then I took out my cell phone and called the Dhamma Sukha Meditation Center. "Yep, they're on the way to pick y'up. Late as usual." The voice was friendly, though the way he said "as usual" was more disparaging than I expected from a member of a Buddhist group. "They should be there in thirty or forty minutes."

I put my phone away. "Good time to meditate," I told myself. I closed my eyes.

A few moments later, I opened them. In the previous thirty hours, I had gotten two hours of sleep. Rather than try to meditate, I gazed absently at the traffic in the intersection.

At nine o'clock every morning, Dave drove the little bus north along Interstate 55 toward St. Louis. Once there, he hung around the Greyhound station until one o'clock in the afternoon. Then he started the return trip to Farmington.

The Dhamma Sukha Meditation Center is nestled deep in the Ozark Mountains about an hour from Farmington. This shuttle is the nearest public transportation.

In order to make the shuttle, I took a red-eye flight out of northern California where I lived. I changed planes in Atlanta and landed in St. Louis in the morning. The Metro Link train took me downtown to the bus station. I found Dave and let him know I wanted a ride. Then I waited around for a few more hours until the shuttle left.

Once in Farmington, I waited for someone from the center to pick me up. After stopping for groceries and other supplies, we drove the hour or so into the mountains. I arrived at Dhamma Sukha in the late afternoon, bleary and weary.

I'm tempted to say, "You can't get to Dhamma Sukha from my house." But that isn't true. It just takes persistence. It felt like traveling in southern Asia, where the connections were complicated and uncertain. All I could do was point myself in the right direction and trust that sooner or later I'd get there (or some other interesting place).

The abbot of Dhamma Sukha is Bhante Vimalaramsi. When I first heard the name, I thought he was from South Asia. Actually, he is a White and grew up in Escondido south of Los Angeles. He'd once been a contractor, building high-end homes in California. He'd been quite successful. But he gave it up and went to Asia.

He spent many years training and teaching in Myanmar (Burma), Thailand, and Malaysia. Now he teaches around the world. But for the past decade, he has focused mainly on bringing his teaching back to his home country. And, if nothing else, the Missouri Ozarks are deep in the heartland of America.

Stubborn Beginnings

I began meditating long before I'd heard of Dhamma Sukha or Bhante Vimalaramsi. In the mid-1970s, I was studying with Ram Dass, another American-born spiritual teacher with an Asian name. I got the impression that learning to meditate would somehow be a good thing. So I tried to teach myself. I sat for fifteen minutes one day, ten minutes the next, and fifteen minutes four days later. Developing momentum was hard.

With a recommendation from Ram Dass, I signed up for a ten-day meditation retreat at the brand-new Insight Meditation Society in Barre, Massachusetts. It was only a few hours' drive from where I was living at the time. I understood that I would be doing nothing but meditating (sitting meditation, walking meditation, eating meditation) or sleeping the whole time. "That should build momentum," I thought.

I was excited when I got to Barre and eager to start sitting. But after about a half hour, it dawned on me that this was all I'd be doing for the next nine days, twenty-three hours, and thirty minutes. A neon sign flashed in the back of my head: *"Mistake! Mistake! Mistake!"*

I stuck with it as best I could. I kept rearranging the cushions and pillows into piles worthy of Dr. Seuss. Still, my mind wandered and my body hurt. Stubbornness was the only thing that kept me going.

Nevertheless, when I left the retreat after ten days, I felt joyful and light. I didn't know if that was meditative progress or just relief to be out of there. I thought, "This is the best thing I've ever done, and I'm glad I won't ever have to do this again."

Back home I found myself meditating forty-five minutes twice a day. And a year later, I went back for another ten-day retreat with Joseph Goldstein, Jack Kornfield, and an Asian master, Munindraji. I was hooked.

The style of meditation was called *vipassanā* "insight meditation."

I also tried other styles of meditation as well. I drove to Providence, Rhode Island, to do a *sesshin* (intensive retreat) with the Zen Master Seung Sahn. As I walked into my first interview, he pointed his finger at me and said, "There it is!" meaning a moment when I was fully enlightened. He was right. My mind was clear and spacious. "Now it's gone," he said. He was right. It was gone.

I realized we must all have those moments. But they go by so quickly we don't see them. His gift was to catch one and point it out to me. I knew it was real.

But trying to stay within the strict Zen customs gave me the worst hemorrhoids in my life. So afterward I did another vipassanā retreat, where the practice is more relaxed.

I studied with Sufi Master Pir Vilayat Khan. I loved the chanting and the sweet energy. But I missed the deep stillness. So I did another vipassanā retreat.

I learned to channel and communed regularly with various disembodied guides. But the practice felt cluttered and busy. So I did more vipassanā.

Then, at the end of one vipassanā retreat, the teacher, Larry Rosenberg, said, "There are many styles of meditation. If vipassanā doesn't appeal to you, by all means try others." I nodded agreement.

Then he said, "But if this works for you, for God's sake, stop looking."

His words hit between the eyes. I got it. This was home for me, not because it was the best for everyone, but simply because it resonated with me.

Calm Abiding

The instructions I heard from a variety of vipassanā teachers were similar: concentrate exclusively on the breathing until the mind stabilizes. Then gradually open the field of awareness to include all body sensations, feelings, thoughts, and finally consciousness itself. If the mind remains steady, stay with this "choiceless awareness"—that is, just be mindful of whatever arises. If the mind drifts, narrow the focus until it steadies.

These instructions made sense to me. They were logical and coherent. I could see how they helped fellow students. But I found them very difficult to implement: my mind would not quiet.

Out of desperation, I experimented. I found that choiceless awareness—that is, just being mindful of whatever arose—was easier. And after a while, concentration came by itself. Rather than concentration being a foundation of mindfulness, mindfulness led to greater concentration. This made less sense at the time than it does now. But it worked for me.

Then a teacher, Corrado Pensa, remarked that the word for "concentration" came from the Pāli word "*samādhi*." A better translation of samādhi was "calm abiding." The English word "concentration" implied too much effort and strain. He said samādhi was the way a mother watched her sleeping child: her attention was steady, but soft and receptive. Corrado said this was the way to practice.

"Hmm," I thought. "Maybe there's more to meditation than stubbornness."

Corrado was helpful. Yet I still found it easier to begin with choiceless awareness than with samādhi, even in this softer form.

One Hundred and Counting

So I arranged a private interview with Larry Rosenberg at the Insight Meditation Center in Cambridge, Massachusetts—about an hour from where I lived. I confessed to him my strategy of starting with choiceless awareness.

He said, "In vipassanā, we don't need that much samādhi before shifting to choiceless awareness. If you can count ten breaths ten times, that is more than enough samādhi."

The interview lasted a half hour, so we must have talked about other things. But what I remembered most clearly was, "Counting ten breaths ten times is sufficient samādhi."

I went home and started a project to count one hundred breaths without letting my mind drift once. I suspected I was taking Larry's words more literally than he intended. But I was seeking tangible affirmation for my practice. This could be it. Besides, it gave me a new way to employ my talent for stubbornness.

Each day when I sat in meditation, I'd start noting: "breathing in" on the in breath and "one" on the out breath. Then "breathing in, two; in, three; in, four," and so on. If I got to "in, fifty-seven" and thought, "this is going pretty well," I'd recognize, "Oh, I just drifted." So I'd start over: "breathing in, one; breathing in, two."

It took me nine months, but finally I could count a hundred breaths without drifting once.

Having achieved my goal, I looked at my mind. It was like a steel trap—tight and clenched. "This is worthless," I realized. "My mind is too tense and dense to see anything."

I never told Larry what I'd done. I imagine him smiling and shaking his head in consternation.

In a strange way, this experience taught me three things: One, I probably did have enough samādhi. Two, all that stubborn strain is truly a dead end. And three, it is okay for me to use choiceless awareness—other qualities will follow.

Jhāna

After practicing for a dozen years or so, I was on another retreat with Larry Rosenberg and Corrado Pensa. Larry gave a series of *dhamma* talks on the "Ānāpānasati Sutta" (the Buddha's talk on mindfulness of breathing). It was the first time I heard an explanation of an actual sutta.

In that sutta, the Buddha described various *jhānas,* or stages of meditation knowledge. I listened attentively until Larry mentioned *pīti,* which means "rapture" or "joy," and *sukha,* which means "happiness."

I'd been chronically depressed all my life. My childhood pictures all have forlorn eyes. As an adult, I didn't know anything was wrong. It was as if all I had ever known was black and white—I'd never experienced color and didn't know what I was missing.

But when my marriage began to sour, I suspected the fault was in me. I sought a therapist who got me fully in touch with the depths of my depression. In pictures from those years, I look like death warmed over.

Fifteen years later with a lot of therapy, bodywork, and meditation, I was beginning to break clear of the depression. But still, I didn't relate to rapture or happiness. They were too colorful. They were for real meditators, not someone as ordinary and stubborn as me. So when Larry spoke about pīti and sukha, I closed my eyes in meditation and barely listened.

Then Larry described in detail the texture of pīti and sukha—not just their names but also the sensations around them. They sounded familiar. I perked up. I'd felt similar things for years but dismissed them. I couldn't believe he was talking about my experience.

After the talk I went up to him: "Larry, I've experienced states for years that may be what you're talking about."

He looked down slightly so he could listen to me more carefully.

I went on: "It's like a white noise comes into my mind, only it's silent. It becomes difficult to think. And I find myself smiling uncontrollably. I call it a 'high-energy calm.' When it is strong, it feels like a non-climactic, non-genital orgasm."

He nodded his head: "Yes, that is pīti."

"After a while I am sometimes able to just let go into it. It spreads out and cools off. It gets very large and peaceful."

He nodded again and said, "Yes, that is sukha."

"Larry," I said. "I thought they were just another distraction. I thought I should ignore them and try harder to stay with the breath."

He looked up at me. "Oh, you can't do that. They're too powerful. When they arise, let go of the breath and let the state you experience be the focus of your attention. After a while, you'll tire of them, and the meditation will go even deeper. In the meantime, they're very healing. You're ready to do real meditation now."

I said to him, "I've struggled with depression for years. I find labels like 'rapture,' 'joy,' and 'happiness' to be confusing."

His eyes twinkled. He put his hand on my shoulder and said, "I give you permission to be a happy person."

I was touched and excited. I had thought my practice was getting nowhere. But some of the states I experienced weren't a problem. They were signs of progress. There were references to them in the Buddha's own words! I was experiencing what he was pointing to. They were early stages, to be sure. But they were part of the path.

I felt encouraged.

Plateau

In the years that followed, I continued going on retreats. I'd sign up with any teacher whose retreat fit my complicated work schedule.

With each teacher, I described the experiences I was having and asked for guidance as to how to work with them.

Mostly I got blank stares. Sometimes a teacher suggested I should stop reading books and just watch the breath. Sometimes there was a hint of disparagement in his voice.

"But I'm not reading books," I wanted to say. "I'm just describing what I see and feel."

But usually I said nothing. I didn't see the point if they didn't recognize what I was talking about.

So I continued to practice as best I could—working with pīti and sukha when they arose. But in truth, my practice plateaued. For ten or fifteen years, it went nowhere.

John Travis

In 2000, my wife and I moved to northern California. A year later, someone showed me a flier for a retreat led by John Travis. I recognized his name from the vipassanā community. I felt drawn.

The retreat was the smallest I had ever been on—only fifteen or twenty people in a house high in the Sierra Mountains.

During my first interview with John, I described my conversation with Larry Rosenberg and my experiences with pīti and sukha. John seemed open. So I told him I felt slightly ridiculed for thinking I might be experiencing these states.

John shook his head and said, "They're very real. They're just what you thought they were."

To my surprise, I began to cry.

John encouraged me to just let the tears flow. As I got to know him later, I understood that he had been through a lot of suffering in his life. It seemed to have just opened his empathy more and more. He was a bit of a wild man, to be sure. But he had a big, wise heart.

John lived about an hour and a half from me. So I began to visit him once or twice a month and went on at least one of his retreats a year. He became my root teacher and my first real spiritual mentor.

He recognized my jhāna experiences and the pull they had for me. And he knew there were teachers who taught the jhānas. But they weren't part of how he taught.

Nevertheless, he was helpful in getting my meditation to open up and deepen. And together he and I looked for a teacher from whom I could learn more about the jhānas.

But there was a problem. Most jhānas were taught in the Burmese style. This style was very severe, involving months of strenuous practice to make the first step. If anything, I already seemed to try too hard. John and I both felt the Burmese style wasn't right for me.

Ajahn Tong

In 2006, I had some sabbatical time from the Unitarian Universalist church I served in northern California. I decided not to go to Burma to train with a jhāna master. But John thought it would be good for me to go to Asia anyway. "It'll pull the rug out from under you and your practice, and that will help."

I found a monk who had studied with Ajahn Tong, one of northern Thailand's most revered meditation masters. But Ajahn Tong didn't work with Westerners. The monk said I could train with him for three weeks. Then he'd introduce me to Ajahn Tong. In this way I'd be considered the monk's student first and a Westerner second. Under those conditions, Ajahn Tong would accept me.

From Ajahn Tong, I discovered a mystical dimension in Buddhism that has largely been filtered out in the West in deference to our more critical mindset. He showed me how to invoke states and visions that I could not explain. I also learned about *nibbāna* (or *nirvana* in Sanskrit), not as a vague, far-off concept but as something tangible and real. In the West, nibbāna is often downplayed as too esoteric. But the Thai weren't shy about it. Ajahn Tong saw nibbāna as quite accessible and had an eight-step program to get there.

Like my first retreat in Barre, Massachusetts, my time with Ajahn Tong was both unsettling and wonderful. It took me six months to reintegrate after returning home.

But still I wanted to learn more about the jhānas.

Tranquility Jhānas

A year after I returned from Thailand, John lent me a copy of a book he'd been given. He thought I might find it helpful. It was a commentary on the "Ānāpānasati Sutta" written by a monk named Sayadaw Gyi U Vimalaramsi.

I didn't find the introductory part of the book helpful. But when I got to U Vimalaramsi's actual commentary on the sutta, I thought I might have found someone who knew what I'd been looking for.

He made a distinction between absorption jhānas and tranquility (passaddhi) jhānas. Absorption jhānas are taught in the Burmese schools. They are so concentrated and strong that while you are in one, the outside world is cut off. Someone could call your name, slap you in the face, or set off a gun, and you wouldn't notice because your mind was so one-pointed on a single object.

The Buddha had trained in the absorption jhānas in his early years as an ascetic. They were commonly taught in his time. He mastered all eight of them. And when he had, he came out of them and said, "These don't work. The underlying imbalances are still in me."

The problem with absorption states is that their depth and power come from blocking out everything but the object of awareness. It takes a great deal of energy to do this. And when we relax, whatever we have pushed down tends to come back up.

Wisdom comes from seeing things clearly as they are, not by pushing them aside.

So when the Buddha sat down under the Bodhi tree to wake up, he took a softer approach: the tranquility jhānas.

The Buddha's descriptions of the various jhānas included thoughts and sensations.[1] He was not describing states of total absorption.

Obsessing over feelings or daydreaming obviously does not lead to awakening. But neither does repression. The Buddha taught a "middle way," a subtle and nuanced balance that was neither of these extremes. This path stressed mindful awareness—knowing what was going on but not using blunt-force control of experience.

Reading the commentary, I sensed that this monk was intimately familiar with the subtleties and nuances of this tranquility jhāna path.

The next time I saw John, I told him I was excited by what I'd read. John said that the monk was traveling in California at that time, and that he knew a person with whom he was going to stay for a week.

I got the number, called, and was able to set up an interview.

Interview

I had understood the monk's proper name to be Sayadaw Gyi U Vimalaramsi. *Sayadaw* means "meditation master" or "monk's teacher." "Gyi" means "deeply honored" or "venerable." These were titles his students had given him while he was teaching in Asia. But he preferred to be called simply *Bhante*, which means "monk."

He said, "*Vimalaramsi* means 'pure' or 'radiant,' and *U* is equivalent to 'Mister.' So my name is 'Mr. Clean.'"

He had a good sense of humor. And he did look a bit like the Mr. Clean of floor-cleaner fame. Bhante was six feet four with a shaved head—except he didn't wear a genie ring and did wear monks' chocolate-brown robes.

At the interview, I sat across from him in his host's living room. I described many meditation experiences I'd had over the years.

There was nothing I said that was not familiar to him. In fact, he could tell me the conditions that preceded my experiences and what came after them. He said some of my experiences had important qualities to be cultivated. Others were distractions to be released. In fact, even the important experiences were best noted and released to keep the meditation going deeper.

I got the impression that he had a roadmap that went from the light, energetic joy of pīti all the way to nibbāna. Later I learned that the jhānas are markers along this path.

I also had the impression that his meditation instructions evolved as one progressed. So I asked him pointedly what he thought I should be doing in meditation.

He asked me a series of focused questions in the form of, "Have you experienced ______?"

At first I answered "yes" to each of these and elaborated on my experience to be sure we were talking about the same thing.

Then after five or six of these, he asked me about something I wasn't certain about. "I've felt that," I said, "but only fleetingly."

"Okay," he said. "From where you are, this is how you might practice." And he gave me specifics.[2]

Off the Plateau

Several days later I flew to Jackson Hole, Wyoming. The *saṅgha* there had rented a dude ranch. It was mud season: the snow had melted or was too slushy for skiing, and the ground was not dry enough for hiking. So they could rent the ranch at off-season rates and use it for a ten-day retreat. They had invited John Travis to come and teach. John encouraged me to ignore the general meditation instructions he was giving everyone else and just follow Bhante's.

Bhante emphasized ease. When the mind's attention was pulled away, I was to first just recognize where my mind had gone. Then I was to release or let go of the distraction, relax, smile, and then return to the primary object of meditation.

He called this "the Six Rs: recognize, release, relax, re-smile, return, and repeat." It was so simple as to sound more like a jingle than serious instructions. I was reminded of the old Burma-Shave roadside commercials from my childhood—I pictured a series of red signs: "Recognize," "Release," "Relax," "Re-smile," "Return," "Repeat," "Burma-Shave."

Jingle or not, the Six Rs worked amazingly well. I didn't fully understand them or use them correctly at the time. But they suggested I needn't fight inevitable distractions. When my attention wandered, rather than stubbornly or even gently pulling it back, I just saw where my mind had gone and relaxed into it. This may have been what Corrado Pensa meant by "calm abiding." But Bhante's technique gave me the practical tools to do it. This was enough to get my practice to take off.

Rather than worrying about my mind getting distracted, I now looked forward to it. Each time I recognized a distraction, let it be, and relaxed, there was a blast of joy. And since I was relaxing, it was easier to sit longer. My mind-heart became so clear and energized that at times I felt like I was on psychedelics.

One of the interesting by-products of this practice was a change in my visual field. For example, in walking meditation I usually kept my eyes down slightly, watching the ground flow through my field of vision. But while doing this practice, there were times when the visual field jerked rather than flowed. It was like watching a movie that projected a rapid series of still images on a screen. The mind normally blended them into a smooth flow. But now, I was seeing each frame.

At first I was startled. As I tightened slightly, the familiar visual flow returned. But when I relaxed, I saw a discrete series of separate images.[3]

Another phenomenon showed up after the retreat. On the return flight, I pulled a Sudoku number puzzle out of the airline magazine. I enjoy math puzzles and am reasonably good at them. But my mind was so relaxed, it wouldn't go into hyper-calculation mode. I couldn't do even the easiest puzzle, though the hardest ones used to be simple for me. (Since then, my old capacity has returned just fine.)

The breakup of the flow of the visual field and the short-term suspension of mathematical thinking were overt and impossible to ignore. But a more important and less definable effect of the retreat was a sense of ease, spaciousness, and irrepressible smiles.

The retreat had been in silence. So at the end, John had us all go around and give our names and where we were from. When it was my turn, I said, "I am Bliss Bunny, and I don't know where I'm from."

When I got home, I contacted Dhamma Sukha and asked if I could come out to Missouri for a few weeks during my summer break.

Dhamma Sukha

Thus it was on that July afternoon that I was sitting in a vinyl chair outside the Ozark Shuttle office where Dave had left me.

Thirty minutes later a big maroon pickup truck pulled up in front of me. The reflection of the sky off the windshield made it difficult to see into the cab. But there was a sign in the windshield—a set of wooden letters painted bright yellow: "Smile." I knew it was either Bhante or his attendant, Sister Khema. It was both.

I put my duffle into the back between gasoline cans, a box of dog food, and some farm tools. We stopped at a big-box grocery store. I was vegetarian. They weren't. They wanted to make sure they had food for me to eat. (The Buddha was not a vegetarian either—but that's a topic for another time.)

A few hours later, the truck pulled off the small country highway onto a dirt road that wound up a small hill into a clearing. We stopped beside an eight-by-twelve-foot barn-shaped shed.

This was to be my *kuti* (meditation hut) for the next few weeks. The inside was unfinished. In fact, the structure had only been delivered a week before. But there was a cot, a chair, a crate for shelves, a few candles, and a jug of water. I was delighted. [4]

Bhante started my practice over at the beginning. I was familiar with most of the elements he taught. I had experience with them through other Theravadan practices of vipassanā ("insight") and mettā ("loving kindness"). But the way he put them together was a little different.

And there were two elements that were new to me, at least in formal practice. These were the relaxing and smiling parts of the Six Rs I mentioned earlier. I had survived many of life's tough spots through grim determination. Relaxing and smiling seemed foreign to something as serious as spiritual practice. As a recovered depressive, the smiling seemed particularly foreign. But he was quite insistent. He also insisted, "Doug, you've got to relax and lighten up."

I was suspicious that he was just making this stuff up. "Where'd you learn this?" I asked.

He smiled in a relaxed way and said, "The Buddha taught me."

Then he opened his thick copy of the *Majjhima Nikāya: The Middle Length Discourses of the Buddha*. "For example, look at one of the best-known discourses, the 'Satipatthana Sutta.'"[5] He ran his finger down to section 4. He read, "'One trains thus…' Anytime you hear this phrase, it means we've come to the heart of the matter. What came before may be important in setting the stage. But what comes after is the essential core of his teaching." He went back to the text, "One trains thus: 'I shall breathe in tranquilizing the bodily formation;' One trains thus: 'I shall breathe out tranquilizing the bodily formation.'"

"Bhante," I said, "when I hear 'tranquilizing,' it reminds me of tranquilizers. I think, 'It's hard to believe the Buddha wants me to dope myself up. I don't get this. So never mind.' So what does this word mean in Pāli?"

He said, "That's one of the difficulties with translations: the word 'tranquilize' has associations in English that don't exist in the Buddha's original language.

"But even in English, the words 'tranquilize' and 'tranquility' have the same root. Tranquility comes closer to the Buddha's intent. He was saying 'Bring tranquility to the body formations or to the bodily experience. Soothe, soften, and open.' In other words, 'Relax.' With each in-breath, relax. With each out-breath, relax."

I knew that in Pāli, the language of the suttas, the word "*passaddhi*" meant "tranquility." So I asked Bhante if passaddhi was the original word used here.

He said, "No. The word is '*pas'sambaya*.' 'Passaddhi refers to a general state. 'Pas'sambaya' is more specific. Pas'sambaya is interesting in that it can be a noun, verb, adjective, or adverb depending on how it's used in a sentence. In this case, it's used as a verb. It's something we do. It's not a noun. It's not a state to be experienced or the quality of a state. It's something we do: Breathing in, one relaxes the body and mind. Breathing out, one relaxes the body and mind. Breathe in, relax. Breathe out, relax.

"When we relax deeply, we tend to smile. And when we smile, we tend to relax. They support each other."

I was beginning to absorb Bhante's instructions. When the mind wandered off, I was to recognize where my attention had gone and release the object that awareness had grabbed onto. Then I was to relax and smile before going back to the primary object of meditation.

The effect of this simple relaxing and smiling was remarkable, as I had discovered in John's retreat months earlier. When the mind-heart was distracted, there was some tension. By relaxing, the tension was released (or at least some part of it). By smiling or at least allowing a lightness to flow into the mind-heart, the quality of attention brought back to the object of meditation was both relaxed and light.

As my body and mind relaxed, I found myself sitting in meditation for three hours or more for the first time in my life. As the mind-heart lightened and brightened, it became clearer and suffused with joy and equanimity. Then it went into deeper states of peacefulness, spaciousness, and silence.

In the "Path" section of this book, we'll look at these states in more detail. For now it's enough to appreciate how simple and penetrating this practice is. And it's all right there in the Buddha's instructions. I wondered how I'd missed it all those years.[6]

When I first arrived at Dhamma Sukha, there was only one other student. He'd been there for a few weeks and had to leave the next day.

A few days later, another guy arrived. He reminded me of Gomer Pyle. He had little meditation experience and goofy ideas about spirituality—like channeling energy from other dimensions. But he followed Bhante's instructions as best as he could. And I could see him quieting and opening in a very deep way.

It was clear that whatever I was experiencing was not unique to me, nor was it due to many years of meditation. The practice worked for all kinds of people.

Easing Awake

John Travis once told me that the only difference between most of us and a fully enlightened being was confidence. The practice the Buddha taught encouraged relaxing into our deeper nature and learning to trust it to emerge on its own.

As I said in the introduction, waking up is not easy. But without ease, it is impossible.

The metaphor of climbing the mountain conveys some of the patience and stick-to-itiveness that are important on the path to awakening. But it may not convey how essential it is to relax and soothe the mind-heart so it can open to its natural spacious clarity.

I call this process "easing awake."

With its emphasis on easing awake, Buddhism is not so interested in what we think or believe. It is interested in how we become more alive right now. After all, waking up in the morning is not about what we think or believe. It is about opening our eyes.

In this way Buddhism is not so much a philosophy or study of ideas. It is a phenomenology, or an exploration of what we actually experience.

So in the next section, we'll begin to explore the Buddha's insights by looking at everything that we can experience.

But first, we'll consider some simple instructions for getting started in this practice.

2

Beginnings

Cavern

Imagine living our entire lives deep inside a mountain. There are seemingly endless chambers and large caverns connected through intricate arrays of tunnels. There are beautiful rock formations and deep pools, and many people living in the mountain; it's pleasant. Sometimes it feels a little confining in a vague way. But since we know nothing outside the caverns, the feeling passes.

We have a friend who is nice, though a little odd. In quiet moments he mentions something called "trees." He says they're green, like some of the rock pigments. Yet the green is deep and soft and delicate. Inside the green are brown pillars, like stalagmites. These "trees" are both strong and soft. He says that if we travel through a certain set of caverns and tunnels, we can actually see them.

We're intrigued. So one day we try to follow his directions. We get lost but find our way back home. We try again. Eventually we come around a turn and see an impossibly bright light. It's beautiful; it's delightful to look at. We sit and gaze. After our eyes adjust to the light, we see deep greens and browns within the light. And the greens sway a little.

Excited, we go back and tell our friend. He listens carefully and says, "Yes, those are trees. You were looking outside the mountain through what's called a 'cave exit.' Rather than just look at it, why don't you try to walk toward it and see what happens?"

This hadn't occurred to us, but it's intriguing. So the next time we find this light, we walk out the cave exit.

Now we see more trees. They are so much taller than we'd imagined: they rise up and up. It's dizzying. And above them there's no rock ceiling—just a tiny patch of…well…nothing. The nothing is a soft light blue. We can't quite focus on it—but it is beautiful. How can nothing be beautiful and have qualities?

We go back and tell our friend, who again listens carefully.

"Yes," he says, "the trees are very tall. And that blue nothing is called 'sky.' It's lovely to look at. But rather than stop there, why don't you walk outside the cave exit to the right. You'll come to some water. Unlike the water in the cavern, this water moves. It's called 'river.'"

Walking outside we come to a wall of trees. The wall isn't rock solid. We can walk through it—slipping between the brown pillars.

Eventually we find the river. It's not what we'd imagined. Not only does it move, it lifts up and down and swirls. It's large and powerful. And the blue nothing above is even broader and lovelier.

We go back and describe all this to our friend. He listens carefully and says, "Yes, that was river and sky. Now you're beginning to see the whole forest. You have gone far—and you can go farther. As you're comfortable, follow the river in the direction from which it flows. You'll come to what's called 'lake.' It's huge and still, and the sky above it is even larger.

Our friend guides us farther and farther. But he can't actually travel with us—we have to do that on our own.

What we find along the way is never quite what we imagined from his descriptions. But when we try describing it ourselves, we can't find better words. It's just something one has to experience to know.

Before we ventured outside the cavern, we could have read about trees, rivers, lakes, and sky. We might have trusted that they existed. We might have believed in them—had faith they were real.

But after experiencing them, we no longer believe in them. We know them. We've seen them directly. This makes belief and faith seem pale and irrelevant by comparison.

Bootstrapping

The path described by the Buddha unfolds in just this way. It begins with experiences we can have from within our caverns. But rather than sit and gaze at how marvelous they are, this path uses them as guides to show us where to go next.

If we tried to go from our mountain chambers directly to the lake, traveling would be as difficult as walking through rock. By going to the cave exit, finding the river, then heading upstream, the journey becomes manageable. From the lake, we get a mountain glimpse that is inconceivable from deep inside the cave.

In a similar way, the Buddha offered instructions on how to travel up to peaks that previously were unimaginable.

The Buddha's instructions came in the form of meditation practices. One of the practices he talked about most has two aspects: loving kindness (mettā) and insight (vipassanā). They aren't separate or even sequential practices. Rather, both are done at the same time and are intended to be integrated together.

In the section three, "Path," we'll go through these interconnected practices in detail. Like traveling up the mountain, engaging them leads to various states and insights. The insights are available all the time, but they're more compelling the farther we go. From inside the cave, we might understand how the river, forest, and mountain interact together. Seeing them from the mountain slope, it's no longer an intellectual understanding. It's direct knowing.

It's specific insights—direct knowing of how things are—that awaken us.

The Buddha described this path in stages (or jhānas). Each leads to insights and states of consciousness that makes the next jhāna more accessible. It's a "bootstrapping"—using the power of each jhāna to help propel us to the next. If we become fascinated with a particular stage and just stay there, progress stops. If we try to move too far ahead of ourselves, progress is very difficult. But if we follow the path, it moves along more quickly than we may have imagined possible.

His discovery of this route is part of what made the Buddha such a master guide.

Insights

The second section of the book, "Insights," looks at the insights that reveal themselves along the way. Some of these, like the view of the sky, are discernible near the beginning. As we travel further, the insights become more nuanced. The sky we see from the cave entrance is real sky, yet the view is obstructed by the trees.

The insights support our progress along the path. And our progress along the path supports the insights. The deeper our practice, the more we'll see. The more we see, the farther we travel.

Before learning in greater detail about the path, it would be helpful to start a meditation practice. If you have a meditation practice already, it would be helpful to see if any of the core teachings of the Buddha might help fine-tune it.

Meditation practice gives an experiential basis from which we might better understand the insights. And later, the insights will help us better understand the stages of practice.

Meditation Practice

Now, let's shift from this metaphorical overview to tangible practice.

Before meditating, it is helpful to find a relatively quiet place to sit comfortably. Sit upright if possible. Lounging invites the body and mind to go to sleep rather than wake up. But the posture should be comfortable. Cushions or chairs are both fine. Sitting cross-legged isn't required. A posture that is familiar to your body will be less distracting and more helpful than one that is uncomfortable.

Now remember what happiness feels like. Perhaps you recently accomplished something that left you feeling great. Perhaps it was the softer happiness of holding a small animal that cuddled into you. Perhaps it was the selfless joy of watching a child play. Perhaps it was the serenity of watching a sunset by the ocean.

All of us have felt happy at times—probably many times—in our lives. The feeling may vary depending on temperament, history, conditioning, and circumstance. The flavor of happiness is not important.

This happiness is the cave exit. This is where this meditation practice begins—not so much with the memory of the situation but with the feeling itself. It's like a glowing in the center of your chest.

To begin, put yourself in your heart. Some people visualize easily. Others don't. It's not important that you clearly visualize. Just imagine holding yourself in the center of your chest.

Then send yourself a wish for happiness or well-being. "May I be happy." "May I be peaceful." "May I feel safe and secure." "May I feel ease throughout my day." Any uplifted state is fine.

The phrases are a way of priming the pump—they evoke the feeling. As it arises, shift your attention to the feeling itself.

Sooner or later the feeling will fade. When it does, repeat the phrase. It's not helpful to repeat it rapidly. This makes the phrase feel mechanical. Rather, say the phrase sincerely, and rest for a few moments with the feeling it evokes. Then repeat it again.

As we do this, three things arise in the mind-heart: the person to whom you are wishing happiness (yourself), the mental phrase, and the feeling. About 70 percent of your attention should be on the feeling, 20 to 25 percent on the person (yourself), and just a little on the phrase used to evoke the feeling.

Spiritual Friend

After about ten minutes, switch the person to whom you are sending kind wishes. Rather than sending loving kindness to yourself, send it to a "spiritual friend."

A spiritual friend is a living person whom you find very easy to wish the best. It might be a favorite teacher who always has your highest interests at heart. It might be an aunt or uncle who always looks out for you. It might be a small child who opens your heart.

A partner is not a good choice for a spiritual friend. You may have a lot of love for him or her. But primary relationships are usually complex. For the purpose of this meditation, simple is better. For the same reason, a teenage son or daughter is probably not a good choice—those relationships have too many textures. A person you find physically attractive is not a good choice either. Physical attraction can become thick, complicated, and distracting. You want the meditation to be light, easy, and uncomplicated.

Once you have settled on a good spiritual friend, stick with that person. It you switch from one person to another, the practice won't be able to ripen or deepen. And if you stay with one person in meditation, the other people around you will benefit even without being the explicit focus of your sitting practice.

So each time you sit down to practice, send well wishes to yourself for ten minutes. Then switch to your same chosen spiritual friend.

Breath Awareness

There is a small percentage of people for whom a spiritual friend is not the best object of meditation. When these people do this practice, they find that most of their attention goes to the friend. Remember, most of the attention should be with the feeling, not the friend. The feeling is the main object of meditation. Nevertheless, they find themselves thinking of the person, wondering how they are doing, wanting to call and check on them. They may become infatuated with their friend. Or they may find themselves continually analyzing their experience—thinking about it rather than simply observing. If this persists, it may be easier for them to use the breath as an object of meditation. Bhante Vimalaramsi has written about the breath practice.[7] But since the percentage of people who get too caught up in their friend is small, using the breath as a primary object falls outside the scope of this book.

The Real Practice

This practice of sending loving kindness or well-being is the storefront. It is something wholesome to occupy the mind-heart. There is a second practice in the back room that is just as important—if not more important.

As you send well-wishing to yourself or your spiritual friend, other things will occur uninvited. Thoughts, images, sensations, and emotions waltz in. This is not your intention. But the mind has a mind of its own.

As long as you're still with the well-wishing for your spiritual friend, just ignore these intrusions. Let them float in the background, as it were, without doing anything with them.

But sooner or later, a distraction highjacks your attention completely. You won't see this happening. One moment you'll be sending loving kindness. The next thing you know, you're rehearsing a conversation, planning your day, reminiscing about yesterday or attending to things other than the object of your meditation.

Rejoice! Now you get to use the second meditation practice. This is a powerful practice that can only be used when the mind wanders. So, now's your chance!

The drifting mind is a symptom of tension disturbing your underlying peace. This side of enlightenment, we all have many tensions. So the distraction points one out—it shows exactly where it is so that you can release it skillfully. This is good news.

The only trick is to do it wisely. An unwise way is to condemn yourself, "Oh, I can't do this!" That criticism creates more tension and destabilizes the mind further. Another unwise strategy is to buckle down and try harder. This too creates more tension and restlessness.

A better approach is employing the Six Rs. As mentioned in the last chapter, these are as follows:

1. Recognize where your attention has gone. In time it will be clear that there is some wisdom that moved your attention to that particular place. It may not be the least bit clear right now what that wisdom is. That's fine. All you need to do is recognize where your attention went.

2. Release your grip on the distraction. Let it be. Don't push it away. Just release the hold it has on your attention.

3. Relax. Let go of any tension in your mind or body. You don't have to search for tension like an enthusiastic detective. Just relax. That's enough.

4. Re-Smile, or smile again. Allow a higher state—any uplifted state—to come into the mind-heart. Having a good sense of humor about how the mind drifts is helpful.

5. Return. Now take the relaxed mind-heart and this brighter/lighter state back to your object of meditation.

6. Repeat. The repetition will happen automatically if you continue meditating—that is to say, the mind will wander again and again. If you haven't released all the tension from a particular distraction, that's fine. It will simply come up again until you have. You can relax in confidence that the mind-heart will let you know if there's more to relax.

This Six-R process contains the practical essence of the Buddha's Four Noble Truths and Eightfold Path. So we'll return to it many times in the context of insights as well as of the practice itself.

To start, thirty minutes a day of meditation is adequate. Forty-five minutes is better. And once you get comfortable, try to not move throughout this period of time. If the mind insists on moving, Six-R the insistence. The Six Rs are very helpful in letting the mind release tension and find deeper ease. Of course, if pain arises from genuine physical harm, you will want to adjust your posture. The way to tell if it is genuine is to notice what happens when you get up from sitting. If the pain goes away very quickly, it was probably not caused by anything harmful. If it returns when you sit, try to remain still and Six-R. If, on the other hand, when you get up the pain lingers, it is best not to sit that way in the future.

If you already have another kind of meditation practice, I encourage you to give this approach a try. Or at the very least, insert a "relax" step into how you deal with distraction: when your mind wanders, rather than pulling your attention immediately back to your object of meditation, relax first.

The Buddha saw that craving or tightness is the root of all suffering. It also gives rise to distractions. So relaxing the tightness goes to the core of his teaching and practice. This simple step can make a huge difference. So give it a try.

These beginning instructions are all you need to get started. In the coming pages, the importance of the Six Rs will become clearer. For now, we're ready to turn to some of the Buddha's core insights. These are the topics of the next section.

Section II

Insights

There is a difference between insight and belief.

Most popular religions in the West define religion by beliefs. If we subscribe to a particular set of tenets, we are said to be of that faith. Beliefs are ideas, concepts, or declarations about the ultimate nature of reality. Often they are metaphysical claims about the afterlife, the nature of God, or other propositions that cannot be proved or disproved empirically. "If you accept Jesus Christ as your Lord and Savior, when you die you will go to heaven and live for eternity with the Divine." In this life, there is no way to check out the validity of this claim. So we're asked to accept this without tangible proof: blind faith.

Buddhism is not based on beliefs, metaphysical claims, philosophical stances, or blind faith. Buddhism is founded on insight.

Walking outside the cave, we see the sky. The blueness of the sky is not a belief. It is an insight we know from experience.

The difference between insight and belief is that insights are grounded in direct experience—they can be verified or refuted by each of us.

Siddhārtha Gautama said that "life has dissatisfaction" (*dukkha*). He didn't say that "life is suffering and nothing but suffering"—only that we all suffer in larger or smaller ways. This is not a belief or a metaphysical claim. It's a verifiable insight which can be experienced directly. To verify or refute it, we ask ourselves, "Have I ever suffered?" Or we can ask aloud, "Will everyone in the room who has never suffered please stand up?"

Siddhārtha Gautama had other insights about the source of suffering and ways to find relief. And he said, "Please don't take my word for any of this. That will be of little value. Explore it in your own life. What you find there will be of great value."

Buddhism revolves around a series of strategies for cultivating insight and testing them. Part of that strategy is the meditative path we'll explore in the next section. It is a way of cultivating direct insight.

But it is helpful to know what we are looking for before we look for it. In this section, we'll explore the insights central to the Buddhist path of awakening.

Understanding these insights without direct experience will not free us. But they will help us fine-tune the practices the Buddha taught. They will help us know what to look for as we travel along.

The Buddha's Eightfold Path begins with right view or wise perspective. He found it helpful for people to have some insight into the practice as a way to begin. Insight, like knowledge, is vast. Not all insights are useful. Not all help wake us up; therefore, in this section we'll consider the insights that the Buddha found most valuable in easing awake.

3

Splinters in the Mind: Cows and Khandhas

I fastened six brightly colored dowels to a piece of cardboard, arranging them from smallest to largest. I showed this model to fifteen kindergartners, one child at a time. I offered each child paper and crayons to draw what they saw.

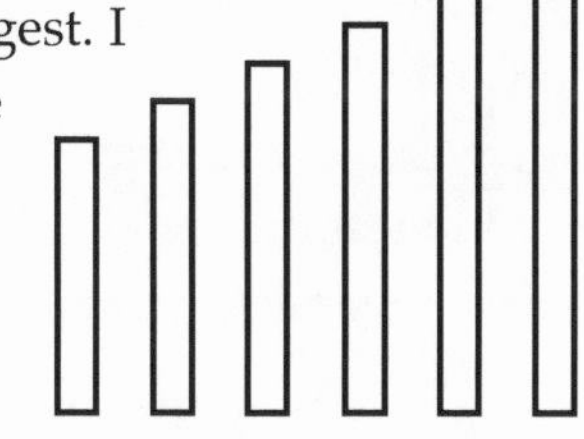

A week later I returned without the cardboard and dowels and invited them to draw what they remembered.

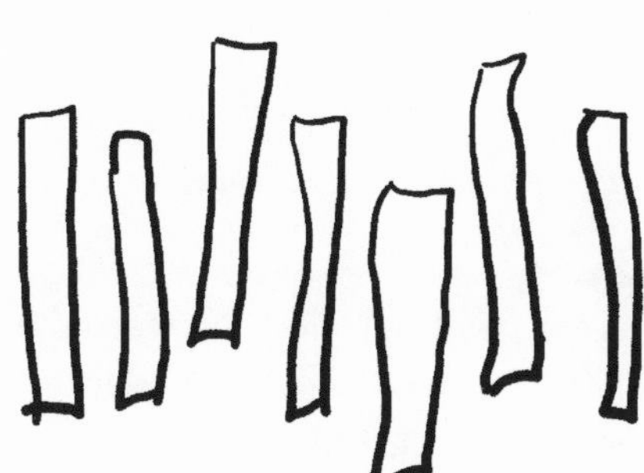

Five months later I returned again and invited them to draw from memory a second time.

The third drawings—the ones done from memory after five months—were the most accurate. After five months, their memory was more accurate than after one week.

This apparent spontaneous memory improvement was what I had hoped for. But it was so counterintuitive that it begged for an explanation.

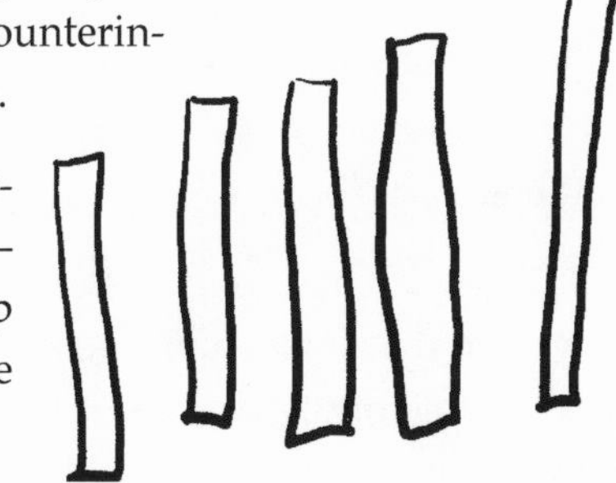

Most of us tacitly assume that perception and memory operate passively—like a digital camera storing a pixel map on a memory card. The reality is far more interesting and dynamic.

Perception and memory involve both raw sensory information and the cognitive structures we use to sort out and interpret that information. The key to the spontaneous memory improvement was not the sensory data but the maturing of the cognitive structures the children used to make sense of it.

But before going further, let me back up for a moment and place my little experiment in context.

In the late 1960s, I was studying psychology at the University of Wisconsin in Madison. At that time, behaviorism and experimental psychology were in vogue at the university. I found them both to be interesting but limited. In my curiosity about the human experience, these areas of study seemed narrow.

In searching for other approaches, I became fascinated by the work of the Swiss psychologist Jean Piaget and his study of the development of intelligence in children. Piaget became renowned for his work. But at that time, he was not well-known in America.

Piaget was not a behaviorist or an experimentalist. He was a phenomenologist. His study did not involve experimental manipulation of behavior as much as astute observation.

He observed that knowing begins at the point of contact between the human organism and the world—it begins with direct sensory experiences. From these raw phenomena, we extrapolate outward to deduce what in the world triggered them. And we extrapolate inward to deduce who is experiencing them.

He was particularly interested in the cognitive structures children use to make these deductions—how they create maps of the world and themselves. He called these structures "schemas," and he catalogued hundreds of them.

Some schemas arise out of our neural physiology. One such schema is the one that understands a series. Looking at six dowels lined up from smallest to largest, we see a series. This is so obvious as to seem unremarkable. But children younger than kindergarten age do not understand a series. We can explain it to them, show examples, and go over it and over it. They just don't get it. Slightly older children get it effortlessly. The schema that comprehends a series appears in most children at a remarkably predictable age regardless of their experience.

Most of my kindergartners did not understand a series when I first showed them the model or a week later when I asked them to draw it from memory. They could see that the dowels were different sizes but had no concept of smallest to largest. Their first drawings reflected this.

Five months later, most of them had matured enough to have the schema for a series. They got it. So when they drew the picture again from memory, they made more sense of the information in their minds. Their drawings were more accurate.

It was as if a person was asked to memorize a sentence in Greek. But she didn't speak Greek, so she memorized a sequence of sounds that had no meaning for her. Then she took a crash course in Greek. At the end of five months, she had a grasp of the language. If asked to repeat the sentence, she now made more sense of the sounds and spoke more accurately.

The point is that perception and memory are not a single, passive process. They are a dynamic, unconscious integration of several different phenomena.

A Picasso story makes this point succinctly:

A woman stood gazing at a large Picasso mural: *Guernica*. Her fists were on her hips. One eyebrow was raised. Finally she muttered aloud, "That is not a cow!"

Picasso was standing nearby and overheard the remark. He wandered over, stood beside the woman, and gazed at the mural with her. Then he leaned slightly toward her and said softly, "Madam, you are correct. *That* is not a cow. That is a *picture* of a cow."

In our minds we create pictures of the world and of ourselves. These include sensory impressions, images, names, feelings, and concepts. Too often we confuse our inner pictures with the external reality. As the Chinese proverb says, "It takes a finger to point to the moon, but woe to the person who mistakes the finger for the moon." After all, a picture of a cow is not a cow.

Phenomenology

Siddhārtha Gautama, like Jean Piaget, was an astute observer of life. As mentioned earlier, Buddhism is a phenomenology—a study of experience. It is based on direct experience, not on our ideas, concepts, or beliefs about that experience.

Most religions define themselves with statements about ultimate reality, the nature of God, what happens when we die, the nature of good and evil, and other beliefs that can't be verified empirically.

Siddhārtha Gautama had little interest in such metaphysical speculations. When asked about them, he usually refused to comment. He steered his students away from questions central to many religious systems. In one talk (or "sutta") he said, "These four imponderables are not to be speculated about. Whoever speculates about them would come unhinged and experience vexation. Which four? What do Buddhas really know? What can meditation ultimately reveal? What are the specific results of karma [e.g., Why do bad things happen to good people? Where did we come from?] What's the purpose of life?"[8]

Buddhist practice does not try to answer questions we cannot answer. Siddhārtha Gautama felt that what we need to awaken can be found in the present moment when it's not cluttered and distorted by concepts and speculations. He developed a practice to help us observe phenomena deeply and clearly.

But in considering the present, he didn't limit exploration to sensory phenomena. He included thoughts because we experience them. The inner world is as real as the outer world—but they aren't the same. Hopefully they correlate. But a picture of a cow is not a cow.

Khandhas

> ***Khandhas***
>
> *Body (rūpa)*
>
> *Feeling Tone (vedanā)*
>
> *Perception (sañña)*
>
> *Concepts and Storylines (saṅkhāra)*
>
> *Awareness (viññāṇa)*

Siddhārtha Gautama was very clear about the difference between sensory experience and mental constructs, between the finger and the moon, between the picture of a cow and a cow. He referred to these as different realms. But he used the word *"khandha"* (or *"skandha"* in Sanskrit). In English, the word literally means "heaps," but is usually translated more genteelly as "aggregates." As the term implies, they are clumps of experience that can group together a variety of similar experiences.

He distinguished not just two but five khandhas. Five is enough to get a handle on the nature of suffering, where it comes from, and how to form strategies for relieving it. He found that suffering has less to do with the splinter in our finger (the raw sensation) and more to do with the splinter in our mind (what we tell ourselves about the sensation).

So to move more deeply into this topic, it would be helpful to look at what each khandha represents. The Buddha used the khandhas to teach about selflessness (anattā). We'll leave that exploration for a later chapter (see page 83). In this chapter, we'll explore the different phenomena associated with each of the five khandhas.

Sensation

The first khandha is the body. The term the Buddha used for body was *"rūpa."* Rūpa refers to more than a corpse. The word *"kāya"* refers to the physical aspects of the body alone. "Rūpa" is the living, breathing, sensing, moving, energetic organism. It is through the living body that we make contact with the world around us. When we're aware of light hitting the eye, we have "eye-contact." When we're aware of sounds hitting the eardrum, we have "ear-contact." The word for "contact" in *Pāli* (the language of the early suttas) is *phassa*. In general, phassa requires the combination of three things: a sensory organ, sensory data, and awareness.

In Buddhism, the mind is considered a sensory faculty that perceives "mind objects" (thoughts). The mind is subjectively located in the body, like the other five senses. And the mind and body are said to arise together. The term *"nāmarūpa"* refers to this mind-body as one thing that may later divide into mind and body.

Note that contact is merely raw sensation without any feeling tone or interpretation. It is just heat, cold, sound, light, tactile sensations, and so forth. It includes the sounds we hear before we recognize that they come from a car or bird or child. It includes the colors and shapes seen by the eyes of the woman looking at the Picasso painting and eyes of the children looking at the dowels on the cardboard. It is physical sensation and nothing more.

Feeling Tone

Contact or raw sensation (phassa) gives rise to the second khandha: feeling tone. The Pāli word *vedanā* is often translated as "feeling." But in English, feelings refer to complex emotions. Vedanā, on the other hand is simple. Perhaps I'm groping in the dark and I touch something soft, cold, and wet. Soft, cold, and wet are feelings in the sense that I know I've touched something but don't yet know what. The feeling tone might be pleasant, unpleasant, or neutral. It may draw me in, push me away, or neither.

The woman looking at the mural found it unpleasant. The children seeing the dowels found it neutral or slightly pleasant.

Perception

Contact (phassa) and feeling tone (vedanā) give rise to the third khandha: perception (*sañña*). Sañña is the names or labels we put on things. For example, I compare the sensations and feeling tone of what I touched in the dark to a mental catalog to see if I find a match: "Ah, yes, the soft, cold, and wet thing is a washcloth." I've now imposed a label on my experience. This helps me figure out what I want to do with this thing I've called "washcloth."

The woman labeled the image in the mural "mixed-up cow." The children labeled the dowels "colored sticks."

To be clear about the difference between contact, feeling tone, and perception, consider going outside on a bright spring day: The sun on our face feels warm (contact or phassa) and pleasant (feeling tone or vedanā). We call it "sunshine" (perception or saññа). This label is not the direct experience—just a label we use to point to it.

Concepts and Storylines

Perception (saññа) often gives rise to the fourth khandha: *saṅkhāra*. Saṅkhāra is hard to translate into English. Often it's called "formations." The root *"khār"* is also the root of the word *"karma,"* which literally means "action." *"Saṅ-"* at the front gives it more emphasis. So saṅkhāra literally means "put together" or "formed."

Saṅkhāra includes concepts, storylines, and meaning that we put together and assign to our perceptions. The woman's storyline might have been, "This guy doesn't know how to paint something as obvious as a cow. There's something the matter with him." The older kindergarteners may have thought, "These are a bunch of sticks lined up from babies to big guys." As we feel the sun on our face on a spring day, we might think, "Mother Nature provides for us if we give her a chance. The sun is melting the clouds, helping the plants grow, and warming us all. I'll hang out here for a while."

These storylines and concepts (saṅkhāra) may be true, but we don't experience them directly. The images of Mother Nature and of the sun shining on the earth are pictures formed in our minds that we hope correspond to some external reality. But it's a constructed image (saṅkhāra), not an external reality. We don't really experience the grass growing. We infer it from observations and arrangements of thoughts. Like labels, concepts are extremely useful in helping us live and enjoy life.

Awareness

The fifth khandha is awareness. The Pāli term *viññāṇa* is often translated as "consciousness." But in English, consciousness often refers to an entity that exists on its own. In Buddhism, consciousness is not an independent entity. It arises only when the conditions are right, and never without a body.

Awareness is part of all the other khandhas. Without awareness we would not know what we see, hear, touch, taste, smell, or think. Without awareness we would not know feeling tone. Without awareness, there would be no perception. Without awareness, we would not know thoughts, concepts, stories, and other formations (saṅkhāra). It is through awareness that we become conscious of all of these.

Our awareness is sometimes clear, sometimes foggy, sometimes soft and receptive, sometimes ragged, sometimes penetrating. We can experience the quality of our awareness directly if we turn our attention to it. The woman's awareness was tight. The children's awareness was apparently light and playful. Lying in the grass on a spring day, our awareness is soft and receptive.

Rapid

Notice that the khandhas tend to flow from one to the next. Often the flow is very rapid. Someone blows a car horn at us. We hear the sound (phassa), find it unpleasant (vedanā), recognize what it is (sañña), think "that guy is a jerk," (saṅkhāra) and our awareness (viññāṇa) turns dark and murky. This happens so quickly that the khandhas seem to blend together as one phenomenon rather than several.

The point isn't that any khandha is better or worse than any other. It's that sensations are sensations, feeling tone is feeling tone, labels are labels, thoughts are thoughts, and awareness is awareness. Confusing one with the other can lead to difficulties. When we place more importance on thought than on sensation or perception, we are in the process of "creating" our reality, not seeing it. If we confuse our thoughts about the world with the world, we are living in illusion. We've confused the picture with the cow.

Splinters in the Mind

The Buddha mentioned the khandhas directly or indirectly in many different suttas, but he rarely explained them. Consequently there are many scholarly disagreements about their exact nature.

I suspect that the Buddha didn't explain them because he wanted us to work with them in our own direct experience rather than adopt his ideas.

The Buddha was not interested in analyzing experience per se. He was interested in helping people relieve suffering and cultivate well-being. To relieve suffering, we must first see its nature.

It's tempting to think suffering arises from the sensation (phassa) or unpleasantness feeling tone (vedanā). It's tempting to think suffering arises from the splinter in our finger, the broken bone, or the death of a loved one.

But the Buddha found that suffering arises most often out of mental constructs, beliefs, and storylines (saṅkhāra)—what we tell ourselves about experience.

For example, I remember having a loose tooth as a child. I loved to wiggle it back and forth with my tongue. It created a sharp sensation (phassa). If I had feared that sensation, I would have suffered. But I interpreted it in a storyline (saṅkhāra) about growing into a big boy and getting a visit from the tooth fairy. So I didn't suffer—I was delighted.

Obviously there is a correlation between the sharp sensations and suffering. But they're in different khandhas. We have less influence over the first khandhas than the later ones. We may not be able to change the sensations, but we can influence our awareness and the stories we tell about those sensations. The splinters in our fingers may cause a sensation, but the splinters in our minds create suffering.

Penetrating Suffering

My first meditation teacher, Ruth Denison, moved with the grace of a young dancer. Part way through the retreat, I learned she had advanced arthritis. Her doctors said she should not be able to walk. I asked her if she was in pain. She smiled sweetly and said, "Of course. But I don't fight it. It's an old friend."

Most of us don't have the years of training or deep calmness to be able to approach such powerful sensations with equanimity. Yet I could see how the desire to be free of something creates turmoil. Without aversion, sensation remains, but the agitation evaporates.

—Anonymous

Let's look at the phenomenon of suffering.

Imagine stubbing a toe. Perhaps you swear or hop around. If it's seriously damaged, you pack it in ice or go to the hospital. But usually, it's not that bad. It's just pain that you know will pass.

It helps to investigate a little. Perhaps you "breathe into it." Rather than contract, hold the breath, and pull away; you imagine breathing out through the hurt. This relaxes the breath and helps open up the direct experience.

You notice the raw physical sensation (phassa). At first there seems to be a solid mass of sensation, an impenetrable, undifferentiated block of energy. But with a degree of inner calm, the sensation starts to break into components as you observe. There's intense burning centered on the first joint of the big toe. The aching spreads out through the toe and surrounding area. It doesn't extend as far as the little toe or ankle. It pulses. You notice tearing in your eyes and subtle vibrations in other parts of your body.

Accompanying these sensations is unpleasantness (vedanā). It's very unpleasant.

You label it: "Ouch!" "hurt," "intense pain." These are perceptions (sañña). If you're patient, you see the labels as labels, unpleasantness as unpleasantness, and sensations as sensations—and don't confuse them with each other. The labels tend to treat it as one object, but you can see that there are many different phenomena arising.

Inevitably, you construct a storyline (saṅkhāra). "I hurt my toe. I don't like it. I want it to stop and go away. I hope I didn't dislocate it. I don't think so. I hope this doesn't last much longer. I hate it." Fear and aversion are often a central component of suffering.

This storyline says the world ought to be different. When your ideas about what the world should be differ from what it is, there is potential for suffering. When you let the world be what it is without fighting it, there is potential for peace and well-being.

As you sit with your stubbed toe, perhaps you see clearly the storylines, constructs, fears, and aversions. This doesn't stop the throbbing in the toe. But if you stop wishing it were different, you stop sending hatred toward the sensation. Resistance to hurt may create more hurt. It's as if the body wants to tighten around the injury, wall it off, and push it out of the body. It cannot. The tightness only intensifies the pain. If you relax your resistance through curiosity, interest, or compassion, the original sensation remains, but the unnecessary hurt dissipates.

The last khandha is awareness (viññāṇa). You notice that we're looking at your toe with a very dense and contracted awareness. This is inherently uncomfortable.

Relieving Suffering

The Great Way is not difficult for those who have no preferences.... If you wish to see the truth, then hold no opinion for or against anything. The struggle of what one likes against what one dislikes is the disease of the mind.

—Seng-st'an, *Hsin Hsin Ming*

If we look at suffering from perspective of the khandhas, it loses some of its solidity. The khandhas suggest that the easiest place to start relieving suffering may be awareness (viññāṇa). Rather than contract around the hurt, we soften, bring a little acceptance, compassion, and caring to it. We don't try to change what is going on. We just open a little more—lessen our resistance. The pain itself may not disappear, but the ancillary misery of resistance does. As much as ninety percent of pain comes from resistance to it. The other ten percent is often manageable with simple awareness.

Curiosity to know more intimately what is actually going on fosters expansiveness and well-being. When the mind is soft and open, happiness and discomfort can coexist.

As awareness softens, the storylines (saṅkhāras) may change. We see the sensation less as a demon and more as just another phenomenon. As our storylines change, we begin to use different labels (saññas), like "sharp sensation" rather than "massive trauma." Perhaps even the unpleasant vedanā shifts toward neutral. Finally, if we go deep enough, the sensation (phassa) may seem to change. Without pouring hatred and dislike onto the sensation, it may lessen. Even if it doesn't, we find it's made up of many different sensations, all of which are shifting bit by bit.

Maybe we begin to suspect that all suffering is ultimately unnecessary. Life brings sensation. We suffer by our response to the sensation. Suffering is the difference between "is" and "ought." It's the difference between how things are and what the mind says they ought to be or wants them to be. When we are openly and calmly with what is, there is experience but not necessarily suffering.

Kindness

Hell is the stiff resistance to what is. Heaven is our loving openness. Hell is resistance. Heaven is acceptance.

—Steven Levine, *Who Dies?*

I'm not advocating masochism. When I had my wisdom teeth out, I was glad for Novocaine. Just because suffering ultimately arises from how we respond to life doesn't mean we should blame ourselves. That just causes more suffering.

Our resistance to pain and our tendency to space out have biological and cultural roots. The conditioning is deep. So it helps to be humble and good-humored.

Since the suffering we create comes out of avoidance and contraction, relief of suffering comes from the opposite: kindness, patience, softness, relaxation, smiling, receptivity, and not taking on more than we can manage.

Awareness is thus the place to begin. The physical sensations and the labels arise doggedly out of our biological makeup and psychological conditioning. We have less capacity to change these at first. If we try too hard, we may just end up fooling ourselves. It's easier to start with the quality of our awareness. We can bring some interest, curiosity, compassion, and other expansive qualities to the way we look at our discomfort. Even this can be hard with strong pain. So we start with a splinter, a mild headache, a small bruise, a minor upset—something that is uncomfortable but not overwhelming, something that stretches our capacities ten percent. There is no need to try something fifty percent beyond what we can manage. We'll just tighten up inside. Instead we ask, "What's really going on here?" We look at the internal qualities and soften.

With care and attention, soon mildly unpleasant events no longer disturb our well-being. Then we can relax with stronger phenomena.

Understanding of the khandhas is helpful in this. They sort out where to focus our attention: How much of the suffering comes from the splinter in our finger and how much from the splinter in our mind?

Meditation

> *I found that the chief difficulty for most people was to realize that they rarely heard new things, that is things that they had never heard before. They kept translating what they heard into their habitual language. They had ceased to hope and believe there might be anything new.*
>
> —P. D. Ouspensky

All this has implications for designing a meditation practice.

When we experience an unpleasant feeling (vedanā), we may want to think about it, understand it, "get a philosophical perspective" on it. But these are just concepts (saṅkhāra), not the feeling tone itself. Many people use thinking to try to overcome a feeling. It doesn't work in the long run. They merely repress the feeling and store it as tension. It is more effective to see things in their own terms—feel feeling as a feeling rather than as a thought.

When meditation gets subtle, we'll experience phenomena (phassa) for which we have no labels (sañña) because they are new to us. We have no language for them. Our first impulse may be to fit them into something we already know. It is wiser to simply sit with the raw sensations and know them on their own terms.

In other ways, it is wise to experience the various khandhas in their own terms rather than translate them into other terms.

Also, in designing a meditation practice, it is important to remember that the fifth khandha, awareness, touches the other four. Without awareness (viññāṇa), we don't know raw sensation (phassa), feeling tone (vedanā), perception (sañña), or concepts and storylines (saṅkhāra). If awareness is tight, murky, or rambunctious, it is difficult to perceive anything clearly.

The Buddha's practice depends on awareness (viññāṇa) that is light, open, clear, and uplifted. This is where it begins, and this is where it returns again and again and again. When the mind's attention gets distracted, it will be important to both recognize where it has gone and to release, relax, and cultivate a lightness of mind.

Dependent Origination

In sum, the khandhas are helpful in recognizing different kinds of phenomena and how they interact. They are particularly helpful in beginning our practice and moving us up through the early jhānas. But in the higher jhānas, they aren't quite enough. For ultimate freedom or full awakening, we need more than the khandhas offer. We need a more refined analysis of the various components of experience. And we need to see better how they interact with one another.

This brings us to Dependent Origination, or paticcasamuppāda—how tension thickens the plots of our lives and how ease can relieve that tension.

This is the subject of the next chapter. From this it will become clearer that Buddhism is not a philosophy, metaphysics, or set of beliefs. It is a phenomenology. It says that awaking arises out of clearly seeing various phenomena and releasing the tension around them.

4

Thickening the Plot: Dependent Origination

Closing the refrigerator door one morning, you notice a piece of strawberry pie. "That would sure taste good," you think. "But not for breakfast."

At work, the pie comes fondly to mind from time to time: "I'd really like some." Walking into the house at the end of the day, you want a taste. You take it out of the refrigerator and hold it in one hand so it won't get away while reaching for a fork. You scoop some up, raise it to your mouth, and close your lips around it. Sweet sensations burst through your mouth. Your mind stops as you savor: "Ah! This is wonderful. This is heaven. This is bliss."

If you're like me, this ecstasy lasts two or three seconds. Then the sensations fade slightly as you think, "Boy, this is great. I want more." You stab for a second piece. The bliss of the second bite only lasts a second. By the third, the ecstasy is gone. But the taste is still pleasant as you gobble down the rest.

What causes that moment of ecstasy with the first bite? What creates that instant of total happiness?

Any fool will tell us, "You were happy because you got what you wanted. You were hankering for the pie all day. When you finally got it, it made you happy."

In our quest for happiness, we have built lifestyles, economic systems, and entire cultures around this philosophy: "Getting what we want makes us happy." We have become proficient at satisfying desires: pies, ice cream, hot tubs, designer clothes, luxury cars, evenings at the theater, varieties of chocolate, three hundred cable TV channels, beds with personalized comfort settings, vacation packages, books, music, and on and on and on. Our technologies for producing comforts surpass anything the earth has ever seen. We are like Gods on Mount Olympus, the envy of the world.

But are we really happy? Most people spend more time earning money to buy the good life than enjoying it. Crime and violence abound. We worry about letting our kids play unattended in the neighborhood. Some level of depression affects seventy-five percent of the population. Teenage suicide. Alcoholism. Domestic violence. Diffuse anxiety. The statistics go on and on.

I have traveled a little in India. I don't envy the poverty. But I can't say they're less happy than we are in America with all our comforts.

What's the matter up here on Mount Olympus? How come it doesn't feel like heaven? Maybe our analysis is wrong. Maybe the fool was foolish when he said, "getting what we want makes us happy."

Let's take a closer look at this strawberry pie. What really happened?

Longing for the pie all day is not happiness. It is an experience of hunger or grasping. It is not pleasant. In fact, it's so unpleasant that we try to take our mind off the actual experience. Instead we fantasize what it might be like to have the pie. "Sweet anticipation," we call it. This takes our awareness off the unpleasantness of the moment. This is unfortunate because without awareness, there is no wisdom. Without wisdom, there is no way to deal with the discomfort of the moment other than fantasy. We have whole entertainment industries—TV, movies, radio, books, magazines, music, and sports—to keep us distracted.

Okay. Wanting the pie isn't pleasant. But what about that first bite? Certainly that's genuine contentment.

It is. But if we look closely, we see that during those few seconds, the desire evaporates. We no longer want the pie because now we have it. The pie does not create happiness. It is the absence of desire that feels wonderful.

Furthermore, the taste sensations are so strong that the mind stops thinking for a moment. We cannot think and experience in the same instant. So with strong sensations, the mind stills. There's no wanting. No holding. No grasping. Just blissful savoring.

We on Mount Olympus confuse having what we want with not wanting. We confuse gratifying a desire with absence of desire. Since we are deeply conditioned to believe that getting what we want brings happiness, we don't notice that the yearning is gone. We focus more on the objects we want than on the state of wanting. As soon as the peace of the moment fades, we leap back into the desire: "Boy, I want another bite," and another and another.

Most of us are sophisticated enough to realize that material items don't give us the deepest well-being. So rather than just collect stuff, we collect as many pleasant experiences as we can. After pie, we have a glass of wine. Then watch a little TV or go to a movie. Then soak in the hot tub for a while. Then listen to music, have sex, read a good book, go for a nice walk, take in a play. Yum, yum, yum. We leap from desire to desire and from comfort to comfort until we are exhausted, frantic, and dying from stress-induced diseases.

Ascetics and fundamentalists of many religious persuasions have figured out that worldly comforts do not bring lasting happiness. Some push them away. Many of these folks seem grim. On the whole, they don't look happier. So avoiding stuff doesn't seem to be the answer either.

You are rich when you know you have enough.

—Lao Tzu

Flow of Events

This analysis of happiness, desire, and absence of desire is not modern. Several millennia ago, Siddhārtha Gautama noticed the same process. But his analysis was subtler and more complete. He saw desire or aversion as just one in a series of events, or just one form of energy in a complex flow.

Let's go back to the pie scenario and trace this flow.

Our story begins with a casual glance into the refrigerator. Light reflecting off the pie strikes the eye. As noted in the last chapter, the Buddha called this "contact" (phassa), meaning the contact between the sensory phenomena (light), the sensory organ (eye), and awareness. The mind automatically interprets the shapes and colors and gives them a label: "strawberry pie." We identify it.

This gives rise to a feeling tone (vedanā). As noted earlier (see page 44), if the feeling tone is pleasant, we tend to lean into it, giving rise to desire, wanting, or attachment. If it's unpleasant, we tend to lean away, giving rise to aversion, dislike, anger, or ill will. If it's neutral, we tend not to notice clearly.

These three responses are collectively called *taṇhā.* Taṇhā literally means "thirst" but is often translated as "craving." Craving can be ravenous, or it can as subtle as wistful wishing. In our pie story, a pleasant feeling gave rise to a wish for a bite of pie.

Craving is a very important player in this plot, so we'll come back to it in the next chapter.

In the story, the desire for pie didn't fade. We found ourselves thinking about it and identifying with it: "I'm hungry." "I'd like some." "I hope nobody takes my pie."

These first thoughts spawned by desire are called "clinging" (*upādāna*). Clinging always manifests as thinking.

If we repeat these thoughts, they start to settle into a pattern or a habitual tendency (*bhava*). Bhava is often translated as "existence" or "becoming." But "habitual tendencies" or even "emotional stuff" gives a clearer and more practical understanding of how it usually operates.

And indeed, thoughts about the pie did recur throughout the day.

Habitual tendencies can give birth to action (*jāti*). Jāti is often translated as "birth" or even "rebirth." But this is confusing, as it seems to imply physical birth. It actually refers to the beginning of any action–physical, verbal, or mental. So a better phrase is "birth of action."

In our story, the habitual tendency gave birth to the action of eating the pie when we got home.

Middle Way

If this outline of events makes sense to you, then you have a good general grasp of what the Buddha called paticcasamuppāda, or the Law of Dependent Origination: everything originates from something else, and there is a predictable sequence to many of these events.

Some traditions make Dependent Origination sound more esoteric or obscure than it needs to be. They apply it only to rebirth—the movement from one lifetime to the next. Or, rather than looking at large stretches of time, they go the other way and look at events that arise and pass in the tiniest fraction of a second.

These macro and micro explanations may be valid, but they weren't the Buddha's main concern. His was a middle way—not the macro or the micro. He wasn't trying to impress scholars or intellectuals but to provide practical guidance useful to anyone in daily life or in meditative efforts to wake up.

Let's take a closer look at this process.

River

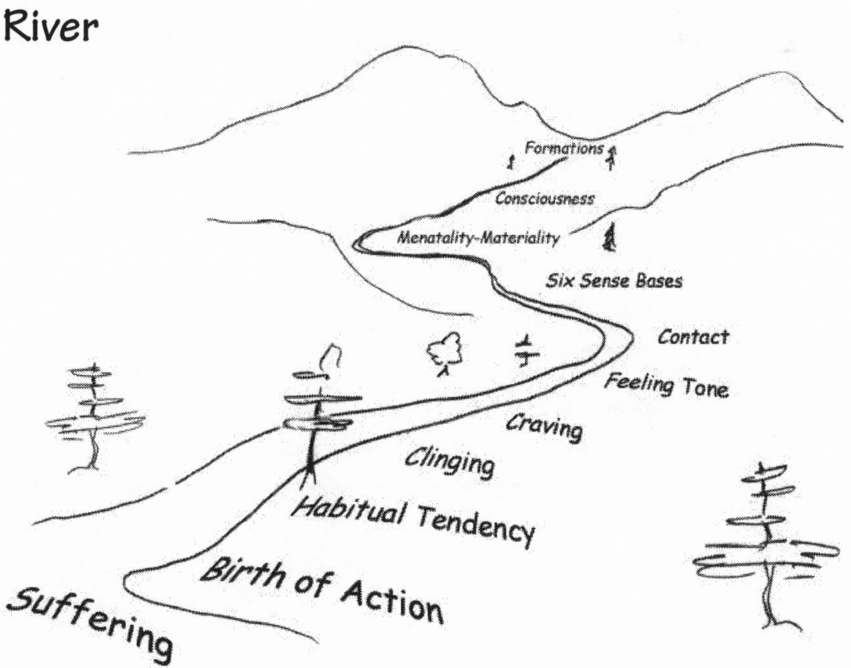

A river is a good metaphor for Dependent Origination. It starts high in the mountains as a tiny trickle. This trickle grows into a brook that becomes a stream that becomes a river that flows into the sea.

A brook is very different from a river. But they are both forms of water in motion.

The names of events along this flow ("brook," "stream," "river") do not describe distinct phenomena. A set of rapids is different from the meandering beyond the rapids, but there is no sharp line where the rapids suddenly stop and the meandering suddenly begins. The river transforms (changes its form) gradually.

So the various events in Dependent Origination (contact, feeling tone, craving, clinging, etc.) are both distinctive and arbitrary. We can lump the process into fewer events or look at it closely and discern many more events. In some places the Buddha described nine events, in others eleven, twelve, thirteen or even twenty-three as he spoke about longer or shorter sections of the river.

Our strawberry-pie story began with the sense-contact: the eye seeing the pie in the refrigerator. When the Buddha described this river of causation to people who didn't meditate, this is where he began. When he spoke to monks with advanced meditation practices, he described subtler events farther upstream. Since these events arise before sense-based perceptions, they cannot be perceived in usual ways. They're below the threshold of ordinary awareness. In most of us most of the time, they occur mechanically and unconsciously. However, as the mind becomes deeply relaxed and alert, it is possible to "see" them.

So a more complete mapping of the river includes upstream events.

The Buddha's most common twelve-event description begins with ignorance (*avijjā*). Avijjā doesn't mean "stupidity" as it can in English. The root of "ignorance" is "ignore"—we don't see something and thus effectively ignore it. The Buddha used the term to refer to not seeing the impersonal nature of phenomena. In the suttas, ignorance means ascribing a sense of self when there is none. Without ignorance, nothing arises. Ignorance is like the mountain slopes before there is even a trickle of water.

Events of Paticcasamuppāda *as they flow "downstream" when the psycho-spiritual system is relatively unconscious and responding mechanically:*			
	English	*Pāli*	*Other Translations*
1	**Ignorance**	Avijjā	Delusion
2	**Formations**	Saṅkhāra	Potential, Fabrications
3	**Consciousness**	Viññāṇa	Awareness, Life force, Mind
4	**Mentality-Materiality**	Nāmarūpa	Mind and body
5	**Six Sense Bases**	Āyatana	Eye, Ear, Nose, Tongue, Touch and Mind
6	**Contact**	Phassa	Perception
7	**Feeling Tone**	Vedanā	Feeling, Valence
8	**Craving**	Taṇhā	Thirst, Desire
9	**Clinging**	Upādāna	Attachment, Grasping
10	**Habitual Tendencies**	Bhava	Existence, Becoming, Emotional stuff
11	**Birth of action**	Jāti	Birth, Rebirth
12	**Sorrow and Grief**	Jarāmaraṇa	Aging, Death, Sorrow, Lamentation, Pain, Grief, Despair

With ignorance, formations arise. "Formations" is one of many ways to translate the Pāli word *saṅkhāra*. Another common translation is "potential." Saṅkhāra arises out of ignorance. The ignorance in each of us is a little different. Therefore the formations in each of us have slightly different potentials. At this stage they have not yet become thoughts, hearing, feelings, or any particular thing. Yet potentially they can become anything. They are like stem cells—they are something in and of themselves and have the potential to become anything. Formations are extremely subtle and cannot be seen unless the mind is very still and receptive.

With formations, consciousness (viññāṇa) can arise. It is a subtle, undifferentiated awareness that has not yet separated into the six senses.

With consciousness, mentality-materiality (nāmarūpa) can arise: mind-body.

With mentality-materiality, the six sense bases (*āyatana*) can arise. These are eye, ear, nose, tongue, touch, and mind (which perceives thoughts).

With the sense bases, contact (phassa) can arise. This is where our story began as you saw the pie in the refrigerator.

Contact can give rise to feeling tone that can give rise to craving that can give rise to clinging that can give rise to habitual tendencies that can give birth to action.

And finally, with birth of action (physical, verbal, or mental), sorrow and grief (*jarāmaraṇa*) can arise. *Jarā* literally means "old age," and *marana* literally means "death." In the suttas, jarāmaraṇa is often translated dramatically: "aging and death, sorrow, lamentation, pain, grief, and despair."[9] But it includes irritation, ennui, and other quieter forms of dis-ease as well.

Going Upstream

There are two ways to view this river: downstream and upstream. The downward flow describes the origin of events. The upward exploration describes their cessation.

The downward flow from ignorance to sorrow is referred to as Dependent Origination—how events are the origin, cause, or condition for dependent events to arise. This is what happens when the psycho-spiritual system is responding mechanically and unconsciously. It's like being in a small boat in a big river without a paddle—we just get swept along.

But we don't have to live mechanically and unconsciously. We can live with deepening awareness. With greater mindfulness, we can follow events farther and farther upstream where it is easier and easier to step out of the flow.

This upward exploration is called "cessation"—how downstream events cease when their upstream causes cease. It's like taking water out of the river so the downstream events cease.

Ultimately, the Buddha was less interested in the truth and origin of suffering (the First and Second Noble Truths) than in the cessation of suffering and the way leading to that cessation (the Third and Fourth Noble Truths).

Paticcasamuppāda *as seen traveling "upstream" with deeper and clearer mindfulness:*		
	English	*Pāli*
1	**Sorrow and Grief**	Jarāmaraṇa
2	**Birth of Action**	Jāti
3	**Habitual Tendencies**	Bhava
4	**Clinging**	Upādāna
5	**Craving**	Taṇhā
6	**Feeling Tone**	Vedanā
7	**Contact**	Phassa
8	**Six Sense Bases**	Āyatana
9	**Mentality-Materiality**	Nāmarūpa
10	**Consciousness**	Viññāṇa
11	**Formations**	Saṅkhāra
12	**Cessation**	Nirodha
13	**Awakening**	Nibbāna

Note that while suffering may be preceded by action, not all action leads to suffering. It's quite possible to act in ways that don't come to grief. If we're free of desire and aversion and simply present to the moment, we eat the pie, enjoy it, and even savor it. Then the next moment is just the next moment without pining for the fading tastes or plotting to get more. Physical, verbal, and mental actions that are free of craving don't cause difficulty.

While there is a strong tendency for upstream events to flow into downstream events, it is not inevitable. There is wiggle room: fate is not sealed. We can step out of the river at any point. Nevertheless, downstream events are always preceded by upstream events. If we experience sorrow or grief, it was preceded by some kind of unwholesome action. Unwholesome actions are always preceded by conditioned habits and tendencies. These habitual tendencies are preceded by clinging. And so on upstream.

We may not see the preceding event—the clinging that precedes the craving, the feeling tone that precedes the clinging, the contact that precedes the feeling tone, and so forth. But with clearer mindfulness, we can begin to see them sooner and sooner. As we do, it is possible to release them and step out of the stream before we get washed away. The whole point of the Buddha's path was releasing and getting out of the flow before it caused suffering.

The Buddha said over and over that the correct way to teach and learn paticcasamuppāda is to start downstream and follow it up river until we can cut it off at the source.

Bliss versus Banana

Let's look at how this works in a real situation.

During my early years of meditation training, I did many retreats at the Insight Meditation Society in Barre, Massachusetts. During one retreat I had several difficult days in a row.

Then one morning, the first sitting was deep and tranquil. The bell rang for breakfast and I stayed on my cushion. Fifteen minutes later I rose slowly and started walking meditation. I went out the front door. The dawn sky was indigo. The air was crisp and invigorating. It seemed the universe was conspiring to keep me in bliss.

After a while I directed my walking meditation toward the dining hall. As I entered, I noticed a banana peel on someone's plate. The retreat food was designed to be undistracting to meditation—it was bland. The sweetest thing they served was banana. In fact, they often ran out of bananas. And I was twenty or thirty minutes late already.

I couldn't see if there were any bananas left on the serving table across the room. Outwardly I looked serene as I pretended walking meditation through the dining hall. Inwardly I plotted how to slip past people and get to the table as quickly as possible.

To this day, I don't remember what happened next. The next thing I remember is sitting at a table with a bowl of oatmeal in front of me. There was half a banana in my hand and half in my mouth. The earlier expansiveness was gone. I thought ruefully, "I just traded enlightenment for a banana."

If I had been more skillful, I'd have simply noticed how the plot of my day had thickened. I'd have recognized the downstream flow from seeing a banana peel, to a pleasantness, to desire, to clinging (thinking about bananas), to a habitual pattern of trying to satisfy craving on its own terms, to a series of actions resulting in a banana in my mouth and a relatively dense consciousness.

Had I known the Buddha's guidance better, rather than falling into my habit of rueful self-criticism, I'd have just recognized where I was at that moment at the table, released the contraction, relaxed, and laughed at myself: "Caught again. Far out."

That return of mindfulness and sense of humor could have given rise to some of the bliss that I'd known earlier. Perhaps I'd have recognized that it had never left—it was waiting quietly beneath the rumble of desire and critique.

With this lighter, brighter awareness, the next time I saw a banana, I might have noticed my habitual tendency as it arose. I could have released it, relaxed, and smiled before it leapt into action. And as I got clearer and lighter, and better at recognizing that conditioned tendency, I might have recognized the clinging—the first thought—as it arose and released it right then.

In this way, with time and practice, I'd work my way upstream until I'd simply notice the banana and the pleasantness it triggered. I'd release, relax, and smile before the pleasantness flowed into desire. The day might have remained light and filled with ease.

The details of the plots of our days are different for each of us. But the underlying series of events is very predictable.

Craving

The strangest and most fantastic fact about negative emotions is that people actually worship them.

—P. D. Ouspensky

Not everyone is interested in getting out of the stream. Not everyone is interested in avoiding grief and sorrow. We hear songs about sorrow, loneliness, heartbreak, and longing (country, jazz, blues, rock—the genre doesn't matter). The singers say they want out of this pain. Listening carefully, it's not so clear. Some would rather milk it than be free of it. Some people find comfort in familiar discomfort. Or they may not realize it's possible to step out of the river.

But if we've had enough, if we've been through the cycle of ennui to the point where we're done, if we're tired of the thickening plot, if we've had enough of the downward course of the river and want relief, the Buddha said the place to begin is craving (taṇhā)—attraction and aversion. This is where it's easiest to step out of the river.

Far upstream from craving, events like formations and mentality-materiality are below normal awareness. It's difficult to work with things we can't see easily. And immediately upstream from craving, normal perceptions and feelings happen automatically. For example, as I write these words, I pause and look out my window. I see birds in the bird feeder, trees, early morning sunlight, and blue-gray sky. The scene is comforting and pleasant. I don't have control over what I see or how it feels. Perception and feeling tone just happen.

But craving is different. Craving may arise automatically, but I don't have to be carried downstream by it. Since the scene outside is pleasant, I'm tempted to stop and go outside. But I don't have to. If the scene were rainy, cold, and unpleasant, I might be tempted to turn away or close the shades. But it's not automatic. I have more control over what I do than what I see and feel.

If I just resist these temptations, I may gain control over my outward actions, but not over the temptation itself. It may spin around inside, causing discomfort.

The beginning of the temptation is craving—a slight tightening and leaning toward what I like or away from what I don't like. If I can experience this leaning clearly, I can relax it. The craving dissolves. The temptation evaporates. Without craving, my actions are not driven by compulsion or tinged with desire or aversion. The mind-heart remains light and clear.

In an interview with Bhante, I once asked, "Is it possible to have aversion without an object?"

He smiled and said, "Of course."

As our minds become open and calm, we may see desire or aversion that has no object. This is pure, free-floating taṇhā looking for some place to hang its hat. But most often, it's already hooked on an object before we see it clearly.

Working with craving (taṇhā) is important enough to be considered as a separate topic. So we'll look at it more deeply in the next chapter.

Thought

If we aren't able to release and relax taṇhā, it "gets past us" (it does more often than not). The next downstream event is clinging (upādāna). Remember, clinging always manifests as thought. Thought can arise very quickly, and all thought has some tension in it.

If the tension in upādāna is not relaxed, the river flows into habitual tendencies (bhava). With habitual tendency, thinking starts to proliferate. Thinking has even more tension in it.

There is a little taṇhā in each event in Dependent Origination. Taṇhā is everywhere in the river of causation. Getting out of the downward flow toward suffering requires releasing the tension.

Incessant thinking is the undoing of many meditators and would-be meditators as they struggle to get control of their runaway minds. But the struggle to stop the thinking puts more stress (taṇhā) into the river and makes thinking increase. The Buddha referred to this strategy as "crushing mind with mind." He said he tried it and it didn't work.[10]

The way to deal with mental proliferation is not force of will, but recognizing the taṇhā, releasing, relaxing, and smiling with good humor. Remember, without ease, waking up is impossible.

In Chapter 18 "No Thing Left: Seventh Jhāna" (see page 219), we'll look at some techniques for working with thinking. But for now it's important to note that all mental proliferation can be traced back to taṇhā. If we deal with the taṇhā, mental proliferation ceases. It's that simple. (It's not easy! But it *is* simple.)

Beyond the River

As our meditation practice matures, there is another more or less predictable series of events that we may encounter. These pick up where flow of Dependent Origination ended in suffering. They are a path of ascent rather than a river of descent. Unlike the downriver flow of events that can arise in a fraction of a second, these spread out over days, months, and years. These events unfold from relaxed and skillful effort, not from unconscious flow.

Let's take a look.

The descending flow of Dependent Origination ends in suffering. The ascending path begins in suffering. But the term the Buddha used is the more general *"dukkha"* rather than *"jarāmaraṇa."*

The word "dukkha" originally referred to a wheel with the axle hole slightly off center—it presses and grinds as it turns. Dukkha is often translated as "suffering," but its meaning is much wider, including everything from deep pain to subtle disquiet. Life in the conditioned world just doesn't work out, because nothing lasts. That doesn't mean life is nothing but suffering—only that life has some suffering in it.

A popular impression is that spiritual practice begins because of inspiration or vision. But most of us actually start to practice because something in our lives isn't working out. Maybe there's great distress. Or maybe everything looks fine, but life feels a little flat or empty. We're looking for some way to improve our quality of living. This sets us on the path.

This suffering can give rise to faith (*saddhā*). It may not be intuitively obvious that faith should arise out of suffering until we see it in action. Dukkha motivates us to try out a spiritual practice. If it works, we begin to trust it. We develop faith in it. So the faith the Buddha spoke of is not blind faith. It is verified faith: something we try and find helpful.

Faith leads to relief (*pāmojja*). We aren't free of suffering, but see that there might be a way to get some relief.

Relief then gives rise to joy (*pīti*).

Joy is a high-energy state that cannot last long. As it relaxes, it settles into a quieter tranquility (*passaddhi*) and happiness (*sukha*).

Tranquility and happiness allow for a deeply collected mind and heart (samādhi). The mind-heart becomes quite still and attentive.

The "higher path" of Dependent Origination *continues beyond the suffering in the first twelve steps*		
English	*Pāli*	*Other Translations*
Suffering	Dukkha	Suffering, Stress
Faith	Saddhā	Faith, Conviction
Gladness, Relief	Pāmojja	Joy, Gladness
Joy	Pīti	Rapture
Tranquility	Passaddhi	Serenity
Happiness	Sukha	Pleasure
Collectedness	Samādhi	Concentration
Knowledge and Vision of Things as They Are	Yathā Bhūtañā Nadassana	Knowledge and Vision of Things as They Actually (or Really) Are
Disenchantment	Nibbida	Disenchantment
Dispassion	Virāga	Dispassion, revulsion
Liberation	Vimutti	Emancipation, Release
Knowledge of Destruction of the Taints	Magga Phala	Ending of the Effluents, Knowledge of the Destruction of the Cankers

Samādhi allows us to see with greater and greater clarity how the conditioned world actually works. This is called "knowledge and vision of how things really are" (*yathā bhūtañā nadassana*).

Knowledge and vision gives rise to disenchantment (*nibbida*). "Disenchantment" sounds sweet—like a character in a Disney movie coming out from under the spell of an evil sorcerer. But the actual experience of disenchantment can be anything but sweet. All our efforts look futile. All our spiritual practices seem ineffectual. All our good intentions seem to have been for naught. Nothing seems to have worked out.

When I was training with Ajahn Tong in Thailand, I came into a huge bout of disenchantment without knowing what was going on. Every time I sat down to meditate, I'd burst out crying. There were no psychological stories around it—just diffuse despair and deep sobbing.

I went to a monk and described what was going on. He listened carefully and smiled. He said, "When I first hit that, I tried to run away. Everything seemed pointless. I ran across the rice fields and ran and ran. Then I gradually realized that there was no point in running and nowhere to run. Life was just how life was. So I stopped and went back to my kuti to meditate."

In the Christian tradition, St. John of the Cross called it "the dark night of the soul." Everything we know and understand falls apart, and a deeper knowing has not yet arisen. As dispiriting as this can be, unlike clinical depression, true spiritual disenchantment never leads to suicidal thoughts or the like. That too would be pointless.[11]

Disenchantment can be quite humbling. As we relax into it, we stop straining so hard. We continue to practice, but with less and less strain to get somewhere. There's no place to get to. We just practice for the sake of practice.

As disenchantment subsides and deepens, dispassion (*virāga*) can rise in its place. There's no pull toward or away from anything. It's quiet and still but not cold. In virāga, kindness is often the only thing that makes sense. Dispassion can be very sweet and peaceful.

Dispassion allows us to truly release not only our sense of self but even the desire to awaken. When dispassion is deep and full, we go into cessation (*nirodha*), nibbāna, and liberation (*vimutti*). Or rather, these just happen. We can't make them happen–they arise on their own.

When nibbāna and liberation are complete, we know they are complete. This is sometimes called "knowledge of the destruction of the taints" (*magga phala*). This means that there are no more disturbances in the mind-heart. All neurosis and imbalances are gone. Our mind-heart is clear and we can see that it is. We are fully awake.[12]

Circles and Chains

General books on Buddhism often describe Dependent Origination as a wheel or as the links in a chain. I haven't used these metaphors because the Buddha didn't. They can be confusing.

The metaphor of the wheel depicts various events as spokes on a wheel that turns round and round. But the Buddha's description of these events was linear, not circular. The first and the last events don't necessarily connect together. Suffering does not inevitably lead to ignorance. And the cessation of ignorance does not lead to suffering. So the metaphor of a river or linear tables seemed more appropriate than circular wheels.

The depiction of Dependent Origination as a wheel is a conflation of two closely related teachings. One is *saṃsāra,* which describes life as an endless cycle of suffering that has no clear beginning or ending. It is resolved only by "getting off the wheel." The other is paticcasamuppāda, which details how suffering arises. It's understandable that some people put them together.

The other traditional metaphor for Dependent Origination is a set of links on a chain. The Buddha never used this metaphor either. It does convey how strongly events are tied together. But it gives the misimpression that each link is a separate thing rather than just part of a current. It also implies that the downstream links pull the upstream links along. As we explore these phenomena in meditation, there is no sense of one pulling on another. It's just a flow.

In addition, the chain metaphor implies that all the links are similar in size and shape. Yet perception feels very different from hunger, which feels very different from opening the refrigerator.

Wisdom and Meditation

Paticcasamuppāda can be mind-boggling in its breadth and subtlety. A boggled mind is not conducive to either wisdom or meditation.

Nevertheless, the Buddha observed that the person who understands Dependent Origination directly from his or her own experience understands the *dhamma* (the way of awakening). And the person who is truly awake understands Dependent Origination. In fact, he used the word "wisdom" to refer specifically to "getting" Dependent Origination. We may use "wisdom" in a more general sense. But in the suttas, when he says "wisdom" he means seeing Dependent Origination.

So the Buddha developed a meditation practice finely tuned to cultivate direct encounter with the reality of paticcasamuppāda. In the next section, we'll explore this practice in detail. For now, it might be helpful to summarize three things that can make it simple rather than mind-boggling: (1) direct experience, (2) the question "How?," not "Why?" and (3) an uplifted mind.

Direct Experience

When the Buddha spoke of causal relationships between phenomena, he was pointing us toward our own direct experience, not toward intellectual analysis. His model was only intended to be a rough map to help guide our attention. A map of the river is not the river. What's crucial is our experience, not the map.

Recall from the previous chapter the insights about the khandhas. Body (rūpa) is a different khandha from feeling tone (vedanā), which is a different khandha from perception (sañña), which is a different khandha from formations (saṅkhāra), which is a different realm from consciousness (viññāṇa).

Dependent Origination shows how events relate to one another. But none is a substitute for another. Contact is contact and thinking is thinking. Thinking arises pretty far downstream. Direct experience arises further upstream.

The meditative process is one of deepening mindfulness, not thoughtfulness—awareness, not analysis.

How, Not Why

Therefore, in looking at your inner process, the important question is, "How is this unfolding?" not, "Why does it work this way?" It's more helpful to ask, "What's going on right now?" than "What will happen next?" or "What just happened?" or "Where does this fit the Buddha's model?"

The question "Why?" puts you downstream in an analytical mode. The question "How?" or "What's the process?" puts you upstream in direct experience.

Besides, there ultimately is no answer to why things work the way they do. Imagine sitting in the woods in the fall. If you are very attentive, you might be able to see a leaf detach from a tree. More likely, it'll catch your attention as it floats to the ground and comes to rest.

In all observations, you don't see gravity. You infer it intellectually, but it's not something you see. You can see how things happen, but not why. And even if you infer gravity is the cause, it begs the questions: "Why is there gravity?"

Asking why things happen is like asking why gravity pulls leaves off a tree or pulls water downhill. There is no reason you can grasp. It just does. All you can say is, "That's the way the universe works." The "Why?" is a mystery.

Similarly, you can see contact followed by feeling tone followed by craving. But you can't see why this is so.

In meditation, the question "How?" or "What's the process?" cultivates wisdom. The question "Why?" does not.

Uplifted Mind

To cultivate direct experience, it helps to have a mind-heart that is uplifted, clear, and relaxed. Mindfulness is receptive. It doesn't lean toward or away from anything. It just sees with balance and ease. A fruitful practice will cultivate a mind that is light and open, not a mind that is trying to grasp, analyze, or control.

For example, if we are plagued by runaway thoughts, trying hard to stop, analyze, or control them is futile. It's like fighting fire with gasoline: it puts more fuel into them. Instead, we can just let the thoughts go on their merry way. We let them be and shift our attention from the content of our thoughts to their feel and notice any tension in our mind and body. Then we can relax tensions without trying to control the thoughts. With relaxation and patience, the thoughts run out of gas. The mind-heart quiets itself.

Tension clouds the waters and thickens the soup—it makes the plots of our lives denser. Ease and relaxing allows us to savor without getting drawn into the thickness. We enjoy and flow on.

Remember, there is a bit of taṇhā in each link of Dependent Origination, in each bend of the river. So learning to work with it skillfully is important.

In the next chapter we'll look at taṇhā in everyday life. Relaxing it is the key to finding ways to thrive even in difficult times.

5

Thriving in Difficult Times: Relaxing Tightness

Imagine a prehuman ancestor—a furry, lemur-like creature living furtively in the primeval forest. He sees something pleasant—food or a potential sexual partner. A wired-in instinct focuses all his attention on it and prepares his body to move toward it. Then he sees something unpleasant—a predator. The primal instinct focuses all his faculties on it and prepares his body to get out of there.

This instinct gives him an evolutionary advantage. To be effective, the instinct must be fast. To be fast, it must be simple. To be simple, it doesn't figure out what to do about the food, mate, or predator. It merely says, "This is good, figure it out," or "This is bad, figure it out."

Notice that it directs attention outward onto the food, mate, or predator rather than inward onto how he feels about them. If he gets absorbed in how good it feels to see his potential mate, she may move on before his DNA gets a chance to reproduce. If he wastes time examining his fear of the predator, he and his DNA will get eaten. So this instinct is the opposite of introspection: it directs attention "out there" rather than "in here."

We humans have such an instinct. I don't have scientific evidence for its evolutionary origins, but it behaves as if these speculations are true. It is fast, simple, preverbal, and non-conceptual. It directs attention away from itself, and it narrows the scope of awareness to the object.

We have many names for it: "desire," "attraction," "attachment," "fixation," "craving," "repulsion," "fear," "anger," "disgust," "uptightness." It's the feeling that generates the thought, "I like it" or "I don't like it," "I want more" or "get me outta here." Yet the instinct itself is precognitive and arises so quickly that we can't control it. It just happens. It arises uninvited out of our neural wiring. Better labels for it might be "getting triggered," "having my buttons pushed, "getting hooked in," or even "the devil made me do it."

In the earliest Buddhist texts, it is called "*taṇhā*." Taṇhā is the Second Noble Truth. The First Truth says that suffering, dissatisfaction, or discomfort (dukkha) is inherent to life. The Second Truth says that the root of our experience of difficulty is this reflexive tightening (taṇhā). The Third Truth says we can release it and know well-being regardless of our circumstances. The Fourth counsels how to do this.

As we saw in the last chapter, taṇhā is also the eighth movement in the downstream flow of Dependent Origination. And there is a little taṇhā throughout the entire river.

The Buddha said that taṇhā is the place where we have the best opportunity to step out of the river as it flows toward suffering.

In short, releasing taṇhā is central to the Buddha's strategy for easing awake.[13]

In the "Path" section, we'll look in detail at how to work with taṇhā in meditation. But given the importance of taṇhā to understanding the entire Path, it would be helpful to know how to recognize and work with it in everyday life.

The question for everyday life is, "How do we thrive in difficult times?" The question isn't, "How do we survive, get by, or manage difficulty?" It's "How do we thrive amidst adversity—how do we navigate rough waters in ways that deepen our lives and open our hearts?" If we can thrive in difficult times, we can thrive in easy times as well.

Taṇhā—this reflexive tightening—is the key. It may be inherited, such as the startle reflex. Or it may be conditioned, such as learning to fear a particular situation. But whatever the case, it can be deceptively difficult to see since it directs our attention away from itself. So first we'll look at recognizing the tightening itself. Then we'll look briefly at dealing with what triggers it. And finally we'll look at the most crucial aspect: releasing it and relaxing until our lives feel enriched even during hard times.

Recognizing

We'll start with simply recognizing taṇhā.

Searching for this reflexive tightening is like my boys searching for Easter eggs when they were little. They'd run out into the yard and look under flowerpots, beneath rocks, and behind wooden boxes and find nothing. My wife and I had hidden the eggs in plain sight: a yellow egg in a bed of yellow flowers, a brown egg on the root of a tree, a blue egg on a blue toy truck in the sandbox, a green egg in a tuft of grass. They were all visible but placed where they'd blend in with the yard. In their excitement, my boys missed the obvious. But once they learned that the eggs were in plain sight, they stopped, looked more carefully, and began to see them everywhere.

The tightening is like that—it's always in plain sight, but its nature diverts our attention away from it. However, when we stop and look carefully, we begin to see it everywhere:

- A car swerves in front of you. Your hands tighten on the wheel.
- You're in a gentle, free-flowing conversation with a friend. Then her eyes cloud over and turn away. "Did I say something wrong?" you ask. She responds curtly, "No. But I have to go!" You've witnessed the unnamed tightening in her.
- You're talking on a cell phone as you cross the street. Without thinking, your eyes turn and look up and down the street as the reflex directs some awareness to check for traffic danger.
- Sitting in meditation, you realize you've been off fantasizing. Rather than Six-R and return to your object of meditation, you think "Oh, it's such a nice story. I'll just daydream a little longer." You're feeling how sweet taṇhā can be.
- You are sitting quietly in meditation. Suddenly you decide to get up. You've felt how subtle the discomfort of taṇhā can be.
- Complaining is always accompanied by inner tightening.
- I approached the grocery checkout lines with a dozen items in my cart. All the lines were long except one. A woman with an overflowing cart

headed toward it. My body tightened slightly as my pace picked up. I got to the empty lane a moment before the woman.

- I was considering going to bed when my wife said she was going to turn on the computer in the bedroom to check her email. I said, "I'll stretch out in the other room." She said, "That's okay. I don't want to push you out. I'll check tomorrow." This may sound like an open exchange. But had you been there, you would have noticed that my voice was a little pouty and my wife's was a little irritated. We were both a bit contracted in taṇhā.

- I picked up a ream of computer paper off the shelf in the office supply store. Then I roamed the aisles looking for something else to buy. "Maybe I need some pens…no, I have plenty. How about labels?… no, I've got more than enough. Maybe…" Then I recognized taṇhā as a vague urge to find something pleasant to buy. I relaxed, smiled, and headed for the checkout counter.

- The Dalai Lama described being driven from a hotel in Los Angeles to a conference center. Each day the route took him past blocks of electronic stores. He said, "Looking out the car window, I wanted things without even knowing what they were." He was feeling taṇhā.

This tightening feels like an urge, drive, or tug. It's uncomfortable. It gets our attention by creating tension and pushing us to do something. If there's nothing to do, we're left with an edginess begging for resolution.

The instinct to tighten and focus our attention may help in situations that resolve quickly or that require fast action—like an oncoming car. It's less help in complex, nuanced modern life. By narrowing our attention, we can get hooked on a detail rather than seeing the broader context.

To a greater or lesser degree, this instinct colors much of human experience.

Dealing with Triggers

Let's turn from how the instinct feels to what triggers it. There are many triggers. Some are obvious: relationship breakdown, job insecurity, disease, death of a loved one, children's difficulties, economic stress, political inanity, war. Some are less obvious: loneliness, annoyance, quiet worries, loss of meaning, purposelessness, yearning for something.

What do we do about these?

The instinct focuses our attention outward. Sometimes it's wise to deal with the world rather than withdrawing from it, to embrace the interdependent web and deal with issues on their own terms. If we're sick or injured, rather than just hoping and praying, we go to a doctor or health-care worker or consider diet, rest, or exercise. If our job is in trouble, we go talk to the boss, send out our resume, advance our education, or network. If a relationship is on the skids, we talk to the person, consult with a wise friend, find a counselor, or seek a support group. If we want something that is easy to obtain without harming anyone, we simply get it.

If this resolves the problem, great. We cure the disease, find a new job, resolve our kid's obstreperousness, or buy the music we wanted. However, there are times when there's no solution. We do what we can, but the difficulty lingers.

When I first moved to Sacramento a dozen years ago, my youngest son, Damon, was about to start his senior year in the charter high school he'd helped found and had poured his heart into. He and my wife, Erika, stayed in Massachusetts that year. I came out alone. Mostly it was okay. I missed them, but I was busy getting to know a new congregation and knew my family separation was temporary.

Still, Friday nights were hard. Fridays had been family time. We played board games, went to movies, or just hung out together. Now, as the twilight settled in on Fridays, my chest ached. I talked to them on the phone, but that wasn't the same. Sometimes the pangs of loneliness seemed intolerable.

Some difficulties resist being fixed. The disease may not have a cure. There may be no jobs around. We may not have the power to solve the political scene. The loved one who died isn't coming back. Our child's problems have no easy resolution.

What do we do then?

Three Strategies

There are three popular strategies for dealing with unsolvable problems: grab something, push something away, or space out. Let's look at each.

Grabbing

The first strategy is to grasp for things or become needy. Unresolved tightening can feel like hunger, thirst, or emptiness. We look for something to fill that void.

When I broke up with a girlfriend in college, I was upset and didn't know what to do, so I bought a Simon and Garfunkel record album: *Bridge over Troubled Waters*. It was comforting. Many people get into a pattern of shopping to feel better. Or they look for other experiences to distract them.

When I was in Sacramento that first year, sometimes I'd go to a movie to get through an empty evening.

A variant of this strategy is to get other people to do things for us. We try to control others as a way to handle our inner discomfort.

Sometimes this strategy is soothing. We relax. But if it doesn't address the true hunger, it has no lasting benefit.

Pushing Away

The second strategy for coping with intractable problems is the opposite. Rather than grasp for things or experiences, we push them away. We become irritable or angry. We've all seen this in others and felt it ourselves. We snap at people more easily, become less tolerant of foibles, lose our temper, criticize more readily. Things that used to roll off our backs get to us. Expressing this irritability may bleed off some of the tension. But if it doesn't solve the real problem, it doesn't lead us to well-being.

Spacing Out

The third strategy is to space out. "There is nothing I can do, so I just won't think about it." We stay busy or medicate ourselves with alcohol, drugs, or food or just don't pay attention to how lousy we feel. We numb out. This too can have short-term benefit and manage a short-term situation. But for long-term issues, it's disastrous.

Resilience

I was a psychotherapist for a dozen years. Most of my clients had been using these strategies until they stopped working. Listening to their stories, it didn't surprise me that they felt messed up. What surprised me was that they weren't locked up on the back ward of a psychiatric hospital. Given what most of us have lived through as children and adults, it's amazing that we are as healthy as we are.

The human spirit is incredibly resilient. It's amazing the depth of pain and suffering we can experience and come through with our hearts and minds open, supple, and alive.

But the thing that brings us down most quickly is isolation. When we aren't alone, our natural wisdom, compassion, and kindness flow even in difficult times.

There is one person whose good attention we need more than anyone else's. It's the one we spend the most time with day and night: ourselves. When we are busy grasping for things, being irritated with others, or spacing out, we're not truly present with ourselves. We've abandoned our hurt, loneliness, fear, or grief. We've abandoned ourselves.

Presence

If we want to thrive in difficult times, it is critical to learn to be present with ourselves more and more.

I remember one Friday night in my apartment. I talked to Erika and Damon on the phone. Then I thought about going to a movie, but that felt empty. I could have called someone in Sacramento, but that would not have been the same as seeing family. I put on music that both soothed and stimulated my loneliness. I began to pace around the apartment feeling more and more frantic, knowing there was no way to assuage the aching I was feeling. There was nowhere to run.

I stopped in my living room and stood still. I realized that at that very moment there were millions of people around the planet feeling as lonely as I. There were hundreds of millions grieving the deaths of love ones. There were countless people worried about their children, concerned about how they were going to make ends meet, frightened by a disease, or cowering before the threat of violence.

Most of us weren't doing anything wrong. Things don't always work out in life. We all die eventually.

Our society does us a disservice in trying to reassure us that we are captain of our ship, director of our fate, controller of our future. That's nuts. We have influence, but bad things happen to good people all the time.

Standing alone in my living room, I thought, "Oh yeah. Right. This is how life is sometimes. I'm not doing anything wrong. I'm not bad for feeling bad. Stuff happens."

I stopped running from the loneliness. I sat down in a chair and just felt it. I didn't try to talk myself into or out of anything. I was just present.

It didn't feel good. But at least I had myself. At least I had one attentive friend in the room: me. With this, the loneliness softened. It didn't go away, to be sure. But the tightness spread out. The heaviness lightened. I didn't have to fight it any more. And I began to feel moist, poignant, and life-filled rather than dry and barren.

Thriving

If we want to thrive in difficult times, it's important to learn to recognize this instinctual response on its own terms. It's not a thought. It's not a concept. It's a wired-in, preverbal, pre-conceptual biological reflex: a mental, emotional, or physical tightening. It focuses our mental faculties on finding a solution out there.

This instinct is simple and not very smart. If there's no solution, it doesn't let go. We lie awake at night worrying about our child, job, health, or relationship in an endless loop of repeating thoughts.

It's important to learn to see the inner holding directly. As we see it fully, it tends to relax. Or we can gently invite it to soften. It's like being with a child waking out of a nightmare. We don't try to talk the child out of the dream. We're just present in a heartful way. Similarly, we don't try to talk ourselves out of our own swirl of emotions or thoughts. We just stay present.

It's very simple. It's also very difficult because this runs counter to the instinct to focus out there. So it's important to be kind, gentle, and patient with ourselves.

As we relax this inner tautness, we won't start thriving overnight. But without that tension, the spinning emotions, thoughts, and feelings start to run out of gas. They begin to slow down a little.

With this, something deeply mysterious and deeply human begins to emerge. We notice a poignant well-being that's not dependent on fixing anything. We touch a wholeness that isn't based on things we try to control. Many people call this well-being "God," "the Divine," or "Spirit." Others call it "Human Essence" or "Buddha Nature." It makes no difference what we call it, because it is pre-verbal and pre-conceptual. We just note the elusive holding, open to it in a friendly way, and relax into it.

This doesn't make us transcend the world or space out into a different realm. But it does give us the courage, heart, patience, and intelligence to come back into this world and our lives more completely, doing what is reasonable for ourselves and our fellow creatures. This helps us to be with things as they are.

With this, we are truly on a path toward thriving even when the times are difficult. We find that we're not the small self we thought we were. Without the instinctual tightening of taṇhā, our sense of self starts to dissolve. This is the topic of the next chapter.

6

Chameleon: Selflessness

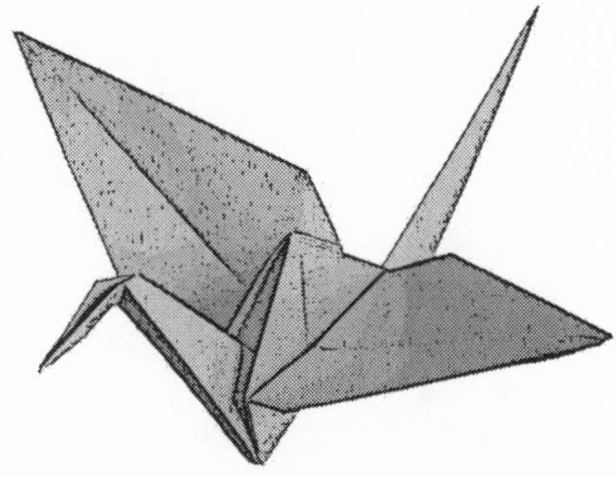

I stepped out from behind the pulpit carrying an origami crane. Earlier I had folded a large piece of colored paper to make the bird. Now I held it in my open palm high over my head so the two hundred people gathered in the room could see it clearly.

"I invite you to imagine you are this bird," I said. "Feel it from the inside. Project yourself into it. Become it."

I kept an eye on a clock in the back of the sanctuary. After twenty seconds I lowered my hand and carefully tore off the wings, pulled out the tail, ripped off the head, crumpled the body, and let the pieces fall to the floor.

There were audible gasps. Some people looked stricken. Some sat with tight lips and stony eyes.

"I'm sorry," I apologized. "Please reassure yourselves that all your limbs are intact. Relax. Take a breath."

After a moment, I went on. "This is a fascinating phenomenon, isn't it? We all knew we weren't that origami bird. Yet with about twenty seconds and an invitation to become the bird, many of us were able to identify with it enough that destroying it felt like an emotional or even physical assault. Fascinating."

We humans have a remarkable ability to imagine that we are what we aren't. We can imagine we are paper birds. We can imagine we are cars (some people describe a car accident as "Someone hit *me*" rather than "Someone hit *the car.*"). We can project our sense of self into cell phones, clothes, food, bodies, thoughts, feelings, ideas about the soul, beliefs, values, and more. If we made a list of everything we've ever experienced, there's probably somebody somewhere who has said of each, "This is me. This I am."

The question "Who am I?" has been contemplated since long before recorded history. Yet after all these millennia, we have no commonly agreed-upon answer. Perhaps the question is flawed. Perhaps we have no solid enduring self.

In one ancient text,[14] the Buddhist sage Nagasema tells King Milinda that self is like a chariot. "Where is the chariot?" he asks. "Is it in the wheel, the axle, the pole, the reins, the frame?" None of the parts contain the essence of chariot. "Chariot" is just a convention for this combination of non-chariot parts. The chariot's existence is completely dependent on elements that are not it. The chariot is said to be "empty" of chariot-ness.

So it is with self. Self is an arbitrary convention for a collection of items (skin, bones, feelings, thoughts, etc.), each of which lacks a self. Self is "empty" of self.

The Buddha went even further. At least with a chariot, there is common agreement as to what the parts are. But our sense of self is a transient phenomenon that waxes and wanes, latches onto one object then another, vanishes and arises again. He called the truth "*anattā*" or "non-self." He wasn't saying that we don't experience something called "self"—we obviously do. But it's a fluid illusion ultimately empty of substance.

And as with the origami crane, when we take this illusion personally, we suffer needlessly. The Buddha referred to this attachment with a litany: "This [phenomena] is me. This is mine. This is myself." He called this "ignorance" ("avijjā"). As we noted earlier, in the *suttas*, anytime he uses the word "ignorance," he's referring to this process of taking personally something that is inherently impersonal. We ignore or don't see a truth that is before us—in this case the truth of anattā or no independent self.

One of the aims of his teaching and meditation practice was to help people penetrate the trance of self and see the deeper reality: "This is not me. This is not mine. This is not myself."

In this chapter we'll explore this phenomenon of self, what it is, how we create it, some of the more convincing objects we mistakenly identify as self, and ways to break the trance. Since self is so deeply embedded in the

Western psychology of personality, we'll venture into that realm and then integrate it back into the core insight of selflessness (anattā).

However, the illusion probably would not have arisen if it served no useful function. So lest we throw the baby out with the bathwater, we'll start by looking at how a sense of self can be useful and is related to one of our greatest gifts.

Evolutionary Advantage

A highly developed sense of self can help synthesize a lot of information quickly. Consider two people standing before a saber-toothed tiger. The first person has little sense of self. He views the situation dispassionately: "This hungry carnivore is looking for a source of protein to assuage its instinctual appetite. He's eying my body to satisfy this urge. Let me consider what is the greater good—feeding the big kitty or getting away?"

The second person has a strong sense of self. His thoughts are focused, simple, and practical: "I want to live!"

Regardless of the philosophical merits of these two perspectives, the first person is more likely to be lunch for the beast while the second is more likely to pass his DNA on to the next generation. His way of thinking is more likely to survive.

A strong sense of self is also helpful in managing less dramatic situations. When I was a kid walking into the kitchen from the backyard, I had to remember to wipe the dirt off my sneakers, close the door, not let it slam, make sure the screen was latched so the mosquitoes didn't get in, wash my hands before I ate, and more. It was a lot to keep track of. But the sense of self helped process the situation quickly. All I had to do was remember, "I'm a good boy," and this shorthand reminded me of all I should do. That sense of self was a synthesis of all that information.

Human intelligence is more general than specific. We don't have a specific instinct that says, "I'm a body," "I'm these feelings," or "I'm a set of behaviors." We have a generalized capacity to identify with everything from origami birds to cars to cell phones to clothes to bodies to memories.

As we mature spiritually and cultivate a mind-heart that is quiet, attentive, relaxed, and engaged, we find more effective ways to process information quickly. Rather than continuing to be helpful, a strong sense of self becomes a distortion of clearer seeing. With spiritual maturity, self-sense and its clumsiness lighten and fade into selflessness.

Empathy

There's another reason self-sense may linger. Even in a highly evolved saint, it's related to one of our greatest gifts: empathy.

When we empathize with another person, we experience them as if we were them. We say, "I feel your pain." We say, "I'm sorry for your loss," meaning, "I feel sorrow inside for the loss I see you have gone through."

Empathy is wired into us. Scientists describe a category of nerve cells called "mirror neurons" that fire in response to seeing expressions or movements in someone else.

For example, when we frown, a particular pattern of neurons fire in our brain. When we see someone else frown, our mirror neurons can trigger a similar pattern—our neural physiology mirrors inside us what we see in another. The same happens when we see a smile or any intentional movement—we experience a neural-physical response as if we had smiled or moved. We can literally feel inside what we see in another. This is why we tend to frown when we see a frown, yawn when we see someone yawn, laugh when we hear a laugh, or open our mouths wide when we have a spoon full of food and want the baby to open her mouth wide.

The Dalai Lama said that empathy is the foundation of ethical behavior. Our capacity to empathize helps us know what is morally right or wrong in how we treat one another. It's the source of the "golden rule" found in all religious traditions: "Do unto others what you would have them do unto you."

This is undoubtedly a good thing. Yet the line between empathy and identification is thin. It's one thing to resonate with someone's experience or to imagine what an inanimate object might feel if it were animate. It's another to slip over the line and think we are the person or object. Yet we have great talent for sliding over that line.

Chameleon

Let's take a look at what happens when we slide from empathy into identification. The process is both fascinating and mysterious. It looks simple: We experience a sight, sensation, or thought and say in effect, "I am that." Our minds coalesce around a perception. Like a chameleon, we take our identity from our environment.

While it's easy to describe the process, it's harder to figure out why we do it. It's as if the eye sees something—let's say a tree—and the eye decides it must be the tree because that is what it sees. The eye cannot see itself directly, so it assumes it is what it sees. The subject (eye) sees an object (tree) and assumes the subject is the object.

It's bizarre: we cannot be what we experience any more than a hand can grasp itself. A hand can grasp an orange. The hand isn't the orange. Similarly, anything we perceive is felt by something that isn't what is perceived. The subject cannot be the object. But we imagine we are the object all the time.

This identification makes our self-sense fluid and chameleon-like. Consider self-sense in different situations: playing with a child; reviewing our job performance with the boss; hiking in the mountains; watching an action movie; dreaming of flying; getting lost in a big city; talking to a pet; feeling heavy emotions like fear, anger, or grief; or feeling light emotions like joy, love, and fun. Our sense of self varies in strength, tone, and texture. We may *think* it's solid, but it shifts throughout the day.

Mountains and Traffic

The dream of my life
Is to lie down by a slow river
And stare at the light in the trees—
To learn something by being nothing
A little while but the rich
Lens of attention.

—Mary Oliver, *Entering the Kingdom*

One of the places where my sense of self becomes light is hiking in higher altitudes. Above eight or nine thousand feet, with wilderness, huge mountains, clear air, and boundless sky, the issues and strain in my life seem trivial compared to the bliss of just being alive on this lovely planet. I melt into selflessness.

Once I was driving through the Sierra foothills toward the higher mountains. I was feeling some of that bliss as I was just present with the road and the forest.

Ahead I noticed a stoplight. There were two lanes going in my direction. The three cars ahead of me stopped in the same lane. So I pulled into the empty lane—I didn't want to get caught behind a slowpoke.

Waiting at the stop line, I noticed that the two lanes merged a quarter of a mile ahead. So when the light turned green, I gave my car a little extra gas to get ahead. The first guy in the next lane had the same idea. His foot was heavier than mine.

I was annoyed to see him get ahead of me. But I thought, "If he wants to be childish, I'll let him have his way." I felt elevated in my forbearance.

As we came to the merge, the second car began to nudge up. I pretended not to notice. With seeming indifference, I squeezed him out. We fell into single file with me in the number-two slot.

Then I realized that my spacious bliss had been supplanted by calculations of speed and distance, and impressive inner monologues rationalizing my competitiveness.

I recognized all this so clearly that the swirl of thinking released. I relaxed and smiled at my foolishness.

Some spaciousness and well-being returned…until the next stoplight. I didn't want to get into that competitiveness and rationalizing, but years of practice had grown strong neural pathways in my brain. Like Pavlov's dog, cars and a red light triggered this sequence of thinking, calculating, explaining, and rationalizing.

However, the more I observed this inner drama, let it be, relaxed, and smiled, the more it seemed like a mechanical, neural reflex—a conditioned pattern. *I* wasn't *doing* anything. I wasn't driving along happily wondering how I could make my mind dense and tight. The yammering just arose on its own.

If I had used willpower to stop the yammering, it would have created an even denser self-sense. This thicker version would have been even more spiritually pretentious and obnoxious.

Instead, I just observed with openness, curiosity, and humor.

If we want the lightness, clarity, and ease of selflessness, we neither indulge nor fight our patterns. We simply recognize, release, relax, smile, and send out uplifting energy. With patience and kindness, our patterns start to run out of gas. But it takes time. In the process, we're less identified with a conditioned reflex. Our sense of self thins out a little.

Private and Enduring

Let's turn from the process of identification to the objects with which we identify.

As noted earlier, we are capable of identifying with almost anything we experience. But some objects are more convincing than others. An experience that is public and transient is less compelling than one that is private and enduring.

Let's go back to the origami bird. It was both public and transient: It was public in that it was shared by two hundred people who saw the same bird. Self-sense likes to be special and unique. It was transient in that it was short-lived. The two hundred people had been aware and conscious for years before seeing the bird and remained conscious and aware after it had been torn apart.

So while it was surprisingly easy to identify with the paper construct, it was easy to break the identification with a little reflection.

But there are many experiences that are more private. Sensations, thoughts, feelings, personal beliefs, and memories can be vivid and powerful yet relatively invisible to others. So when we take these personally, it's more compelling. If an experience is both private and enduring, it's even easier to believe, "This is me. This I am."

For example, if a child is mistreated occasionally, he'll have a transient experience. If he talks about it to a sympathetic person, it is somewhat public. He says, "I *feel* bad." But if he's mistreated often and has no sympathetic ear, it will be long lasting and private. He'll say, "I *am* bad."

If an adult feels sad and isolated upon occasion, she'll say, "I *feel* lonely." If she feels isolated most of the time, she says, "I *am* lonely."

Recurring, private feelings and thoughts more easily fuse with self-sense. Since they happen a lot, we believe they must be what we are.

Ironically, we are usually at least partially unconscious of this identification. If the woman consciously said, "I am loneliness," she'd realize that the statement was absurd. She's not loneliness—she's someone experiencing loneliness. Yet without being fully conscious of what she's doing, she may organize her day as if she were loneliness incarnate. To deeply identify with an experience requires not being totally aware that we're doing it.

False Self

To make this process even more complex, we often don't identify directly with the feelings or thoughts. Sometimes we identify with reactions we have to them. Consider the boy feeling upset and the woman feeling lonely. The boy might find the upset and the thought, "I am bad," to be intolerable. So he projects the thought onto others: "They're bad, and I'm better than them." This bit of narcissistic inflation covers the pain. The woman might find the loneliness intolerable. So she imagines she is a spiritual adept who has evolved beyond the need for human support. She identifies with a persona that doesn't have to deal with loneliness.

None of us makes these adaptations easily. But when our natural needs are frustrated too often, we find some means of compromise. The influential psychiatrist D. W. Winnicott[15] calls these compromises the "false self." The boy's false self is, "I'm better than them." The woman's false self is, "I'm holier than thou."

There are many different kinds of adaptations we make. Traditional psychology studies these maneuvers. It calls them "personality," "character structure," "neurosis," "ego ideals," and so forth.

Some spiritual practices leverage our propensity for identification by using affirmations that replace a negative self-identity with a positive one. Rather than unconsciously say, "I am a miserable wretch," we consciously say, "I am a loving child of the universe." The fact that this can be uplifting underscores the power of this identification mechanism.

If affirmations help dissolve old identifications, they can be helpful. But if they just cover negative feelings with positive images, they create a thicker, more complicated sense of self.

Healing ourselves psychologically and waking up spiritually involve sorting through these layers of thoughts and feelings. Let's look at what's involved in easing out of these entanglements and waking up to simple truth.

Real Self

For D. W. Winnicott, beneath the false self is the "real self."[16] The real self consists of the natural, biologically based feelings that arise spontaneously in a healthy human: hunger, sex drive, love, yearning for contact, and so forth. The real self also includes feelings that arise when these natural needs aren't met. These feelings aren't always pretty. When our needs are frustrated, we might feel sadness, anger, hurt, pain, grief, or rage.

The false self is what we experience when our real needs are overwhelmed to the point that we fool ourselves into thinking we don't feel what we feel. The "real self" is what we experience when we don't fool ourselves. It is the organism's uncompromised experience.

Psychotherapy may help us de-identify with this false self and identify with our "real" self. Awareness is crucial to this process. The unconscious wall built around repressed feelings is broken down, and we feel more. As we become better able to tolerate the feelings that arise when our needs aren't met, we're more able simply to be with what we feel rather than fool ourselves into thinking we aren't hurt. As we become more aware of our basic drives, we become more adept at satisfying them. The false self of adaptation and compromise fades. We identify with the natural body and its emotions. From the traditional psychological perspective, the identification of "self" with body-instinctual processes is the culmination of emotional healing.[17]

I-ness

Is identification with the natural body the end of the line? Some people find the gradual freedom from the tyranny of the false self is such a relief that they're delighted. They seek nothing more.

Others of a more contemplative bent don't stop here. They explore this "real self" and its simple drives and needs. "If I am this mind-body process, what is it exactly?" "Who am I really?"

If we think, "I am this body," there is a problem. Almost every molecule in our body is replaced at least once every seven years. Our bodies recycle themselves with the environment. Even our capacities change. For example, when I was younger I could run for miles. Today, a knee injury makes it difficult for me to run for more than fifty yards or walk on hard surfaces for more than half an hour. If we are our bodies, we are different beings than we were a few years ago. But it doesn't feel that way—we feel we're the same person.

If we think, "I am my thoughts. I am my history. I am the sum total of my memories," there's a problem here as well. I used to think my father was pretty great. Then I thought he was a borderline psychotic. Then I thought he was just an injured heart stumbling through life. Our memories today aren't the same as our memories of a few years ago. History is an interpretation, and the interpretation drifts. If we are our memories and history, then we're a different being than we were a few years ago. But it doesn't feel that way. We feel like the same person.

And so it is with any mind-body process we might try to identify with. Feelings come and go. Aspirations and worries change. Failures and triumphs arise and pass. If we identify with any of these processes, then we're a different person each day. But it doesn't feel that way—we feel like the same person.

We may see a deeper sense of self that lies beyond these processes. For lack of a better term, we could call it "I-ness." It's not the false or real self.

It's neither an adaptation to frustrated needs nor simple body feelings. We may notice a sense of self independent of these other forces. This I-ness is quiet but enduring. It's been called "soul," "Higher Self," "essence," and "inner self."

As our self-identification shifts away from body and instinctual processes to I-ness, we've left the realm of traditional Western psychology. Psychology is suspicious of the claim of anything like I-ness. It sounds too metaphysical. And I-ness is difficult to weigh and measure. There are many strategies for testing and measuring false and real selves. But I-ness is subtle.

There is a more serious reservation traditional psychology has about I-ness. The false self would like to believe that it's above ordinary feelings and body needs. It uses repression, dissociation, projection, and other mechanisms to deny feelings. To downplay the importance of body-based experience sounds suspiciously like dissociation. If we stop identifying with our anger, aren't we just shoving it under the carpet and strengthening a false self?

But the real shift of attention to I-ness isn't through repression or denial. We make no attempt to deny feelings. We open and embrace the sensations that arise inside without taking them so personally. We deal with them openly without so much fanfare. They lose their grip on our identity.

> *The seeker is he who is in search of himself.*
>
> *Give up all questions except one: "Who am I?" After all, the only fact you are sure of is that you are. The "I am" is certain. The "I am this" is not. Struggle to find out what you are not.*
>
> *Discover all that you are not—body, feelings, thoughts, time, space, this or that—nothing, concrete or abstract, which you perceive can be you. The very act of perceiving shows that you are not what you perceive.*
>
> *The clearer you understand that on the level of mind you can be described in negative terms only, the quicker will you come to the end of your search and realize that you are the limitless being.*
>
> —Sri Nisargadatta

Process

Have we reached the end of the line? Have we found the true self behind the false and real selves? Is this sense of I-ness who I truly am?

Perhaps we don't find this totally satisfying. For one thing, we still look like chameleons as we identify first with the false self, then the real self, and now I-ness.

Furthermore, I-ness is elusive. If we try to fix our attention on it, it slips away unless the mind is very still. But it is observable. If we sit quietly enough, we can begin to sense it directly. This raises the question, "Who is the I who experiences this I-ness?" If I-ness is something we can experience, how can it be the one who is experiencing it? Can we be both the observer and the observed, both the subject and the object?

There is one last place where we can turn our attention. We can set aside the question of who is identifying with what, and look at the process of identification itself. What do we notice when we quietly observe this process?

The most obvious thing we see is that we identify a lot. Much of our idle thought takes the form of the mind trying to define itself. But identifying does stop at times. When we're truly open, moments arise containing no grasping or identifying. During those moments, there is no sense of self or other. As we watch the sunset from the mountaintop at the end of a long hike, we may feel so peaceful and satisfied that there's not a whisper of "I am that" or "I am not that." There's just is-ness which is no longer divided into me and not me. Self-sense fades—at least until the process of identification starts up again.

Does this mean that the sense of self *is* the experience of identification? Is "self" just another word for identification? Is self a verb rather than a noun: "selfing" rather than "self"? Selfhood is born in the process of identification. Maybe the attempt to find "self" has been focused in the wrong place. We keep looking at what "I" identifies with and trying to decide if it's the true self. The true "me" may not be a thing so much as a process: the process of identifying.

Can there be identification without a separate self who is identifying? Can identification just arise out of nowhere? Is there really an eye (I) or just seeing? Is there some separate thing identifying, or is there just the grasping of identification?

The Buddha encouraged us to look directly at the process of experience: not *why* things happen (that's philosophical speculation) but *how* things happen (the process). And the best tool for clarifying our observation is meditation practice—the topic of the next section.

Proving Nonexistence

Before moving on, let's pause for a moment and notice how difficult it is to logically prove the nonexistence of anything.

For example, imagine our neighbor is convinced we have elves in our closet. We tell him, "There's no such thing as elves and certainly not in the closet."

He smiles and says, "I understand. You just want to keep them to yourself."

We invite him to come look. When he finds none he says, "You probably hid them in the attic before inviting me over."

"Search the house from roof ridge to basement floor," we say.

He looks behind every door, under every bed, inside every drawer, beneath every rug, behind every book, and in every nook and cranny. Afterward he concludes, "Just shows how quickly elves slip from room to room every time I turn my back."

No matter what we do or say, he's never convinced, because not finding evidence does not mean they don't exist, only that he hasn't found the evidence. They may exist someplace else.

Self-sense is like an elf. After thousands of years of contemplation, humanity hasn't been able to pin it down. But it's such a deeply ingrained concept that finding no evidence isn't totally convincing that it doesn't exist.

Six Sets of Six

Nevertheless, doing a thorough search can weaken our conviction. So the Buddha encouraged looking for self everywhere from the rafters to the basement floor.

In the "Chachakka Sutta" (*Majjhima Nikaya* 148), [18] he catalogs every kind of phenomenon in Dependent Origination from the six sense bases to craving. With each phenomenon he asks, "Is there a self here? What happens when we think there is? What happens when we see there is not? How do we get fooled? How do we get free?"

For example, verse 10 begins: "If anyone says, 'The eye is self,' that is not tenable. The rise and fall of the eye are discerned, and since its rise and fall are discerned, it would follow: 'My self rises and falls.' That is why it is not tenable for anyone to say, 'The eye is self.' Thus the eye is not self. If anyone says, 'Ears are self,' that is not tenable..." and so on through all six internal sense bases (eye, ear, nose, tongue, skin, and mind), the six external sense bases (sights, sounds, odors, flavors, touch sensations, and thoughts), the six consciousnesses (eye-consciousness, ear-consciousness, etc.), the six "contacts" (eye-contact, ear-contact, etc.), feeling tone (pleasant, unpleasant, and neutral), and craving (grasping and aversion).

From the perspective of popular culture, the "Chachakka Sutta" is tedious and repetitive. Most translations use ellipses to cut out as much of the repetition as possible. Listening to the entire sutta read out loud can take an hour!

Nevertheless, if we stay open and present, reading or listening to the whole sutta can weaken our identification. Intellectually we know that our self is not our eyeballs or sights or seeing or feeling or grasping. By going through the entire list, we may start to take these phenomena less personally.

When Self Ceases

Cutting the last traces of self-sense requires more than looking at the various parts of self or the various experiences we identify as self. It requires seeing clearly the process of how self arises. To do this the Buddha recommended meditation.

As the practice deepens, the mind-heart gets quieter. Sensory and mental distractions become sparse. Each phenomenon can be seen from the first flicker of its arising until its complete disappearance. The flow of experience appears less personal and more mechanical.

In the seventh jhāna,[19] there may still be a sense of I-ness observing the flow. But it is easier to observe the observing I-ness. Awareness turns back on itself. The "eye" does see the "I." This is called "pure consciousness" because there are no objects of consciousness other than consciousness itself.

Subjectively, the distance between observer and observed gets smaller and smaller until they blend together. There's just the flow of experience. No observer. No observed. Just phenomena arising and passing. No self. No god. Just the interactions, arising and passing.

This is difficult to put into words because language is so embedded with the concept of self that anything we say implies a self. Our syntax demands a subject and object. However, beyond thought and language there is the experience of subject and object being the same thing.

In this subtle flow, a tension may arise, and with it, a sense, "I am watching something." For many people, the sense of "I" resides in the middle of the head behind the eyes. From there we seem to look at the world or "down" into our body. For other people, the sense of "I" may reside lower in the body—maybe as far down as the heart area.

But wherever it is located, if we mindfully attend the sensation itself, we see a subtle tension. Feeling it clearly is often enough for it to release. As this tightness softens, I-ness fades.

There is no "I" creating the tension. Rather the tension arises and gives birth to I-ness. When it fades, self-sense evaporates.

And when mind-heart comes into complete balance, we wake up. Attachment to self is severed completely.

There is no way to force this awakening, because force creates tension, and tension is the core of self-sense, the core of I-ness. But we can relax into it when the mind-heart is clear, relaxed, and attentive. Then there is just the flow of experience. And none of it is personal.

Taking things personally is a great hindrance—it blocks clearly seeing how things really are. It hinders our progress toward awakening. Yet hindrances of all kinds can help us pinpoint where we need to bring more mindfulness. This is the topic of the next chapter.

The rabbi came down to the altar and began beating his chest, "I'm nobody, I'm nobody, I'm nobody."

The cantor knelt down next to the rabbi and began beating his chest, "I'm nobody, I'm nobody, I'm nobody."

The janitor saw them and knelt down next to them and began beating his chest, "I'm nobody, I'm nobody, I'm nobody."

The cantor turned to the rabbi and said, "Look who thinks he's nobody."

7

Hindrances Are Your Friends

Every morning a new arrival.

A joy, a depression, a meanness,
some momentary awareness comes
as an unexpected visitor.

Welcome and entertain them all!
Even if they're a crowd of sorrows,
who violently sweep your house
empty of its furniture,
still, treat each guest honorably.
He may be clearing you out
for some new delight.

The dark thought, the shame, the malice,
meet them at the door laughing,
and invite them in.

Be grateful for whoever comes,
because each has been sent
as a guide from beyond.

—Rumi

In my late twenties, I spent five months hitchhiking around the United States and Mexico. While I was staying in a spiritual community high in the mountains of northern New Mexico, a couple, Mark and Pat, approached me. They planned to get married, knew I was a minister, and hoped I'd officiate. I agreed. As we made plans, Mark told me a story from their relationship.

Several months earlier, the community had created a Kali ceremony. Kali Durga is a Hindu Goddess. She's portrayed as a Medusa's Medusa with snakes for hair, human skulls for a necklace, and blood dripping from her fangs. However, to the pure hearted, she appears as a beautiful, radiant Goddess. Kali loves to devour impurities. If we try to hold on to ours, she seems like a monster. If we are free of attachments, she appears radiant.

The Kali ceremony included a late-night bonfire in a mountain meadow, Sanskrit chanting, and an invitation to offer Kali something about themselves that they didn't want any more.

Mark was inclined toward jealousy. He knew it was irrational and created difficulty, but he couldn't shake the feeling when it arose. So he symbolically threw his jealousy into the fire and asked Kali to remove it from him. He didn't say anything to Pat.

The next day she started an affair with another man. Mark was shocked. He didn't say or do anything overt. But over the next several days, his jealousy rose to a fevered pitch. It was driving him nuts. He became so overwhelmed that he couldn't hold onto it any longer. He released it—let it go entirely.

The next day Pat lost interest in the other man and came back to him. A few months later, they decided to get married.

He said, "The moral of the story is, don't mess with Kali. If you really want to change, she's a great help. But if you aren't committed, watch out. If you secretly try to hold on, she'll rip you apart."

Prevalence

In Buddhism, hindrances are the functional equivalent of Kali. There are differences, though. Kali is dramatic; hindrances can be fierce or they can be a whisper encouraging us to mosey off the path. Kali is scary; some hindrances are just beguiling. And Kali comes by invitation only, while hindrances feel free to drop in uninvited—they may walk into our lives unsolicited.

Yet Kali and hindrances both go after our weaknesses, and both have a dark side and a bright side.

In Pāli, the language of the suttas, the term for hindrance is "*nīvaraṇa*." Nīvaraṇa literally means "covering"—it covers something valuable. This is the dark side, the obstruction.

The bright side is that the hindrances show us exactly where to look for wisdom and guidance. They effectively say, "It's right here. Just take a look under this cover." In this way they are friends and allies.

Hindrances can be thought of as a personal trainer. They know us well—perhaps better than we know ourselves. Like a true friend, they don't care what we think of them. They have no ego. They will show us what we need to attend to whether we like it or not.

If we are deeply committed to our spiritual growth, we welcome hindrances. If we aren't so committed, if our faith in ourselves is weak or if we are more interested in superficial happiness than deep happiness, then hindrances are a nuisance. And if we are merely confused, it's all too easy to mistake these friends for enemies.

We all have places where we hold on or hold back. No matter how strong our commitment, we can expect many hindrances to visit us.

In fact, on the eve of enlightenment, the Buddha had a hindrance attack. He sat down under the Bodhi tree determined not to move until he woke up completely. He was assailed by ten thousand demons. Then he was assailed by ten thousand seductive maidens. Then Mara—a sophisticated trickster—tried to lure him away.

So if we feel burdened by many obstacles, it helps to know that the Buddha had to deal with them as well—we are in good company.

In fact, long after the Buddha's enlightenment, Mara kept visiting him. "I see you," the Buddha said to Mara. The implication is that hindrances appear even to an enlightened being. The difference is that he saw their nature immediately and was not thrown off by them.

Unless we imagine we should be in better shape than the Buddha, the presence of hindrances is a normal part of living and an expected part of spiritual practice.

Let's take a closer look.

Chatter

A common example of a hindrance is a chatty mind. We sit down to meditate or enjoy a sunset and find ourselves thinking about a problem at work, a fight with our partner, or an inanity like a grocery list. We think, "If my mind would just shut up, I could enjoy this quiet moment." The most common reason non-meditators say they don't meditate is that they can't stop their minds from thinking all the time.

A traditional image of the mind is a bunch of drunken monkeys stung by bees—they swing from branch to branch in uncontrolled yelling. I prefer the metaphor of coyotes howling at the moon—they joyfully party through the night. Mind chatter seems to be an obstacle to peace of mind.

Busy mind is only one hindrance; there is an infinite variety. We each have ones exquisitely designed just for us—they are tailored to our temperament. They know just where to get us.

This is because they arise out of us. They may seem to hop over the fence and creep in the backdoor, but in truth all hindrances are homegrown. They are a reflection of our blind spots, tightness, holdings, and confusion.

Big Five

Despite their infinite variety, the Buddhist literature gives special attention to five hindrances: desire, aversion, agitation, sloth and torpor, and doubt. These show up often in most people, so it is worthwhile to keep an eye out for them. We can expect to have to deal with one or two or all five of them.

Desire

There are only two tragedies in life: one is not getting what one wants, and the other is getting it.

—Oscar Wilde

Desire is a move toward something. The mind wants to shrink-wrap around it and hold on. Desire comes in many flavors: wanting, greed, pining, lust, grasping, envy, and more. The object of desire can be almost anything, from food to sex to good books to wonderful experiences.

Not all desires are problematic. The desire to be kinder, more generous, or more awake can move us in a good direction. Desires such as these are sometimes called *chanda* or *dhammachanda*, which means "wholesome desire." However, to enter nibbāna or to fully awaken, even these must be released.

When a strong desire arises, it's helpful to see it clearly, then release it and relax and move on. Indulging desires or dwelling on them gives them more energy.

Aversion

Aversion is a negative desire—a desire to not have something like balding, obsessive thinking, or physical pain. It too comes in many flavors: dislike, anger, hatred, annoyance, irritation, boredom, ill will, and more.

The rule is, "We get what we put our energy into." If we put energy into holding a desire, it will get stronger. If we put energy into pushing away an aversion, it will get stronger. With aversion, it is important not to push it away or try to control it. See it, let it be, and relax. As we develop a little more equanimity toward aversion, it will begin to fade on its own.

Sloth and Torpor

Sloth is an absence of energy. We feel tired or lethargic. The body may feel heavy or weary. Torpor is a loss of interest. The mind drifts in a dream-like state without clearly seeing anything. Together, sloth and torpor can feel like slogging through mud.

It is important to notice that the mind actually contracts in sloth and torpor. It gets tight and dense. This may not be obvious at first because sloth and torpor make perception fuzzy.

The antidote is usually to bring in some more energy, curiosity, or joy to enliven the mind-body system. However, if the root problem is being physically depleted, it may be best to take a nap.

Agitation

Agitation is usually the result of too much energy or, conversely, not enough equanimity, tranquility, or collectedness. The mind-heart get scattered in several directions at once. This can show up as irritability, anxiety, worry, restlessness, and more.

The mistake some people make is try to bring the mind under control. This is like trying to beat a hive of bees into submission: it rarely works. It puts more energy into a swarm that already has too much.

It's more helpful to feel the tension within the agitation and invite it to soften. Soothing the mind is more effective than trying to force it into submission.

Doubt

Doubt is lack of faith or confidence in our path or ourselves. There are times when it is healthy to question—it can lead to deeper investigation and insight. But doubt can also be a more generalized worry with no productive strategy. Investigation tends to bring clearer energy, while doubt is more of a cloud in the mind-heart.

Mindfulness

Notice that chatty mind is not among these five hindrances. However, excessive thinking can be a symptom of any of them. If the hindrance is desire, thoughts tend to be, "I want this," "I'd like a little more of that," "Wouldn't it be nicer if…," or "It was better when…" If the hindrance is aversion, thoughts are more likely to be, "I don't like it when this happens," "I wish he'd go away," "If only she wouldn't do that, things would be better," or "Why does this always happen to me?" If the hindrance is sloth and torpor, the thoughts might be, "Oh well, now where was I…," "I think I'll just rest a little," or "Nothing really matters anyway." If the hindrance is agitation, there may be lots of thoughts going in lots of different directions. And if the hindrance is doubt, the thoughts may be, "Am I doing this right?," "I always get things wrong," "This seems to be going well, but it can't be that easy," or "I'm not sure my teacher knows what's right for me."

Complex thoughts can point to a simple hindrance. Excessive thinking itself is not among the big five, because it is too far down the chain of causation in Dependent Origination.

As we saw in earlier chapters, habitual thought patterns (bhava) don't arise unless there is clinging (upādāna). And clinging doesn't arise unless there is craving (taṇhā—desire, aversion, or confusion). And craving doesn't arise without a feeling tone (vedanā—pleasant, unpleasant, or neutral feeling). And feeling tone doesn't arise without contact (phassa—physical or mental sensations).

The classical hindrances do not include mind chatter because in the flow of Dependent Origination, there are many things that come before it—too many dominos have already fallen.

If our mindfulness is strong, then we notice the preceding phenomena long before they develop into mind chatter. We see the desire or aversion and release the tension in it before we identify with it and start thinking about it. Or we notice the pleasant or unpleasant feeling tone and release the tension before it gives rise to liking or disliking.

However, when mindfulness is weak, we may find ourselves lost in thought or unbalanced actions.

P. D. Ouspensky, a student of the Russian mystic Gurdjieff, was once walking down the streets of Paris when he decided he would remain mindful from then on. A few minutes later he noticed his favorite tobacco shop. Three days later he remembered his determination to be mindful.

A lapse in mindfulness is the common thread that runs through all hindrances. Hindrances show us precisely where our mindfulness needs strengthening. This is what makes them so annoying. And this is what makes them so helpful.

As the Ouspensky story illustrates, sheer determination to be mindful is generally not helpful. Some intention can help mindfulness, to be sure. But too much effort causes agitation and intensified thinking!

On the other hand, ignoring a hindrance or trying to get rid of it is like throwing the proverbial baby out with the bathwater.

So it is helpful to remember that hindrances, obstacles, and distractions cover things up that may be very helpful. The trick is to figure out how to see what the hindrance is hiding.

When we come to the "Path" section of this book, particularly the chapter "The Six Rs," we'll look at ways to let hindrances make us wiser.

But before we get to that, we should look straight at the topic of suffering. Suffering in subtle and not-so-subtle forms shows up in hindrances and in other places in life. Finding a balanced way to deal with life's inevitable suffering is a key to happiness.

8

Be Kind, Pay Attention, Relax: A Blue-Collar Hologram

If dukkha (suffering or dissatisfaction) is the disease and we are the patients, the Buddha's diagnosis is sobering: the illness is incurable. Dissatisfaction is inherent in the relative world in which we live. It's unavoidable.

Since we can't get rid of the malady, his cure was to get rid of the patient. If there is no one who suffers, there is no more suffering.

This elegant solution is not appealing to most people. They would rather fix the disease or fix themselves. Few are enthusiastic about getting rid of themselves. They may even wonder, "If I get rid of myself, won't I still have the 'I' that got rid of me?" Paradox abounds.

So the Buddha's diagnosis went further: he said this self that we are so fond of (even though it gives us trouble) is a trance. It arises out of a confusion that tries to hold onto or hold off fleeting experiences or changing opinions. The confusion and holding create tension. We interpret this tightness as a self. Since we tighten a lot, we think this self must be permanent.

Self is composed of real and transient phenomena—sensations, feelings, thoughts, consciousness, etc. The glue holding them together in a self-identity is tension (taṇhā or craving).

The Buddha's treatment plan was simple: relax. If we release our grip on the trance state, we wake up. If we relax the tension deeply enough, self fades and there is no one who suffers.

The relaxation he prescribed was not grabbing a beer, putting our feet up, and watching TV. It was opening our eyes, minds, and hearts, and paying careful attention to what's going on and relaxing at the same time.

So the Buddha's treatment—the whole of his teaching—could be summed up: be kind, pay attention, and relax.

Hologram

In this chapter we'll look at the whole of the Buddha's teaching as a blue-collar hologram. Though we won't find the words "blue-collar" or "hologram" in the suttas, these analogies capture the essence of his approach.

If we paint an image on a piece of glass and break it, each fragment of glass contains a different part of the image. But if we embed an image in a holographic plate and break it, each fragment contains the whole image from a different perspective. So when all the fragments are together, we can turn it and view it from many angles: each piece contains that whole from a specific vantage point.

The Buddha's teachings are similar to a hologram in the sense that no matter where we enter it, if we go deeply enough we'll find the whole of it. Every teaching is in every other teaching. The various aspects are just different ways of viewing the same whole.

Blue-Collar Teachings

The Buddha's teachings are blue-collar in two respects: he spoke to everyone and was interested in direct experience.

His family came from the aristocratic warrior class, to be sure. He knew how to speak to kings, priests, and scholars. But his language and message were couched in words and metaphors that appealed to milkmaids, cow herders, and untouchables as well as the educated elite. The suttas were recorded in everyday Pāli rather than the erudite Sanskrit. He spoke in common vernacular.

And his subject matter was blue-collar in the sense that it was not abstract speculations. It was concrete and immediate. He didn't want us to believe what he said because he said it. He wanted us to explore our own lives and discover in our own experience what is most real.

Three Realms

When we explore our own experience, there are three different places we can look—three different realms. These are the internal realm (what we experience inside ourselves), the external realm (what we see around us when we observe objectively and dispassionately), and the relational realm (how we relate to ourselves, other people, creatures, and life itself).

> ***Three Refuges***
>
> I take refuge in the Buddha.
>
> I take refuge in the dhamma.
>
> I take refuge in the saṅgha.

All languages contain references to these three realms: "I," "me," and "mine" (internal), "it," "him," "her," and "them" (external), and "we," "us," and "our" (relational).[20]

In Buddhism these are alluded to in the "Three Jewels": the Buddha (our true inner nature), the dhamma (the objective world around us and the laws that govern it), and the saṅgha (the relationships that make up the community of seekers). Most Buddhist meditation retreats I've been on began by taking refuge in the Buddha, the dhamma, and the saṅgha.

Depending on temperament, different people may prefer one realm over another. Some people seek happiness by looking inside and cultivating inner peace and well-being. Others try to look objectively at the external world. They use science and reason to discern what is most real and important. Others look to the relational realm to make their connections with people as fulfilling as possible. Or they work to bring relational qualities—like justice, compassion, and fairness—into the world.

Ultimately, no realm is superior to any other. We all live in all three all the time. We all have an inner life, observe the world around us, and relate to other people and creatures.

The phrase, "Be kind, pay attention, and relax" points to all three realms. In the relational realm it encourages kindness. In the objective world it encourages paying attention to see clearly what is actually there. In the inner world it encourages us to release and relax.

In earlier chapters we explored the second two of these three ("pay attention" and "relax") but not the first ("be kind"). In chapter 3, we saw the aggregates (khandhas) as a way of recognizing (paying attention to) the flow of actual phenomena. In chapter 4, we saw how Dependent Origination (paticcasamuppāda) recognizes the way phenomena progress from one to the next, thereby creating suffering. We saw how relaxing out of the progression (cessation) wakes us up. In chapter 5 we saw how important it is to relax the instinctual tightening of taṇhā. In chapter 6 we saw how inner identification with transient phenomena creates a "false self," a "real self," and "I-ness." Recognizing and relaxing these three lead to selflessness. In chapter 7 we saw how the hindrances bring attention to where we are tight and need to relax.

However, we haven't looked at the relational realm or the importance of kindness. Nevertheless, one of the foundations of Buddhism is kindness and generosity. We can't go far in meditation without bringing it off the cushion into everyday life. In daily life we interact with people. If we hurt others, it disturbs the mind's deeper peace. Without non-harming as a way of life, the mind remains too restless to settle into deeper jhānas. The only peace possible is to force the mind into stillness. And forced stillness is, by nature, temporary and unsustainable.

However, with the addition of kindness to our practice, we get a fuller feel for the hologram. So before going further, let's look at what the Buddha had to say about relationships. It's another way to engage the whole of the practice.

Five Precepts

I undertake to keep the precept to refrain from killing or harming living beings on purpose.

I undertake to keep the precept to refrain from taking what is not freely given.

I undertake to keep the precept to refrain from wrongful sexual activity.

I undertake to keep the precept to refrain from telling lies or harsh speech.

I undertake to keep the precept to refrain from taking drugs or alcohol.

—first five precepts as translated by Bhante Vimalaramsi

Kindness

After the Buddha's awakening, a community formed around him. As members of the growing saṅgha interacted, problems arose. To keep relationships supportive of awakening, the Buddha recommended precepts. Over the years, 227 precepts were created for monks and 311 for nuns. The first five were used by lay followers. They are still used today in Buddhist meditation retreats and by lay practitioners.

Several years ago I heard of a situation in a Zen community that illustrates how the precepts are meant to be used.

This community took seriously the precept of non-killing—they vowed not to destroy any sentient creature. Then the zendo was invaded by cockroaches. They got into the rice. They crawled through the flour. They ran across guests. It was horrible. The residents knew that moral codes didn't need to be followed blindly. They served a practical purpose. Maybe this was a time when that practical purpose might be better served by poisoning a few bugs.

So they went to their Zen master and asked if it was okay to kill the cockroaches.

His response was, "I'm not going to tell you."

This wasn't a cop-out. He didn't want his students to cop-out of taking responsibility for their actions and their hearts. If he had told them either "yes" or "no," they would have been off the hook. They could blindly follow his authority and not struggle with the issue.

From the perspective of spiritual development, cockroaches were not the issue. The issue was the minds and hearts of the residents. If they were left on their own to figure out what to do, then they would be forced to look deeper into themselves in order to decide.

The problem with killing is that it is hard to imagine doing it without anger. Even swatting a mosquito involves some irritation. Anger and irritation are painful mind states. They are not bad in a moralistic sense—they just hurt. Of course, we might kill while oblivious to what we're doing. Oblivion is not conducive to well-being either. Vowing not to kill makes us more aware of what is going on inside when the urge to swat something arises.

The point of the precepts is to live with more awareness, not to sign up for a behavior code. The Native American tradition has a long history of killing animals for food. But they do it honoring the animal for the gift of its body, humbly honoring the needs of their bodies for food. This can be done consciously, without anger and with great respect. But killing needlessly, blindly, or out of anger or irritation is not conducive to well-being. When we live with greater awareness, most killing becomes unthinkable.

Stated positively, non-killing is trying to live in harmony with all life—living with kindness and generosity. It is in our enlightened best interest not to kill, steal, misuse our sexuality, lie, gossip, chatter idly, and so forth because these disrupt outer and inner peace and harmony.

The precepts are worded as negatives to flag behaviors that tend to arise out of unwholesome states. It's valuable to be aware of these states rather than just trying to fix our behavior.

Precepts are not magical incantations. Staying within their bounds doesn't earn divine approval or mysteriously win us favor. If we are about to act contrary to a precept, it is a reminder that this is a time to pay attention to our inner states and relax.

Finally, most precepts are an elaboration of the phrase, "Be kind." But kindness shouldn't be confused with niceness. The Buddha described a previous life when he was on a ship with five hundred people. The captain was a pirate who was going to sink the ship and kill everyone on it. The only way the Buddha-to-be could prevent this was to kill the captain. So he killed him to save the lives of five hundred people and to save the captain from the karma of all those deaths. It wasn't nice. But it was the kindest course of action available.

This type of logic can be a slippery slope, to be sure. But it shows that no code of behavior gives a literal answer to every situation. If we want to deepen our consciousness, we have to attend to our outward actions and inner states by cultivating kindness, paying attention, and relaxing.

Five Precepts (stated positively)

I vow to cultivate compassion and learn ways to protect lives.

I vow to cultivate loving kindness and learn ways to work for the well-being of people, animals, plants, and minerals.

I vow to practice generosity by sharing my time, energy, and material resources with those who are in real need.

I vow...to engage in sexual relations only with love and a long-term commitment.

I vow to cultivate loving speech and deep listening...and to speak truthfully, with words that inspire self-confidence, joy, and hope.

—Condensed from *The Five Wonderful Mindfulness Trainings* by Thich Nhat Hanh (http://dharma.ncf.ca/introduction/precepts.htm)

First Teaching

With kindness fully in the picture, we can return to the blue-collar hologram.

The interaction between kindness, paying attention, and relaxing can be seen in Siddhārtha Gautama's first successful teaching. It wasn't the first time he tried to teach after his enlightenment. But it was the first time that it had an immediate effect.

After his enlightenment, the newly realized Buddha hung out around the Bodhi tree for a month absorbing the insights he'd gained. He thought they were too rarified for anyone to understand—look at all he'd gone through to get there. But he became convinced that some people could hear him. So he set out toward Varanasi to teach.

The first person he came across on the road was an ascetic named Upaka who basically said, "Whoa, brother. Something sure happened to you. What was it, man? Who are you?"

The Buddha answered, "I am one who has transcended all, a knower of all, unsullied among all things, renouncing all, by craving's ceasing freed..." and went on like this in verse for several minutes.

Upaka tried not to roll his eyes, but he was sure Siddhārtha had gone off the deep end. The suttas say it this way: "When this [the Buddha's description of who he was] was said, the ascetic Upaka said: 'May it be so, friend.' Shaking his head, he took a bypath and departed."[21] In other words, Upaka didn't get it. The Buddha's first teaching appears to have flopped.

A little farther down the road, he came to the Deer Park at Sarnath. There he came upon five ascetics who knew him from training together before his enlightenment. They asked him to teach them what he had learned. Fresh from his meeting with Upaka, the Buddha tried a different approach. He laid things out systematically in ways that bridged the everyday world and deep practice.

This worked better—all five ascetics soon became enlightened. It was said that these teachings "set the wheel of dhamma in motion." They made the dhamma accessible to the world.

This first successful teaching is known as the "Four Noble Truths." Let's look at them more closely.

Four Noble Truths

To the modern ear, the fact that so much in Buddhism is numbered (Four Noble Truths, Eightfold Path, Five Enlightenment Factors, Four Brahmavihāra, Twelve Links of Dependent Origination, and so on) makes it sound like scattered lists of independent parts rather than a hologram. But the numbering was just a mnemonic device. In the Buddha's time, writing was considered too crude for sacred wisdom. Writing was for legal contracts and inventory lists. Spiritual teachings were learned by heart and passed on by word of mouth—or heart to heart. So the numbering and structure of these teachings were to make them easier to memorize.

"Four Noble Truths" is a translation of the Pāli term *cattāri ariyasaccāni*. It's a little misleading in English because "noble" does not refer to the truths but to the one who understands them. The First Truth is suffering. There is nothing noble about sickness, grief, or failure. The fact that we suffer does not make us grand or glorious. But the person who truly understands the nature of suffering is wise. To have full insight into the nature of reality is to have a noble mind-heart.

The format of the Four Truths was already used in medicine during the Buddha's time. Each disease had (1) a name, (2) a cause, (3) a cure, and (4) a treatmen t. Anyone in any class of society would have recognized this format. It made it obvious that the Buddha was talking about a malady of the mind and heart. It made it easier for them to grasp.

Following this medical formula of his day, the Four Noble Truths are:

1. Name: Dukkha (suffering or dissatisfaction). Ultimately, things don't work out.
2. Cause: Samudaya (origin). Craving (taṇhā) is the origin of suffering.
3. Cure: Nirodha (cessation). We release and relax.
4. Treatment: Magga (path). The Eightfold Path (*ariyo aṭṭhaṅgiko maggo*) outlines his treatment plan.

Notice that these Four Truths are concrete, tangible, and verifiable. Christian truths are usually speculative statements about ultimate reality: "I believe in one God the Father almighty, maker of heaven and earth and in all things visible and invisible..." This creed is to be taken on (blind) faith. There is no way to verify it empirically.

The Four Noble Truths, in contrast, are a hands-on, blue-collar invitation to examine our own experience and see for ourselves if they hold up. They aren't invitations to blind acceptance. The Buddha suggests where to look more than suggesting what we'll see.

And when we look, these Four Truths are found in every aspect of the dhamma and every aspect of life. We find them in the links of Dependent Origination, where each aspect has (1) a name, (2) a cause or origin, (3) a cure in cessation, and (4) a way leading to its cessation.[22]

In the next section, as we look in detail at the meditation practice, we'll see these truths again and again. When a hindrance arises, we recognize it (First Noble Truth), see the tension in it (Second Noble Truth), and relax (Third Noble Truth). This strategy is a path leading to cessation (Fourth Noble Truth).

The meditation practice is one aspect of a larger way of living that frees us. The Four Noble Truths also apply to this larger context.

The first three truths—suffering (dukkha) caused by tension (taṇhā) and cured by cessation (nirodha)—give the whole story in very broad terms. The third truth (cessation) describes *what* the cure is without much hint of *how* to get there. The Fourth Truth, the Eightfold Path, gives a more comprehensive treatment plan for everyday life as well as meditation.

Eightfold Path *(Ariyo Aṭṭhaṅgiko Maggo)*		
Pāli	*English*	*Other Translations*
Sammā Diṭṭhi	Harmonious Perspective	Right View
Sammā Sankappa	Harmonious Intention	Right Thought, Aspiration
Sammā Vācā	Harmonious Communication	Right Speech
Sammā Kammanta	Harmonious Conduct	Right Action, Movement
Sammā Ajīva	Harmonious Lifestyle	Right Livelihood
Sammā Vāyāma	Harmonious Practice	Right Effort
Sammā Sati	Harmonious Mindfulness	Right Awareness, Observation
Sammā Samādhi	Harmonious Collectedness	Right Concentration

The Eightfold Path

The eight folds are commonly called right view, right intention, right speech, right action, right livelihood, right effort, right mindfulness, and right concentration.

The Jesuits were among the first to translate the suttas into English. They translated the Pāli term "*sammā*" as "right." They naturally viewed the text through the lens of Christianity, where right and wrong play a prominent role. But in Buddhism, right versus wrong is foreign. A better translation of the various "sammā" might be "wise view," "wise intentions," "skillful speech," "skillful action."

Bhante Vimalaramsi prefers to translate "sammā" as "harmonious" because that comes closer to the meditation experience. When we experience genuine *sammā diṭṭhi* ("right view"), we have a perspective on life that feels harmonious. When we exercise *sammā vācā* ("right speech"), we are communicating in a way that is harmonious.

Bhante also translates the other words in the Eightfold Path in ways that more closely fit our experience in life. For example, *sammā ājīva* ("right livelihood") becomes "harmonious lifestyle" because it pertains to more than just what we do to earn money. It's about how we carry ourselves in the world and how we treat other beings. *Sammā vācā* ("right speech") becomes "harmonious communication" because it pertains to more than just vocalizing. It's about writing, e-mail, nonverbal gestures, and other ways we communicate.

The Whole of the Hologram

There are many commentaries that analyze the eight-folds in great detail. Some are useful. But what's more important than analyzing the details is noticing how all work together intimately with each other as a whole and with the Four Noble Truths.

For example, sammā diṭṭhi ("harmonious perspective," "wise view") sees that all life is impermanent. If we identify with any phenomenon or take things personally, we tighten up. The result is suffering (First Noble Truth) caused by tightening (Second Noble Truth) and relieved when we see clearly enough to let go (Third Noble Truth). Sammā diṭṭhi sets us on a path (Fourth Noble Truth) by inspiring *sammā sankappa*—the harmonious intention to pursue the path of awakening (Fourth Noble Truth). Sammā diṭṭhi also motivates us to be kind in speech *(sammā vācā)*, conduct (*sammā kammanta*), and lifestyle *(sammā ājīva)*. These provide a balanced mind and heart that enter meditation practice in a balanced way (*sammā vāyāma*).

Kindness is important in how we relate to other people and how we relate to ourselves: being clear and kind with our hindrances, wandering minds, and habitual tendencies. This cultivates mindfulness (*sammā sati*) and collectedness (*sammā samādhi*). In deep collectedness, the mind is quiet enough to see how mechanical and impersonal phenomena are *(sammā diṭṭhi)*.

In a similar way, if we reflect deeply on any of the Four Noble Truths or any part of the Eightfold Path, we eventually discover all the other elements because they are a hologram.

Other Teachings

The Buddha lived forty years beyond his enlightenment. With different people and different circumstances, he elaborated and refined the Four Noble Truths, offering us additional teachings and insights. If we go deeply enough into any of these truths, we find the others.

Three Characteristics

Dukkha: dissatisfaction

Anicca: impermanence

Anattā: selflessness

For example, the "Three Characteristics" are a CliffsNotes version of the Four Noble Truths and the Eightfold Path. They say that the most essential things to pay attention too are dissatisfaction (dukkha), impermanence (anicca), and selflessness (anattā). It is shorthand for saying that suffering arises when we try to hold onto impermanent phenomena or the impermanent self.

On the other hand, the "Five Characteristics" are a more nitty-gritty way to look at the essence of what's most important. Monks contemplate these each morning, which helps them focus on the obvious forms of anicca (old age, illness, death, and losing everything we cherish). Seeing anicca encourages using the Eightfold Path because "I am of the nature that the only thing I own is my action."

Contemplations on the Five Characteristics

I am of the nature to grow old.

I am of the nature to become ill.

I am of the nature to die.

I am of the nature that all I cherish will be taken away.

I am of the nature that the only things I own are my actions.

None of these or other teachings adds anything brand-new to the Four Noble Truths. But they add texture, depth, and multiple ways of viewing the whole of the Buddha's teaching: be kind, pay attention, and relax.

And this is best done with lightness—the topic of the next chapter.

Everything put together
Sooner or later falls apart

—Paul Simon

9

Lightness of Spirit: Uplifted Mind

I walked through the ornate temple entryway of Wat Phra Doi Suthep and past the row of huge bells until I came around back. A group of five teenagers were laughing, joking, and carrying on. Each had a long pole with a crosspiece at the end. A large, square rag hung from the crosspiece. With a flick of the pole, the rag wound around the crosspiece, turning it into a large mop. With a different flick, the rag unwound and could be hosed and cleaned.

Wat Phra Doi Suthep is perched on the side of a large mountain range in northern Thailand. A marble terrace with a breathtaking view of the city of Chiang Mai surrounds the temple. Every day, hundreds and hundreds of people take buses or taxis from the city up the mountain to worship, make offerings, ask advice, hear monks chant, ring the bells, gawk at the gold and jade Buddhas, photograph the valley, or just hang out in the mountain air.

Those five teenagers were supposed to keep the marble terrace sparkling for the visitors. But they didn't seem to take their work seriously. I couldn't understand their language. But from their laughter, gestures, and loud voices, I surmised they were goofing off.

I sat on a marble bench beneath a tree of magenta flowers. I could see the entire Chiang Mai valley. And I could surreptitiously observe these teenagers.

I was surprised. The kids wound the rags into mops, pushed them across the marble for fifty or sixty feet, ran to a hose, cleaned the rag, rewound it, and wiped another fifty-foot swath. They worked hard and efficiently. The way they joked and carried on would be a sure sign of laziness in America, but here it was a sign of something else. It was a sign of what the Thai call "*sànùk*."

I spent the month of March 2005 in Wat Chom Tong, about thirty miles south of Chiang Mai. Midafternoons I often took a break from meditating to stretch my legs and walk along the rice fields.

Typically it was 90 degrees with 90 percent humidity. The workers in the fields sloshed through mud to their ankles and water to their calves. It was backbreaking labor. Not speaking Thai, I couldn't understand what they called out to each other. But by their tone and gestures it seemed like jokes and amusing stories.

These were signs of sànùk.

The wats charged nothing for food, clothing, shelter, meditation instruction, or anything else I needed. But I wanted to make a donation. I made out several traveler's checks to one wat and belatedly found that they weren't allowed to cash them. They returned them to me.

So one afternoon I went into a bank to see if they could cash these checks that had already been signed and made out to someone else. The clerk made phone call after phone call up through the bank hierarchy and eventually through the American Express hierarchy. Finally she found a way to cash them for me. All the while she was wrestling with these bureaucracies, her boss was watching from several desks away. Their exchanges were polite, professional, and often playful.

Even in the bank there was sànùk.

Fun

"Sànùk" is a Thai word that translates roughly as "fun." Something with sànùk is enjoyable, pleasant, or playful.

For the Thai, sànùk is not a conscious philosophy or belief. It's an unconscious frame of reference which says that anything worthwhile has fun or playfulness in it. The Thai understand that valuable endeavors may require effort, discipline, hard work, sacrifice, and even pain. Nevertheless, anything worthwhile will also have some element of play in it.

Sànùk is not something we bring to a task. It's not grafted onto an onerous job. It's not making lemonade out of lemons. It's already inherent in anything that is wholesome. It's there to be noticed or discovered.

To call something "mai sànùk" or "not fun" is to condemn it. Someone who sticks with a task that is never enjoyable must be mentally unstable or spiritually unbalanced. The person must be arrogant or misguided. The gods don't intend us to stick with something that is never fun.

America

In America we have the opposite of sànùk—sometimes called the "Puritan ethic." It says that anything worthwhile is heavy to bear: "Take up your cross and follow me." If something is valuable, we must suffer for it. If we are having too much fun, we must be goofing off. We're probably irresponsible.

The majority of Americans may reject Puritanism as a set of beliefs. But the attitude is so deeply engrained in our psyches, institutions, and habits that secular Puritanism is an unconscious frame of reference. It's a secret traveling companion that pops up as an inner critic if we are too lax. The Thai say, "No fun, no value." We say, "No pain, no gain" or "It's good to stay busy."

Middle Way

He who binds to himself a joy
Does the winged life destroy;
But he who kisses the joy as it flies
Lives in eternity's sun rise.

—William Blake, "Eternity"

We can approach wisdom and spiritual practice with a range of attitudes. On one end of the spectrum is loose, go-with-the-flow, whatever-is-easiest laissez-faire. On the other end is taut, focused, grim determination.

One of the central insights of Buddhism is that wisdom is not found in extremes. It's found in a "middle way." It's found in balance. The Buddha explained this in a conversation with a monk, the Venerable Sona, in the Cool Wood near Rajagaha:

"Now what do you think, Sona? Before, when you were a house-dweller, were you skilled at playing the vina?"

"Yes, lord."

"... when the strings of your vina were too taut, was your vina in tune and playable?"

"No, lord."

"... when the strings of your vina were too loose, was your vina in tune and playable?"

"No, lord."

"... when the strings of your vina were neither too taut nor too loose, but tuned to be right on pitch, was your vina in tune and playable?"

"Yes, lord."

"In the same way, Sona, over-aroused persistence leads to restlessness, overly slack persistence leads to laziness. Thus you should determine the right pitch for your persistence...[23]*"*

The Thai culture is gentle, mellow, and relaxed. Thai people can be industrious, but they rarely forget the importance of fun. Western culture by comparison is stressed and driven. We can enjoy ourselves, but we are more likely to approach spirituality with fortitude than lightness of spirit.

When Thai go "out of tune," they are more likely to be too loose. So Southeast Asian meditation masters speak more about diligence, persistence, and resoluteness than laughing and smiling. These help the mellow Thai come into a truer pitch and find the middle way.

When Westerners go out of tune, they are more likely to be too taut. I first learned meditation from Westerners who had learned stricter approaches from Southeast Asia. They didn't emphasize relaxing or having fun. It took me a while to learn to lighten up. It was not until I trained with Bhante Vimalaramsi that I learned that when I was stuck in the practice it was almost always because I was trying too hard, not because I was trying too soft.

Meditation does require effort, and at times it is hard work. But effort can be saturated with humor, smiling, and ease. It can be practiced with sànùk.

In contemplating the insights of this section of the book or engaging the practices in the next section, remember the old saying: "Angels can fly because they take themselves lightly."

Wisdom and spaciousness are inherently suffused with joy. Diligence in practice is helpful only if balanced with sànùk. Enjoyment is not goofing off. When balanced, meditation is fun.

Section III

Path

When I was in college, a fellow psychology major undertook an experiment. Every time his roommate moved his hand toward his ear, he smiled. He never told his roommate his scheme. The smiles were never broad or obvious—just a subtle show of approval. Within two weeks, his roommate developed a habit of pulling on his earlobe.

A number of years ago, a psychology class at a large university conducted an experiment on its professor. It was one of those large lecture classes with three or four hundred students. When the professor was out of the room for a few minutes, they agreed that every time he walked to the right side of the stage, they would be very attentive and take lots of notes. When he walked to the left side, they would drift off, gaze out the window or look bored. Very quickly the professor was glued to the right side of the stage.

These examples involve one behavior, subtle reinforcers of that behavior, and a short period of time. Consider the impact of targeting many behaviors and attitudes, using obvious as well as subtle reinforcers, and continuing the process for years. We would expect large changes in the person's actions, underlying attitudes, feelings, and even thought processes. We might expect changes in who they thought they were.

Hypnosis

The ease with which we can be influenced has long been demonstrated by hypnosis. Hypnosis is an unremarkable procedure that can produce remarkable results. If we were interested in being hypnotized and were at least somewhat susceptible (most people are), there are basically two things a hypnotist would tell us. First, he'd ask us to fix our gaze on a single object, such as a candle flame. After a while, he'd suggest that our eyes were getting heavy and our vision was getting distorted. This is a predictable result of staring fixedly at one point, but we might take it as a sign that the hypnotic suggestion was working. Second, as we stared at the object, he'd say, "Think about what it's like to relax. Allow yourself to relax. You're becoming relaxed. You're feeling sleepy." Interspersed with these statements would be reassurances that hypnosis is easy and normal; that since we are allowing him to hypnotize us, we must be willing; and so forth.

After ten to twenty minutes, we'd probably go into a light hypnotic trance. In such a state, he could suggest that our arms have gotten very heavy. We'd be unable to lift them.

If we had a talent for hypnotic states, we might go into a deeper trance in which more fundamental perceptual distortions were possible. For example, if there were three glasses on the table, and he said there were two, we would swear there were only two. This is called a negative hallucination—not perceiving something that is present.

He might suggest that someone wanted to talk to us on the intercom. We'd listen and respond to questions from the intercom despite the fact that it was turned off. This is called a positive hallucination—perceiving something that is not there.

Another well-known hypnotic phenomenon is posthypnotic suggestion. For example, he could tell us that after coming out of the trance, every time he used the word "button" we'd walk to the window. If we were responsive to hypnosis, he could bring us out of the trance and weave the word "button" into the conversation, and each time, we would get up and walk to the window.

A fascinating aspect of this phenomenon is that people responding to posthypnotic suggestion make up explanations for their behavior: "I'd like a breath of air," "I hear someone calling me," or "I love the way the sky looks this time of day." They're unaware of why they are doing what they're doing and spontaneously come up with reasonable though spurious rationales. They construct a reality.

But there are limits to hypnotic suggestion. It is difficult or impossible to get somebody to do something that clashes with strongly held values. Still, it is amazing how drastically our thoughts and perceptions can be altered by such an innocent-looking procedure. And it doesn't take a lot of training to learn to hypnotize people. Standardized procedure can simply be read out loud.

Child Rearing

Child rearing uses all the techniques of hypnotic induction and many more. We don't tell our children that their eyes are getting tired as they stare at a candle, but we do tell them over and over what they might experience as they grow. When these predictions come true, children magically believe that what we say must be true. And we suggest to them over and over who they are, what they can do, what is "normal," and how to get along. Good parents tell their children they're wonderful, capable, and talented. Other parents tell their kids they're no good and will come to nothing. But even the most laissez-faire parents give signals more obvious than the quiet smile given to the roommate as his hand moved toward his ear or the look of attention as the professor moved to the right side of the stage.

Not only does child rearing use the techniques of hypnotic induction, but it uses them in ways that are hundreds of times more powerful. Unlike formal hypnosis, child rearing isn't confined to ten to twenty minutes but extends over ten to twenty years—and the most impressionable years at that. While the hypnotic subject usually has no special relationship to the hypnotist, the child is very dependent on his or her parents. While formal hypnosis is voluntary, a child doesn't have the option of choosing parents. While hypnosis subjects may feel indifferent toward the hypnotist, children usually want to please their parents. While formal hypnosis doesn't use reinforcers, child rearing applies positive reinforcements like touching, holding, stroking, and praising, and negative ones like disapproval, guilt, and sometimes physical punishment.

On top of this, media, advertising, friends, and family tell us who we are directly or by implication. And in fact, if we listen closely to the thoughts inside our minds, most of them are suggesting who and what we are. We have become our own hypnotists!

The most reasonable conclusion is that we're in a kind of hypnotic state and responding to posthypnotic suggestions. Charles Tart,[24] an expert on hypnosis, has come to exactly this conclusion. He calls our normal state the "consensus trance" or the "sleep of everyday life." Spiritual teachers from many traditions say we walk around half asleep in a trance of inner words.

The Buddha agreed. His path to awakening wasn't designed to wake us out of nighttime slumber. It was designed to wake us out of our daytime trance.

No matter how deep and compelling the trance, it's never total. We always have the capacity to wake ourselves up.

For example, let's say we've been hypnotized into thinking there are two glasses on the table. We glance and report confidently, "There are two."

Then someone we trust says, "Take another look. Relax. Examine carefully with fresh eyes and tell me exactly what you see."

We look openly for a few moments and notice, "Oh, there are actually three glasses."

The way we stay hypnotized is to not pay careful attention, to brush over things lightly, to assume we already know what is real. If instead we suspend our preconceptions and gaze receptively, we start to see more deeply what is true. In *Pāli*, this quality of mind is called mindfulness or heartfulness (*sati*).

Requirements

The Buddha understood keenly and in detail the nature of the trance we're in and the importance of mindfulness for waking up. The path he laid out focuses only on what is essential and leaves everything else aside. These essentials include the insights from the previous chapters. In the coming chapters we'll see how these are integrated into an optimal meditation practice. But first, let's review them. They include the following:

- Mindfulness (*sati*)—It's not enough to learn ideas, doctrines, or beliefs. Awakening comes through direct experience. The practice must emphasize attentive, receptive, open, clear, and relaxed awareness.
- Aggregates (khandhas)—The practice must distinguish thought from perception, labels from feeling tone, consciousness from mental constructs, and any aggregate from any other aggregate. It must encourage de-identification with these.
- Dependent Origination (paticcasamuppada)—The practice must see the details of the trance: how phenomena affect each other. And it must see them so clearly that the chain of causation ceases (so-called "cessation").

- Craving (taṇhā)—Craving is where we can most easily relax out of the trance. So the practice must give special attention to this aspect of Dependent Origination.
- Dispelling ignorance (avijjā)—Self-sense is a key aspect of the trance. It confuses what we see with what we are. The practice must see through the tendency to personalize and must help the mind shift from "my pain" to "the pain" and from "my happiness" to "all-pervading happiness."
- Hindrances (nīvaraṇa)—The practice must not push hindrances away, because this just strengthens them. Instead, the practice must use them to show where to attend more mindfully.
- Three characteristics (tilakkhaṇa)—Dissatisfaction (dukkha), impermanence (anicca), and selflessness (anattā) are fundamental elements of existence. The practice must see these deeply and directly to help us see reality beyond the trance.
- The Four Noble Truths (cattāri ariya saccani)—They are central to diagnosing the trance and to breaking out of it. Seeing these must be part of the practice.
- Stages (jhānas)—To be efficient, the practice must unfold in stages. It must utilize the insights and qualities we've developed along the way. And it must not depend on them before they've been developed.
- Lightening up—When the mind-heart is light, it sees and knows with more agility. The practice must cultivate uplifted states.
- Simple and easy to follow—The simpler the practice, the easier it is to engage in it.

Taken together, this might seem like an impossible list. But the meditation the Buddha taught actually includes all of these in ways that are remarkably accessible. In the coming chapters, we'll look at the specifics of the meditation he taught.

This meditation has two practices that work together. The first is the jhānas or stages of meditation that unfold as the mind-heart gets quieter and clearer. The second is the Six Rs which are used when the mind-heart is noisy or foggy. We use the jhāna practices when we're on track. We use the Six Rs when we drift and need to get back on track.

The next chapter introduces the jhānas by describing the first one in detail. The following two chapters describe the Six Rs in depth and some other supporting practices that can be used at any stage and with any jhāna. The following chapters go up through the other jhānas and peek at what lies beyond.

10

Joy: First Jhāna

A man stood in the strip of land between the river levy and the backyard fences. Holding one end of a three-foot piece of purple plastic, he pressed the other end over a yellow tennis ball on the ground. The ball fit perfectly. Holding the purple gadget over his shoulder, he flung the ball into the air. It rocketed a hundred feet before falling and bouncing on the ground.

Meanwhile a dog focused on this tennis ball. As the ball sped through space, he leapt into the air, spun around, and hit the ground running so fast he left puffs of dust behind him.

The ball zigged and zagged as it bounced over the uneven ground. The dog zigged and zagged in perfect unison until he pounced on it and, in one economical snap, gripped it in his jaws.

Without slowing, he wheeled around and ran enthusiastically back to his human. He dropped the ball at the man's feet and backed away. His eyes remained locked on the ball. He didn't look at the ground, the levy, the fence, the birds nearby, or his human. His eyes glistened with joy. To the dog, the entire world was BALL.

The man picked up the ball with the purple plastic and pitched it in the opposite direction. The dog leapt into the air in pursuit. But this time, the man had only gestured. He hadn't actually released the ball. As soon as the dog was off on his misdirected chase, the man threw the ball in the opposite direction.

It took the dog two seconds to realize he'd been tricked. He stopped dead in his tracks and scanned. Where's the ball? There it is! He was off again—no time to feel failure, disappointment, humor, or anger. He honed in on his quarry. In the whole universe there was nothing more important. He was in the chase and nothing but the chase.

I could imagine how such rapt attention on rodent-sized moving objects had given his ancestors an evolutionary edge in capturing a meal. Now all these genetic instincts were trained on a lime yellow sphere of rubber and felt—an object with zero protein.

I felt bad for the dog locked into an inbred reflex. And yet I couldn't help but smile at his ecstasy.

When I first began meditating, I tried to cultivate what the dog had in abundance. His attention was completely absorbed on his object of meditation. His object was the ball; mine was the breath. His concentration was rock solid; mine was wimpy.

And when he lost contact with his object, he didn't beat himself up, dwell on his failing, become depressed or disturbed. He simply returned to his object with vigor and without melodrama, and he had no trouble maintaining interest in his object. He was filled with energy and joy. He was mindful. He had great concentration—had a cat jumped onto his back, I doubt he would have noticed.

And yet, despite all his yogic achievements, the combined effect was not exactly what I was yearning for. I saw no wisdom, spaciousness, proportion, peacefulness, or balance. There had to be a better way.

The Buddha called his path a middle way. It brought into balance not just one or two qualities, but many. Yet in my early meditation training, I was encouraged to develop concentration first and choiceless awareness later. I learned to strengthen determination and not be concerned with joy (for which I was too depressed to relate to anyway). I was taught to bring more energy to the practice and not relax or rest. I was told to stay with simple concrete experiences like body sensations and not to worry about spaciousness or nibbāna.

In fairness to my early teachers, I'm not sure whether that's what they meant or just what I heard.

The Buddha described his path as "complete in the beginning, complete in the middle, and complete in the end." In other words, it was meant to be a middle way balanced in the beginning, balanced in the middle, and balanced in the end.

Since we come to the practice with different temperaments, inclinations, and gifts, what we need in order to find balance may be different. Some may need more energy, some more relaxation, some more curiosity, some more tranquility, some more joy, some more equanimity.

In reading the suttas, it's clear that the Buddha approached different people in different ways. But he was always looking for balance.

Nevertheless, the way he most often recommended starts with joy. In Western culture with so much striving and stress, joy and kindness seem particularly important.

So as we turn to specific instructions, we're going to start with joy and see how the path unfolds from there. Other starting points are also effective, but joy brings a lightness that helps balance many of us right from the beginning of practice.

Instructions: *Pīti*

(If you haven't read the section "Meditation Practice" starting on page 28, you might do so now. The following elaborates on those instructions.)

The Buddha talked about four qualities of mind that were particularly wholesome. They are called the four *brahmavihāras* and consist of loving kindness (*mettā*), compassion (*karuṇā*), joy over others' good fortune (*mudita*), and equanimity (*upekkhā*). What's most important in starting the practice is not these states precisely but any states that help the mind-heart feel expansive, light, or uplifted. The practice begins by creating phrases that resonate with any of these qualities: "May I be happy," "May I be peaceful," "May I have ease." No quality is necessarily better than any other. They're just a way of getting a foot in the door of the brahmavihāras in general. We use whatever works best for us—whatever comes most easily and naturally.

We say the phrases sincerely with clear intentions. They aren't said quickly or rapidly like a mantra. We use one phrase per breath at the most so we can relax into its meaning.

We send or wish these qualities to ourselves because we cannot truly send to others what we don't already experience. The Buddha said that if we searched the entire world for the person most deserving and most in need of our love and kindness, we'd find no one more deserving than ourselves.

And we send these qualities to our spiritual friend to cultivate a consciousness that extends beyond a sense of self. Selflessness (anattā) is one of the "three characteristics" of all things. As we send uplifted energy beyond ourselves, a personalized sense of self may start to weaken.

As we relax into the phrases, there may be moments of joy (pīti)—soft bursts of well-being that have nothing to do with self or other. The attention may be drawn here. It's very healing. As we relax into this joy, it spreads out and softens into a less focused and lower-energy happiness (sukha). As we relax into happiness, it may spread out into a more spacious equanimity (upekkhā). Equanimity does not have much energy to hold our attention. It is so quiet that the mind may lose contact with it.

This little cycle from joy to happiness to equanimity may pass in just a moment. It can happen so quickly that we don't notice the various phases—just a little burst of well-being that fades quickly. This is fine. With time and patience, it will lengthen on its own.

This short cycle is a sign of the first jhāna (stage of meditation). It's a toe in the door. It draws and focuses the mind, bringing more collectedness (samādhi), even if only for a moment.

We don't hold onto it—holding creates tension. In the beginning it is easier to connect with this joy, kindness, or uplift than it is to sustain contact with it. But each time we contact it, collectedness strengthens a tiny bit. So as we relax into it, it will strengthen itself.

Jhāna Stumbling

I have seen people go into the first jhāna just as gracefully as I described. But that's not how I did it. My first experiences were more like stepping sideways, tripping over a bench, falling through a door into a room, and running out because I didn't think I belonged there.

When I began meditating, I was sure the first step was to develop enough concentration to make my mind stay put on the breath. Once I had enough of this one-pointedness, I could shift to "choiceless awareness" whereby I let my attention go wherever it wanted as I stayed completely mindful. Concentration first, awareness second: my early efforts in this were not particularly pleasant or successful.

But I stuck with it because I was stubborn and because when I stopped meditating, I felt so much better. The quip says, "I'm hitting my head against the wall because it feels so good when I stop." I didn't think that was what I was doing. When I got up from my zafu, my spirits were lighter than before sitting down. The experience on the cushion wasn't great, but the aftereffect seemed genuinely good.

Looking back, I suspect my mind was getting more collected. But since I was forcing it, there was no ease or balance. The balance came when I stopped "meditating" and eased up a little.

But my practice didn't go any deeper than this.

After a year or two, I wondered if I really had to start with one-pointed concentration. I felt drawn to choiceless awareness. So I tried it even though I judged my concentration to be weak. I felt guilty—like I was being a bad student. But I wanted to see what would happen.

Choiceless awareness felt less forceful than concentration. I didn't push so hard; I relaxed a little. I used just enough effort to notice where my mind was wandering next. I was surprised that my mind quieted down on its own. It became more collected.

On a retreat I ventured to comment to a teacher, "It seems that practicing choiceless awareness helps me develop concentration rather than concentration being a prerequisite for choiceless awareness." He listened carefully and said, "Concentration and awareness are opposite sides of the same coin. Most people need more stillness in the beginning. But a quarter of the people find what you describe: they start with mindfulness, and this helps still the mind. So use what works best."

I was relieved to get this confirmation and began to practice with less emphasis on strengthening concentration.

However, when my mind did wander, I wasn't sure what to do. It wandered a lot. So I just let it drift unless it seemed to be drifting too much, in which case I went back to focusing on the breath.

By shifting back and forth between these two practices, my meditation went a little deeper. After several years, I noticed times when my mind was so quiet that it was difficult to think if I tried. Thoughts were very slow in coming. As I described earlier, I experienced this as mental "white noise" in which thinking was foreign. This state felt effortless, joyful, and peaceful.

When I described this to various teachers, they frowned: "Be careful. You don't want to get attached to those pleasurable feelings. They are a trap—or at best a dead end. So if they arise, just go back to the breath."

I did as I was told. But sometimes the joy and peace became so intense that I did not want to ignore them. I called it a "non-genital, non-climactic orgasm": an intense and self-sustaining feeling of well-being.

And sometimes it was overwhelming. I'd feel myself spinning around like I was in a whirlwind. If I tried to stop the spinning, it just got more intense. Finally, not knowing what else to do, I gave in to it. Surprisingly, when I relaxed into the whirlwind, it slowed and spread out into a deeper, wider, subtler feeling of peace and happiness. I smiled.

Most of the time in retreats, I flopped back and forth between bare attention (mindfulness) and concentration on the breath without coming into balance. I had no way to bring up these peaceful, joyful energies, but they arose on their own more and more often.

It was during this time that I heard Larry Rosenberg's talk on the "Ānāpānasati Sutta"—the Buddha's talk on mindfulness of breathing—in which he described some of the signs of the first and second jhānas. Larry confirmed my experience as being jhāna related. It was the first time I heard the word (see pages 12–14).

I was delighted that these experiences were not symptoms of wandering off the path but of going further along it.

Still, I didn't know what to do with them.

It was many years before I found a teacher—Bhante—who understood how to work with the jhānas.

The difficulty with one-pointed concentration was that it created too much tension. Without the relaxation step that the Buddha taught, the tension built and built, making the practice more and more uncomfortable.

The difficulty with choiceless awareness or bare attention was that I didn't know how to work skillfully with the wandering mind. All I knew was forcing the mind into stillness or letting it run amuck. There was no balance.

It wasn't until I learned how to use the Six Rs that I found a way to both honor the joy, happiness, and equanimity (pīti , sukha, and upekkhā) as they arose and how to work with distractions without tightening up.

In the next chapter we'll go more fully into the Six Rs.

Many Paths

When I look back on my experience in those years, it is clear that there are many ways to enter the jhānas. I found my own way into them with some sensitive flopping around. It took me five or six years.

I've seen people use the breath awareness with the relaxation step and the Six Rs and move into the first jhāna in a matter of days or weeks. And I've seen people with very little meditation experience use mettā with the relaxation step and the Six Rs and move into the first jhāna in a matter of a day or two.

Many report feelings of intense joy. At first it is tentative. But when told they are on the correct path, they relax and it becomes more powerful. Then it passes. With this they've gone through the first and are on to the second or third jhāna—topics for later chapters.

The Buddha was an incredibly gifted teacher. Following his instructions closely moves us along the path very quickly.

In the Buddha's Words

Let's look at what the Buddha actually said in the suttas about this first stage or jhāna.

A sutta is a single thread in the whole cloth of the Buddha's teaching. The word "sutta" literally means "thread." Each sutta is a single discourse or fragment of a teaching passed down to us from the Buddha himself. Some of the threads are probably closer to the Buddha's original words than others. But when we weave them all together, we get a better feel for the whole of what he wanted to teach us.

He described the first jhāna in many suttas—sometimes succinctly, sometimes in more detail, sometimes about his own experience, sometimes about another's.

In the "Anupada Sutta: One by One As They Occurred" (*Majjhima Nikaya* 111), he described the experience of one of his students, Sāriputta. Picking up at verse 3:

> *(3) Here, quite secluded from sensual pleasures, secluded from unwholesome states, Sāriputta entered upon and abided in the first jhāna, which is accompanied by thinking and examining thought, with joy and happiness born of seclusion.*
>
> *(4) And the states in the first jhāna—the thinking, the examining thought, the joy, the happiness, and the unification of mind; the contact, feeling, perception, formations, and mind; the enthusiasm, choice, energy, mindfulness, equanimity, and attention—these states were defined by him one by one as they occurred; known to him those states arose, known they were present, known they disappeared. He understood thus: "So indeed, these states, not having been, come into being; having been, they vanish." Regarding those states, he abided unattached, unrepelled, independent, detached, free, dissociated, with a mind rid of barriers.*

Let's go through this passage.

Sāriputta was one of the Buddha's most accomplished students. He became fully enlightened and was gifted in his wisdom. The monks who were followers of the Buddha would have been very interested in how Sāriputta practiced.

The first thing Sāriputta did was to find seclusion—some quiet place with few distractions. We can count on the world intruding on us from time to time. But when we meditate, it is helpful to do what is reasonable to have some external peace: turn off the cell phone, shut off the TV, close the door, find a time when we have no immediate obligations, and so forth.

Seclusion also means an intention not to indulge distractions when they arise in the physical world or in the mind's thinking. And when something grabs our attention anyway, as soon as we realize it we Six-R it: recognize where our attention has gone, release it, relax, smile, and return to our primary object of meditation. This cultivates inner seclusion.

Meanwhile, there is a lot going on in this seclusion. Sāriputta experienced thinking and examining thought—discursive thinking. He also experienced all five khandhas: contact, feeling, perception, formations, and consciousness.

As noted earlier, some schools of meditation describe the jhānas as states in which the external world and thinking are completely shut off—the mind is totally absorbed in one-pointed concentration. But here the Buddha uses jhāna to refer to something far more dynamic and accessible.

Amongst this inner activity is the cycle of joy (pīti), happiness (sukha), and equanimity (upekkhā) mentioned earlier. And there are other wholesome states as well: enthusiasm (wise effort), energy, mindfulness, attention, unification of mind, and so forth.

What's crucial is that Sāriputta does not get lost in the phenomena. He doesn't identify with them or call them "self." Rather he sits back and observes the process—he doesn't indulge them or try to make them go away. He's neither attracted nor repelled; he simply watches them arise and vanish.

Meditation is not about entering a specific state and having it remain unchanged. That goes against a basic characteristic of all phenomena: impermanence (anicca).

Awakening arises from seeing things as they are, not controlling them or trying to fit them into some mold of what we think should be. It arises from a detached, clear, and unencumbered observation of the flux and flow of inner events. This relaxed attention cultivates the "unification" of mind that is hinted at in the first jhāna.

The "Kāyagatasati Sutta: Mindfulness of the Body" (*Majjhima Nikaya* 119) verse 18 includes a metaphor for the first jhāna:

> *Just as a skilled bath man or a bath man's apprentice heaps bath powder in a metal basin and, sprinkling it gradually with water, kneads it till the moisture wets his ball of bath powder, soaks it and pervades it inside and out, yet the ball itself does not ooze; so too, a monk allows the joy and happiness born of seclusion drench, steep, fill, and pervade this body, so that there is no part of his whole body unpervaded by the joy and happiness born of seclusion.*

In other words, joy (pīti), happiness (sukha) and equanimity (upekkhā) first run through quickly. But as the jhāna deepens, they begin to spread softly through the body and mind like moisture through a ball of bath powder.

The reference to a ball of bath powder was probably more familiar to people in the Buddha's day. The ball of powder is small. We'll see that the next verse describing the second jhāna uses the metaphor of a lake—a much larger object. So the joy and happiness of the first jhāna is only a hint of what's to come.

Distractions

As noted before, the mind in the *jhānas* is not free from distractions. They arise frequently and don't need to be suppressed. As long as we retain some contact with the object of meditation, we can let them float in the background.

But sooner or later they take our attention away completely. We are lost in thoughts or images. And then, wisdom asserts itself. We suddenly remember where we are and that we've been lost in a distraction.

What we do next is crucial to cultivating balance. We'll take this up in the next chapter as we explore the Six Rs in depth. In the following chapter we'll look at supporting practices which, like the Six Rs, can be used along side any jhāna. After this we'll come back to the jhānas themselves.

11

Six Rs: The Real Practice

After the British were comfortably in control of India, they looked around for entertainment. They decided India needed golf—a game that emphasized skill and control more than chance. So they built a golf course in Calcutta.

India has different fauna than Great Britain. It has monkeys—lots of them. The monkeys were fascinated by the little white balls popping around the tidy, green lawns. They chased the balls, carried them, bit them, and threw them around—great fun.

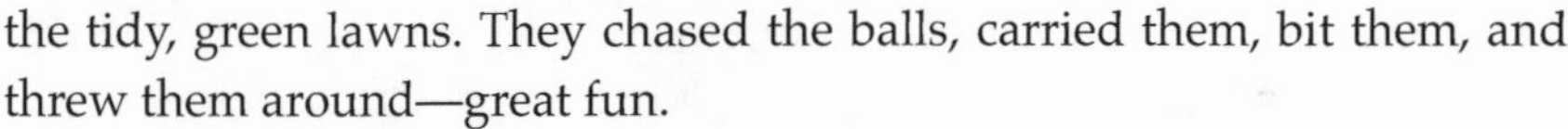

But not for the British: "This will never do!" So they built a high fence around the course to keep the animals out.

The monkeys were delighted. Now they had a wonderful new climbing structure as well as little white balls to play with.

So the British trapped the monkeys and carried them far into the jungle. But that amusement park had become so popular among the monkeys that for every one they sent away, two more showed up.

So next the British created alternative entertainment to entice the monkeys away. But to the monkeys, nothing was as enticing as seeing humans in white shorts and white shoes jump up and down and yell every time they picked up a little white ball.

Finally the British found a solution: they modified one rule of the game and posted it at the golf course entrance. The sign read: "You must play the ball where the monkey leaves it."

Sometimes we approach meditation as if it were a nine-hole golf course: eight jhānas plus enlightenment. And we'd like to go straight down the course with as few strokes as possible.

But we soon discover that meditation is like the rest of life—there are monkeys we can't control. In fact, trying to control them makes them misbehave even more. The mind has a mind of its own that is not interested in what we'd like it to do. Distractions abound.

To say this more prosaically, the wandering, lively mind is a symptom of tension, too much energy in the mind-body system. It darts around to work off some of its energy. Trying to control the flow of attention puts more energy (and tension) into the system, causing it to wander more.

To say this poetically, fighting the monkeys invigorates them.

In the short run, it is possible to still the mind with force of will. We clamp down on wandering thoughts, creating an artificial stillness. But it's like pushing the monkeys into a closet and holding the door shut. When we relax or step away, they burst forth with more vigor than ever.

In the long run, a more effective strategy is to play the ball where it lies. This is valuable in life in general. Reality is what it is, whether we like it or not. Fighting reality doesn't work for long.

In meditation, playing the ball where it lies means using the Six Rs: recognize, release, relax, re-smile, return, repeat.

This is a middle way between two extremes. On the one hand, it doesn't indulge the monkeys and let them run loose. On the other hand, it doesn't fight them. We accept reality as it is in the moment. Rather than fight the moment, we relax tension so the mind-heart can move organically and without force toward a natural peace.

In the beginning, we use the Six Rs only with big distractions that cause us to lose complete contact with the object of meditation—a spiritual friend or the feeling of mettā. As we saw in the first jhāna and will see in many of the later jhānas, the monkey mind will continue. Distractions will arise. If we try to Six-R everything, we'll be jumping around like a monkey. Instead, we let them play with the ball in the background. As long as we keep some connection with the mettā practice, we let the excess energy run out on its own.

There will be hundreds and thousands of times when our attention forgets the mettā practice completely. We'll be sitting in meditation and suddenly realize we've been planning the day, replaying a fight, or otherwise swinging through the trees.

This is where the Six Rs are very helpful. Let's look at them more closely and see how they work.

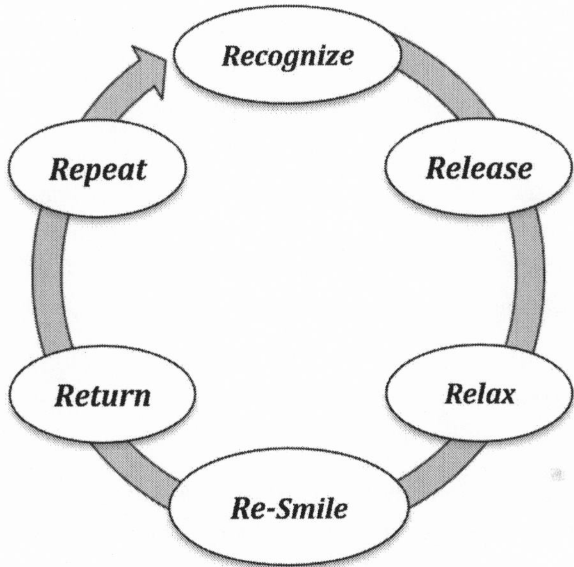

Recognize

When the mind's attention wanders from the object of meditation, we may take it personally: "Oh, I messed up. My mind is supposed to be on loving kindness and compassion, but instead I'm fantasizing about how to get even with my irritating neighbor." So we want to fix it—bring our attention back to where it's supposed to be.

In reality, when the attention wanders, it's because of tension. For several days in one retreat, anytime a distracting thought arose, I saw immediately how it related to a conversation, disagreement, feeling of guilt, or unmet desire I quietly held from the past. Sometimes the source of tension was many years ago. As I saw each of these, the tension in them softened and slowly released.

But usually I don't see so clearly where the tension came from. It seems to be just a thought that came along to annoy me and disrupt my peace. However I've come to appreciate that there is wisdom in every distraction, something valuable in every hindrance. I may not know what it is, and I may never know what it is. But I don't want to dismiss it without first at least recognizing it.

Awakening arises from a deep and thorough understanding of how life is. When we recognize clearly, the mind-heart releases and relaxes into its natural state. It's not general intellectual understanding that liberates but in-the-moment direct experience—recognizing how things are right now.

If our hand hurts, it will tighten—the body reflexively defends against pain. But if we look at our hand and see a hot coal, the hand releases. We don't have to think, "Hmmm. Maybe the burning sensation is coming from this coal. What should I do? Hold on? Let it go? Ask for advice?" Instead, the body releases faster than we can think, "Ouch."

To ignore a distraction that has fully stolen our attention is like tightening our hand around a hot coal and putting it behind our back to ignore it. It just doesn't work in the long run.

So when the mind's attention is fully pulled away, it's kinder to just recognize where it went. This doesn't mean thinking about it or getting involved in the content of a distracting thought. It's enough to just note "thinking."

Vipassanā is called "insight meditation." Insight comes from seeing how things are. When we recognize distractions and hindrances as they are, they offer helpful insights.

Release

On the other hand, we don't want to indulge hindrances either. We don't want to nurse them along by getting too involved in them. So after recognizing what the distraction is, we release it. This doesn't mean "push it away." It means letting it be so it can stay or leave or float in the background.

The Zen Master Suzuki Roshi once said, "The best way to control a cow is to put it in a very large pasture." "Release" means to give it some space.

As we release it, it may wander across the pasture and out of our lives. Or it may come back and stare us in the face with big brown eyes as it chews its cud and shakes flies off their ears. Either is just fine.

Releasing isn't a euphemism for "getting rid of." It's not trying to control it. It's just releasing our grip on it. To truly let something be means it can do what it wants. We no longer hold it close or hold it off. This way we are taking it less personally. It's okay for it to be here or not.

The best way to control a cow is to release it into a large pasture.

Relax

Recognizing and releasing are basically passive steps. Relaxing is the first active thing we do. Recognizing and releasing are about the object that has grabbed our attention. Relaxing is about the tension inside us that arises with the grabbing: we relax the tightness.

Early in my practice, I noticed a lot of tension in my shoulders. But I never seemed to be able to relax it. I would soften my shoulders or even push them down, but they stayed tense. Then I noticed that my hands were tense. When I relaxed them, my shoulders began to soften on their own.

I've also noticed that if I drive off into a lengthy mental ramble, when I "come to," the bottoms of my feet are usually slightly contracted. I have no idea what that means. But when I relax them and let them flatten out against the floor, my whole body relaxes a little more.

Another place I can hide tension without knowing it is around the eyes. I like to check and see if I can let the eyes soften—let them float in their sockets.

You may have your own special ways of quietly holding tension. It's good to get to know these so you can give them special permission to relax.

In this phase we relax the body. We also relax the emotions and the mind. This is what the Buddha meant by "tranquilizing the formations." In teaching the breath meditation, he advised using both the in breath and the out breath to tranquilize the formations—to relax. In the mettā practice, we don't pay special attention to the breath, but do actively relax as a way of working skillfully with distractions.

This step distinguishes the Buddha's practice from others of his time. Most of the practices in his time were "warrior" practices of forcefully controlling the mind. He found that this ultimately didn't work. "Crushing mind with mind" did give some temporary relief by suppressing hindrances. But he could see they were still alive in him and would pop up again.

So he taught himself and then taught his followers a different strategy which relaxes instead of tightens. Whether you use the mettā practice or a different one, without the relaxation step, you are not really following the Buddha's instructions. It goes to the essence of what he taught.

Re-Smile

By the time I met Bhante, I was free of the clinical depression that had haunted me for four decades. But his insistence on smiling all the time still felt foreign and a little extreme.

Fortunately, my time in Thailand in 2006 had introduced me to what the Thai call "sànùk" or "fun." As described earlier (see pages 121–125), sànùk is an attitude which says that anything worthwhile in life, including meditation, has some fun or playfulness as a natural part of it.

Sànùk speaks to the essence of the fourth of the Six Rs. The fourth R invokes an uplifted state. The Buddha knew that an uplifted mind-heart is calm, peaceful, and mindful. Enlightenment is an uplifted state.

As we use the Six Rs to release and relax, we leave a void inside where the tension had been. If we do nothing, the momentum of old habits may fill it with unwholesome tendencies. Old distractions may pop up again. And again. And again in a habitual cycle. Or a different unwholesome state may appear.

Instead, we fill the void with kindness, compassion, joy, ease, or any elevated quality.

Often I resist this. If I've been caught up rehashing a fight, I may not want to relax and feel good. I'm more interested in proving someone wrong than in feeling good. If I feel guilty about how I treated someone, I may want to nurse the guilt. I may not want to feel better yet.

In these situations, I've personalized the feelings—identified them as me or mine. Losing them feels like losing a part of myself. I don't see these states as temporary clouds in the sky—things that arise impersonally from causes and conditions.

This tendency to identify with inner states can be so strong that it isn't helpful to be harsh with ourselves about it. But we don't want to encourage the old habit either.

Instead, we invite in a more wholesome state—we don't force it but just invite it. If this feels foreign, we can just lift the corners of the mouth whether we feel like smiling or not. Physiological smiling tends to trigger the psychological smiling.

If we just don't want to smile, we're taking it all too seriously. It's time to lighten up, laugh at ourselves, take it easy, not try so hard, find some balance, and look for sànùk. And smiling is the best way to not take ourselves so personally. It creates some objectivity and a sense of distance from issues that we may have over-identified with.

Return

After recognizing, releasing, relaxing, and re-smiling, we return to the object of our meditation.

As simple as this sounds, it is the first place where I got into an argument with Bhante. It was on my first retreat with him. I'd been practicing choiceless awareness—letting my mind go where it would for as long as I could remain mindful. If I lost mindfulness or got distracted, then I'd return to the primary object. Otherwise, I found it best not to interfere.

So when I started working with Bhante, if a disturbing memory came up, I'd recognize it, release it, relax, and smile. Then a related memory would come up. I'd recognize, release, relax, and smile without returning first to sending mettā. If this memory reminded me of an upcoming situation that I feared, I would recognize, release, relax, and smile with that fear.

On my third or fourth day at Dhamma Sukha, I sat at the kitchen table in the old farmhouse after lunch insisting that this kind of choiceless awareness was very valuable. "I've had many insights from this over the years. They've been very helpful."

Bhante quietly shook his head, "Choiceless awareness without returning to the mettā easily leads to mental proliferation and lots of unnecessary thinking."

This was a dilemma. I trusted Bhante. But I trusted my own experience more. So finally I said, "Okay. I've come all the way to Missouri to see what I can learn from you. So I guess I should withhold judgment until I've given it a try."

Bhante said, "That's all that I'd suggest. Try it for yourself for a while and see what effect it has."

So I did.

And two days later I said to Bhante, "You were right, mostly. And I was wrong, mostly. I see how the Six Rs are more effective than I'd realized. But I think occasionally something may come up strongly and repeatedly, and then it may be helpful to follow it for a while and see where it leads. But most of the time it's more helpful to stick with all six of the Rs, not with choiceless awareness."

Bhante nodded. "There are times when it is helpful to contemplate a difficult issue. But not as a regular practice."

Unfolding the First Five Rs

Before looking at the sixth R, let's pause and look a little more carefully at how these first five work closely together.

I was sitting in my home office meditating early one morning. At least if you'd stuck your head in the room, that's how it would have looked. Actually, I was thinking, "What would be a good example to use to illus-

Recognize:	*Be aware of*
Release:	*Let it be*
Relax:	*Soften*
Re-Smile:	*Invite uplift*
Return:	*Radiate Well-being*
Repeat:	*"Ah yes"*

trate the Six Rs? It shouldn't be overly complex or overly simple. Something personal would engage the reader. Yes, personal would be good... Oh, I'm thinking. I'm supposed to be meditating. I've been rambling on here for several minutes." I recognized "thinking," released, relaxed, smiled vaguely, and returned to sending out mettā.

Within a few minutes I was rumbling along, "It's got to be a good example people can identify with. Personal is good... Oh, I'm thinking again. And these aren't even new thoughts..." I Six-R'd again. And then again. And again.

After a while, that thought pattern was familiar. It wasn't novel or exciting—just repetitive. So I caught myself after a few sentences rather than after a few paragraphs. I Six-R'd and returned to the mettā more quickly. And I stayed there a little longer before running off again.

As my mind became more collected, I noticed the first words that arose, "What about..." and Six-R'd them immediately.

I also noticed a feeling of urgency that came up with the thinking—a mixture of excitement, worry, and wanting to write.

After a while I was able to Six-R these familiar feelings even before a single word emerged.

Then, as I was sending out mettā, I'd notice a slight tightening in my field of awareness—just a bit of aversion. I Six-R'd this, and the sense of urgency did not arise.

By this time, I was no longer losing contact with the mettā. The slight tightening and even the urgency arose from time to time but no longer captured my attention. There was no need to Six-R them—I just let them recede into the background.

Eventually they faded on their own. My mind was peaceful and quietly joyful for long stretches of time.

Mettā, Samādhi, and Sati

This experience illustrates how loving kindness, collectedness, and mindfulness—mettā, samādhi, and sati—are cultivated at the same time. The brightness and clearness of loving kindness and the stillness of equanimity helped my mind become more collected. That stillness helped me see subtler and subtler disturbances. At the same time, the stillness helped loving kindness flow more easily and increased mindfulness. And the mindfulness supported the kindness and stillness. And these created the conditions that allowed insight to arise—I saw more easily and clearly what was going on.

The Buddha did not intend mettā, samādhi, and sati to be separate practices. When they are done together using the Six Rs, these qualities arise together.

Cessation

Also notice that Dependent Origination (paticcasamuppāda) and cessation (nirodha) are also integral to this practice. Dependent Origination flows from contact (phassa) to feeling tone (vedanā) to craving (taṇhā) to clinging (upādāna) to habitual tendencies (bhava). Cessation reverses this order: habitual tendencies relax, revealing clinging, which relaxes, revealing craving, which relaxes, revealing feeling tone, which relaxes, revealing raw sensation (contact).

The habitual tendency in my meditation was the familiar way I overworked, thought, and puzzled things out. The clinging was the first few words that set off this thought pattern. Clinging always manifests as thought. As I relaxed the first thought (the clinging), the habitual tendency stopped. I didn't push it away or hold it down. But without clinging, the habitual tendency ceased. That's an aspect of cessation.

The sense of urgency was a form of craving. Craving has many guises, and they all have a sense of tightening. As I relaxed the craving, the clinging ceased. No more thoughts.

Since my mind-heart was quieting down, it was easier to see the feeling tone of aversion or unpleasantness that subtly triggered the craving.

The Buddha said that one who understands Dependent Origination understands the dhamma, and one who understands the dhamma understands Dependent Origination. And he said that the way to learn Dependent Origination was to go "upstream" in the direction of cessation rather than downstream in the direction of suffering.

As I sat that morning, I wasn't analyzing my experience or putting Buddhist labels on it. I was seeing the flow of phenomena in their own terms.

As I do this day after day and year after year, the common elements in this flow become more and more obvious. On that particular day, the thoughts about writing and urgency were like leaves and sticks floating on the surface of a river. They were the most obvious manifestations that day.

But as I practice this process, I see more and more clearly the channel in which this river flows from contact to feeling tone to craving to clinging to habitual tendency and so on to suffering. As I see this process happening over and over, it looks more mechanical and less personal. Rather than think, "Oh no, I've messed up again," I think, "Oh of course, that's how things work. It's no more personal than gravity. It's just the dhamma. It's just the way things are."

Four Noble Truths

Notice that using the Six Rs is also a way of practicing the Four Noble Truths. I see dissatisfaction (dukkha) more clearly—the First Truth. I see how it arises out of craving and clinging and tightening—the Second Truth. It becomes clear that there is a little bit of craving in each link. The Four Noble Truths are part of the whole flow of Dependent Origination. By relaxing the tension, I'm practicing the cessation of suffering—the Third Truth. And taken together, the practice is a way of learning to live and work skillfully with the dhamma. This is an expression of the Eightfold Path—the Fourth Truth.

Three Characteristics

Notice that using the Six Rs is a way of practicing the three characteristics. They are imbedded in Dependent Origination (paticcasamuppāda).

They include dukkha (seeing suffering more clearly), anicca (seeing how things arise and pass away), and anattā (seeing the impersonal nature of it all).

Repeat

The final R of the six is Repeat. We go back and do the first five Rs again the next time our attention is completely taken away.

At first I thought this Repeat phase was redundant. If we do the practice, we will be repeating. We don't need a reminder of it.

But I came to appreciate that the Repeat step is not so much a reminder as a supporter. It's so easy when we have to Six-R over and over to think that we aren't doing well. The process is so simple and yet so difficult to maintain at times.

Having the Repeat step included is a reminder that we aren't alone. Everyone has to repeat this process over and over. The process may be simple, but it cuts to the core of so much of our conditioning that it needs to be done over and over. Repeating is not part of failing. It's part of the progression along the path laid out by the Buddha.

Rolling the Rs

As we repeat again and again, the Six Rs may feel less and less like six steps and more like different aspects of one smooth flow. We call this "rolling the Rs." It's a natural result of practice.

In fact, in the higher jhānas, this flow is important. Doing the six steps one at a time is too coarse. However, in the earlier jhānas it's helpful to practice them separately until they flow together on their own.

And when they do roll together, I've found it helpful to stop every once in a while for what I think of as a "checkup." This involves slowing them down and seeing if one phase has been subtly left out. Over the years I found that sometimes I gradually left the Release aspect out so that the remaining five Rs rolled past: I was ignoring distractions rather than letting them go. Sometimes I left out the Relax step. Sometimes I wasn't smiling any more. When this happened, progress in meditation invariably slowed down.

Therefore, after we find ourselves rolling the Rs, it's important to check up on them from time to time and make sure they are still the complete process and not shortchanging anything.

12

Supporting Practices

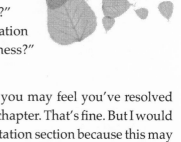

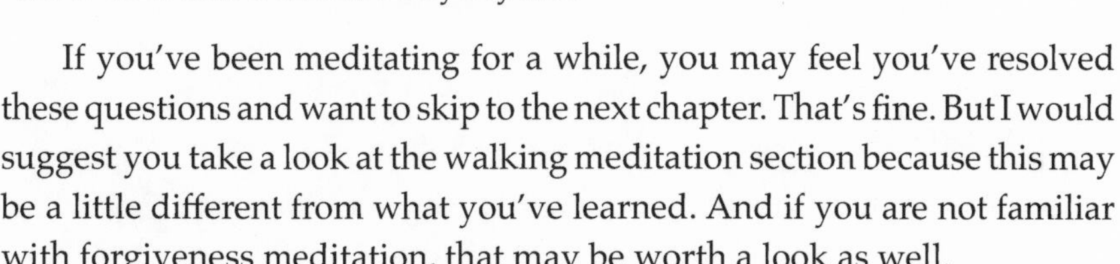

There are some practical concerns that aren't addressed in the suttas. They were probably so broadly understood that the Buddha didn't feel he needed to mention them. These include questions like, "How long do I sit in meditation?" "What postures are best?" "Can I move?" "How does walking meditation work?" "What other practices are helpful?" "What's the difference between contemplation and meditation?" "What about forgiveness?" "How does this work in everyday life?"

If you've been meditating for a while, you may feel you've resolved these questions and want to skip to the next chapter. That's fine. But I would suggest you take a look at the walking meditation section because this may be a little different from what you've learned. And if you are not familiar with forgiveness meditation, that may be worth a look as well.

For the rest of us, let's look at these questions, starting with how long to sit.

How Long?

If we sit in meditation too long, we create undue strain. If we sit too short a time, we don't progress and get discouraged. So we need a middle way.

For beginners, thirty minutes is a reasonable length of time—longer if we're comfortable. It takes about twenty minutes for the mind to begin to settle itself. If we sit for half an hour, we'll feel the benefits. The quieting may not be apparent while we're sitting. As the mind quiets, it becomes more sensitive to subtler disturbances. Subjectively it may not seem we're getting more collected. But as we get up and go about the day, the results are noticeable.

Of course, this won't be true of all sittings. Sometimes the mind settles deeply and quickly. Sometimes it runs around like a drunken coyote, no matter how skillful we are. But if we're sitting for thirty minutes a day or longer, we'll notice changes over time.

The Zen master Suzuki Roshi said that meditating regularly is difficult and meditating irregularly is impossible. So it helps to sit every day. In the beginning, we might experiment with various times of day—see what fits our schedule and biorhythms. Once we've figured that out, it's best to sit at the same time each day when possible. This way the mind anticipates the quiet time and starts to settle before we meditate—we start from a stiller place.

If we have days when we truly don't have time to sit for a half hour, it's best to sit for at least five or ten minutes. It's hard to sincerely convince ourselves we don't have that much time. And it's enough time to strengthen the daily habit.

Habit is stronger than will. So we want our practice to rely more on a habit than on willpower.

As the practice settles in, it is natural to feel like sitting longer than thirty minutes. This is helpful.

Posture

Sitting posture is not crucial. It helps to sit in a way that is both relaxed and alert. Sitting on the floor, a cushion, a chair, or couch can all work fine. Lying down is more difficult because most of us are conditioned to go to sleep when we lie down. If we have physical problems that require lying, it can be done. If not, it is usually easier to sit up.

Sitting cross-legged is a style that came out of Asia where people were used to sitting on the ground. Their bodies were accustomed to it. They could sit this way relatively effortlessly. This is not so true for Westerners. Not knowing this, I trained myself to sit on the floor on a zafu (meditation cushion). After many years of practice, I could usually sit for an hour and a half or two hours.

When I started training with Bhante and my collectedness got much stronger, I wanted to sit for two and three hours. My body protested. Now I sit almost exclusively on a chair.

I don't find either postures better or worse except that in longer sittings, a chair is easier for me.

Not Moving

Not moving is more important than the specific posture. We want a posture we can remain in for a while. I allow myself a few minutes to wiggle when I start sitting. If something is physically uncomfortable right away, it's best to adjust. But after a few minutes, it's best to not move. The mind's restlessness will come up with many excuses to move. It's best to Six-R these and remain still.

Even though I'd been told this, it took me a while to really believe it. I sometimes feel a sensation like a single hair from a brush pushing lightly into my cheek as it spins—it tickles like crazy. When I rub the spot, the sensation leaves immediately. A few minutes later, the sensation appears on my arm. If I brush it away, it appears on my hands. Pretty soon I'm rubbing and wiggling all over.

On the other hand, if I Six-R the tickle—let it be there and relax—it gets more intense, subsides, and doesn't reappear elsewhere.

Sometimes I get intense pain in my chest or elsewhere. If I move in the slightest, it disappears. From this I know it's not an actual physical problem but what's called "dhamma pain" or "meditation pain." If I don't move, it may hurt for a while. But when it subsides, I'm free of it.

On the other hand, if I have physical discomfort after I get up, then I could be overstraining. Pain that lingers after a sitting is a sign not to sit that way. It's wisest to adjust the posture in the next sitting.

Walking Meditation

The only difference between sitting meditation and life in general is that meditation has less stimulation and a slower pace. Everything that comes up in our daily life comes up in meditation: thoughts, fears, longing, pleasure, boredom, worry. With less stimulation and more time, it's easier to observe these clearly. This makes a huge difference.

Walking meditation is halfway between sitting meditation and normal living. It can be helpful in several ways:

1. If we're very restless, walking meditation can release some of the restless energy while remaining relatively mindful and collected. If we feel we really have to move, it's better to just get up and walk rather than wiggle.

2. If we're sleepy, walking meditation can bring more energy and wakefulness.

3. If we're sitting for longer stretches or several times a day (such as in a retreat), walking meditation can give the body some needed exercise while continuing to build meditative momentum.

4. Walking meditation can provide a bridge between life on the cushion or chair and life on the street. It builds mindfulness in a more active setting.

For all these reasons, I don't find slow walking helpful. I trained in slow walking meditation for years. When I was in Thailand, I noted eight different precise movements in each step. Slow walking doesn't alleviate restlessness when we're tired or build more energy when we're sleepy. It doesn't give the body good exercise. And it doesn't translate into everyday settings like walking in the grocery store or down the street.

In this style, walking meditation proceeds at a normal speed. If we've been sitting for longer stretches—a few hours or more—it can be helpful to walk fast enough to get our heart rate up. The circulation and energy will help the next sitting.

Ordinarily, we want to find an area about twenty to forty feet long where we can walk back and forth. The mind is tempted to check out new surroundings, so going back and forth over a small path reduces this temptation.

The mind tends to follow the eyes. If we look around at the scenery, the mind will wander off. Therefore it's helps to keep the eyes lowered.

As we walk, we continue the mettā practice: sending out kindness, love, tranquility, uplift, or ease to our spiritual friend. We do the same practice that we were doing while sitting, only now the body is moving.

It's likely that our mind won't stay as collected, because of the added stimulation of movement. That's fine. As always, stay with the object of meditation. If the mind's attention wanders completely, then Six-R.

This both builds the momentum of the meditation and gives us some experience in a setting that is closer to everyday life. It will make it easier to carry the benefits of meditation into other aspects of our lives.

Other Practices

In "The Greater Discourse to Sakuludāyin," (*Majjhima Nikāya* 77) beginning in section 15, the Buddha gives a catalog of various practices other than jhāna meditation. These show up in other suttas as well. They include reviewing past lives, visiting other realms, developing paranormal powers, and meditating on round disks called *kasiṇas*. None of these practices are to be engaged until we've reached the fourth jhāna. I've engaged in some of them over the years. However, they lie beyond the scope of this book for several reasons:

1. I'm not certain the Buddha actually endorsed them all. There is obvious corruption in many of the texts. These other practices were part of the Brahmin (Hindu) tradition and may have been inserted in later years.

2. There are problems with mixing practices. Jhāna development is a very complete path. Mixing it with other practices can dilute it and slow progress.

3. Some of these practices appeal to the ego. Western culture hyperstimulates our sense of self (either positively or negatively). These practices can encourage ego inflation or deflation.

4. It's not wise to engage in many of these practices until we're in the fourth jhāna or higher. But it's possible to read this book without ever entering a jhāna. The reason for this precaution may be most obvious in past life visitations. All of us have done terrible things in the past. Reliving such events is unwise without the equanimity of the fourth jhāna.[25]

5. It is impossible to empirically verify most of these practices. I don't want to be in a position of defending their validity. I often say, "Rationally I don't believe any of it. But I know they are true."

Nevertheless, I do want to mention them because they are found in the literature and they may spontaneously appear in our practice. This is possible at any stage. This is particularly true of the upper jhānas when the sense of self lightens up or loses cohesion, or there are flashes of images that seem to be from other lives or other realms.

Whether we are deliberately developing these abilities or avoiding them, what we do with these experiences is the same: we recognize the perception without analyzing, release it without pushing it away, relax, smile, return to our core practice, and repeat as needed. We Six-R. Even the most fascinating insights can be impediments if we hold onto them rather than going deeper.

Contemplation

There is one exception. There are times when contemplation can be helpful.

I was feeling stuck in my practice at one point. I couldn't figure out what was holding me back. I "asked" for guidance, for insight as to what was stopping me.

A short while later a distinct sentence appeared in my head, "I'm special." It jolted me. I saw how much of my practice was motivated by trying to prove that I'm special. I could feel the insincerity in it—a cover for feeling ignored or ridiculed as a kid. I saw how it motivated me to try to develop expertise so I could explain things to people and prove I was special. I saw the role it played in getting into the ministry, in working too hard, in pushing my kids too hard. It went on and on, insight after insight.

So I let these revelations unfold without Six-R-ing. They kept flowing in for an hour and a half. Then, some started to repeat. My experience shifted from revelations to repetitive thinking. So I began Six-R-ing the repetitive thoughts. This didn't work so well, so I shifted into walking meditation.

There are times when contemplating a particularly powerful insight can be helpful, especially if we are powerless to stop it. After his enlightenment, the Buddha spent almost a month hanging around the Bodhi tree contemplating the implications of what he'd realized.

We don't want to get into the habit of contemplating everything. Most insights are clear and full in a moment and need little more than to be recognized and released.

However, when an insight has many implications, spending some time with it can be helpful. But when thoughts start to repeat themselves, we know it's time to Six-R again.

Forgiveness

There are times when our meditation becomes laden with sadness, fear, worry, grief, anger, frustration, struggle, or other heavy emotions. We Six-R these. Yet they arise again and again so quickly and deeply that we become discouraged. It may be a time to shift to forgiveness meditation.

The comedian Lily Tomlin said, "Forgiveness means giving up all hope for a better past." This is as good a working definition of forgiveness as I have come across. It sounds so obvious when expressed this way. But there are many other ideas about what forgiveness is. Before looking at forgiveness as a meditation practice, it may help to consider what forgiveness is not.

Condoning and Forgetting

Forgiveness is not condoning or forgetting.

When I was working as a psychotherapist, several of my clients were incest survivors. As children, they had been raped repeatedly by their fathers or other relatives. When they learned I was a minister as well as a therapist, they invariably asked, "Do I have to forgive him?"

My short answer was, "Absolutely not." I said this because they were usually asking, "Do I have to condone what he did as if it were okay? Do I have to forget what he did to me?" Many had already spent years blaming themselves or trying to forget what had happened. It didn't work. It never does.

After developing some trust, I could give a longer answer: "You and I both wish it had never happened. But it did. It need not ever happen again. But we can't get rid of the past.

"In the present, you still have hurt, anger, and grief. As you explore these and find safe ways to recognize, express, and release them, you'll find a place that is deeper than these feelings—a place that he was never able to touch. As you trust your deeper essence, you'll lose interest in putting attention into what he did years ago. You'll find a wholeness that just wants to live fully now.

"This doesn't mean that what he did was okay. It wasn't. It doesn't mean that you have to forget it. How could you? It merely means that the past will feel more like the past. And you'll be with your life unfolding today.

"That is the essence of forgiveness. Nothing more and nothing less."

Few of us have had the horrendous abuse of incest. Yet most of us have suffered things that were not right by any reasonable standard. Forgiving is not saying these things were okay or that we have to live as if they hadn't happened.

Most of us have done things we regret. Out of hurt, fear, or confusion, we've done things we wish we hadn't. Asking for forgiveness or forgiving ourselves does not mean that what we did was okay. We recognize our remorse, do what we can to make amends, and figure out ways to help us not repeat the same mistake. Then it is possible to be with what is now without having to try to forget or condone the past.

Naïveté

This suggests something else that forgiveness is not. True forgiveness is not naïveté. If someone hurt us, it may be naïve to believe they could never do it again. If we did something we regret, we may be kidding ourselves if we think we're incapable of doing it again. It is naïve to think that forgiveness magically changes another person or changes us.

We can forgive a person and still be mindful. We can do reasonable things to not put ourselves in a position where they could hurt us again consciously or unconsciously. We don't have to throw away our defenses.

It is wise to protect ourselves reasonably from other people's unskillful habits.

And it is wise to figure out how to attenuate our own unskillful habits.

In fact, resolving to take reasonable steps to deal with these difficulties may help forgiveness arise more easily.

Reconciliation

And finally, forgiveness is not reconciliation. Reconciliation is a meeting of minds and hearts. It is usually preceded by both people being open about what they did, taking responsibility, making amends where possible, taking credible steps to assure they won't do it again, expressing genuine remorse, and forgiving the other person and ourselves.

Reconciliation requires that both people do these things.

We cannot reconcile with someone who is unwilling. We cannot reconcile with someone if they don't want to reconcile with us. Yet we can still forgive that person regardless of what he or she does or doesn't do. Reconciliation requires forgiveness, but forgiveness does not require reconciliation.

Forgiveness comes more easily with reconciliation, though it is not a prerequisite. We let go of trying to change the past and come fully into the present.

Three Arenas

There are three arenas of forgiveness: forgiving those who have harmed us, asking for forgiveness from those we have harmed, and forgiving ourselves. In our relationships with the people in our lives, each of these arenas has special considerations. They are rich arenas that go beyond the scope of this book. But none of them requires condoning, forgetting, naïveté, or reconciliation. Knowing these are not required is enough to turn to forgiveness meditation itself.

Forgiveness Meditation

Like mettā meditation, forgiveness meditation begins with simple phrases. In choosing phrases consider three things: (1) not fully understanding a situation is the most common source of mistakes. We act out of partial ignorance. Or we're blinded by emotion. (2) Remorse and guilt are stronger when we harm someone or ourselves than when no harm results. And (3) our inner critic is the most unrelenting when our behavior violates our values.

These considerations lead to four forgiveness phrases:[26]

I forgive myself for not understanding.

I forgive myself for making mistakes.

I forgive myself for hurting myself or others.

I forgive myself for not following my deepest values.

We can begin by saying our version of one of these phrases. We choose a phrase that has some pull for us. I like to begin with: "I forgive myself for not understanding." Whatever phrase we start with, we repeat it slowly until it becomes real. As we feel the forgiveness, we let it radiate from our heart as a soft, kind acceptance. We let it surround us.

The mind may wander off on all kinds of errands. Often we resist forgiving ourselves. So if the mind wanders to blame or distractions, six-R and gently come back to repeat a phrase.

Depending on our situation, the mind may naturally go to the person who hurt us or made us angry or who left us. If this happens we can shift the focus to them:

I forgive you for not understanding.

I forgive you for making mistakes.

I forgive you for hurting me or others.

I forgive you for not following my deepest values.

In our mind's eye we look directly into their eyes and really forgive them. It's best not to get involved in storylines. We just use the phrases.

Sometimes things may turn around so that we're looking into their eyes and asking for their forgiveness:

Please forgive me for not understanding.

Please forgive me for making mistakes.

Please forgive me for hurting you.

We keep asking until we can hear them forgive us.

It helps to carry the practice into everyday life, forgiving everyone and everything that comes along. Most of us have a zealous inner critic. To soften the inner judge we can forgive ourselves for everything we do:

I forgive myself for stubbing my toe.

I forgive myself for bumping into the table.

... for burning my finger.

... for being distracted.

... for making a mistake.

... for getting angry.

...for breaking a shoelace.

...for repeating that bad joke.

As the mind-heart gets lighter, we understand more clearly, make fewer mistakes, cause less harm to ourselves and others, and live more gracefully by our deepest values.

The forgiveness practice does not get rid of distractions, change other people, or stop us from experiencing hindrances. However, over time, it changes our relationship to them. We can let them be what they are. We release them. We let the past be in the past. And we experience whatever is in the present with less and less judgment.

After a while, the phases may become very simple. We may not need to name the distraction. We simply say "I forgive myself," "I forgive you," or "I ask your forgiveness."

With this we come into a more loving acceptance of the flow of life as it is. We continue with the forgiveness mediation until the mind and heart feel lighter. Then we ask, "Is there more I need to forgive?" If there is, we continue. If there isn't, it is time to move back to the regular mettā practice.

This practice may be useful no matter where we are in our meditation. I've seen it used effectively by people who were having difficulty getting into the first jhāna. Bhante recommended it to me when I was having trouble getting into the eighth jhāna—and it made the difference that allowed me to get past some subtle blockages.

However, it is important not to move quickly in and out of the practice. If forgiveness meditation is to be most helpful, we use it for several days before switching back. If we try switching back and forth often, figuring out when to switch becomes another hindrance. So it's best to stay with it for a while.

Everyday Awareness

Whether doing sitting meditation, walking meditation, contemplation, or forgiveness, the point of developing a meditation practice is not to become a good meditator. It is to cultivate heart and wisdom in our everyday life. It helps to remember to cultivate mindfulness, send mettā, and Six-R distractions everywhere we are. One thing I love about this practice is that it is relatively easy to bring it into everyday life. We can even be in the midst of an argument and recognize, "Oh, I'm really mad. Far out." After recognizing, we release, relax, and even smile a little. As we do this, we may even continue arguing. But we aren't so attached. And with this, the exchange may move into a wiser, more heartful place.

When I was running a counseling center for street kids, one day one of the adolescents took advantage of me. Even though we were closed, I had let her come in to use the phone because she said she had to let her mother know where she was.

I left the room as she was talking to her mother. Ten minutes later, I came back to find her gabbing with a friend on the phone. I felt anger rising in my body. I was just back from a retreat, so I saw this anger with some dispassion. I realized that if I gently expressed my disappointment, this young woman would not get it. Anger was needed to break through her street-tough exterior. I had no attachment to the anger, but I didn't push it away. It seemed appropriate to the situation. I recognized and released it in a relaxed way. The anger didn't fade, so I let it flow out of my mouth as I spoke strongly and forcefully.

She looked up at me. Then she smiled. It was an open, genuine smile. She got it. For about two seconds, we had a deep connection of minds and hearts. Then she apologized sincerely and got up and left. This was a kid who usually argued about everything and never apologized. At that particular time, anger was a skillful means to make a meaningful connection. It got through to her.

Most of the time when I'm angry, it indicates attachment or confusion. But not always. Living in the world with awareness, heart, and wisdom doesn't mean we'll look serene and emotionless. Living wisely in everyday life is enhanced by sending mettā and releasing tightness. But from the outside, it can look very different.

13

Confidence: Second Jhāna

Navajo Mountain is a volcanic bubble that formed when magma from deep in the earth pushed the surface into a dome without actually breaking through. Over the centuries, water cut through the sandstone along the mountain edges forming canyons. The same natural forces carved Rainbow Bridge in one of those canyons. It is one of the world's largest natural bridges.

When I was fifteen, getting to Rainbow Bridge was difficult, requiring a drive over a long dirt road in southern Utah followed by a thirteen-mile hike through hot canyons.

A dam on the Colorado River would soon create a lake and make the bridge accessible by boat. My father, my older brother, Reynold, and I were determined to get there while relatively few people had seen the natural wonder.

The hike in was hot and difficult, though it was mostly downhill. The next day, the hike out was uphill and more strenuous. My father began to run out of energy. This was a new phenomenon for me to witness—he was a powerful man, and I had never seen him at his limits. Yet I still had energy to spare.

Reynold and I conferred and decided that he, Reynold, should hike ahead to the ranger station at the trailhead. The station sold a little food. We needed some and didn't think my father would make it before the station closed. So my older brother left us.

An hour later, my father said he could go no further and wanted to stop for the night. I said I would go ahead and get some food from Reynold and bring it back. I left my water with him and headed out.

After a half mile, I came upon two other men who had collapsed and built an overly large fire in the middle of the trail. They pressed me for water. I said I had none and went on.

The men pointed me in the wrong direction. I lost the trail completely. The sunset gave way to a moonless night. The sky was clear and brilliant with stars, but there wasn't enough light to see the ground around me. I knew the dangers of groping around the desert at night, including the possibility of falling off a steep embankment or cliff.

The wisest course was to do nothing, just wait for daylight. I trusted that my father would be okay. I knew I was fine and could find my way out easily in the morning.

Confident, relaxed, and patient, I got a ground cloth and sleeping bag out of my pack and lay down. I felt the timeless mountain beneath me. I listened to the whispers in the desert silence. I watched the stars slowly circle around the North Star. I felt how small I was compared to the mountain, the desert, the stars, and the turning universe. I was serene, knowing I was a tiny part of this web of life.

During the night the forest ranger hiked in with flashlights, food, and water and got my father and the other two men out safely. But he couldn't find me—I was too far off the trail.

In the dawn light, I saw that I had stopped about twenty feet from a cliff. I was glad I had trusted my instincts to stop the night before. From the cliff edge, I spotted the trail a quarter mile below, climbed down, and hiked out in good shape.

Many decades later, I still remember the quiet joy of being alone in the stillness of the desert night. Despite the drama around me, I trusted the natural forces. If I respected them, relaxed, and waited patiently for the dawn, things would be fine. And they were.

Subtle Shift

The second jhāna is about confidence, stillness, and patience. These are states we've all experienced. They can arise in the midst of a drama if we instinctively relax into the flux and flow of forces around us. And they can arise sitting quietly in meditation if we relax into the flux and flow of the forces within us.

Confidence is not a belief that we will prevail over a difficult situation; it's trust in how things are unfolding. Stillness is not holding ourselves in check; it's relaxing softly. And patience is not waiting in anticipation; it's comfort being with things as they are.

Confidence, stillness, and patience are states that arise and pass. We don't necessarily achieve them and own them forever. Rather they arise when the conditions are right.

They arise in the second jhāna. However, we may not recognize them, because they are quiet and don't draw attention. Most people don't recognize this jhāna when it first arises.

I didn't recognize the jhāna at first partly because I was floundering around without a knowledgeable teacher. I didn't know what to look for or what to do.

When I started training with Bhante, I didn't recognize it, because I was waiting for him to tell me and he didn't. He saw it and suggested changes to my practice to utilize it. But he didn't label it out loud, because thinking about "What jhāna am I in now?" can be a distraction more than a help.

And most people don't recognize the second jhāna, because it is so similar to the first. We send out mettā to our spiritual friend. Then our attention drifts off somewhere else. We recognize the distraction. Almost by itself the mind releases and relaxes, giving rise to joy and a spontaneous smile. This spreads out into a quieter comfort and sense of well-being as we return to sending out mettā.

This cycle from joy to happiness to equanimity (pīti to sukha to upekkhā) is the same as in the first jhāna. But it takes less effort to remember the Six Rs. And going through this cycle over and over, the joy may become more intense and last longer. The happiness and equanimity stay longer before fading. And when we go back to sending out mettā to our spiritual friend, the body and mind feel lighter.

We may not immediately recognize that we're sending mettā longer before drifting away. However, looking back, we realize we've sometimes spent five or ten minutes without drifting. There is less discursive thinking. And it is easier to sit for longer stretches since the body is more relaxed.

I remember sitting in a retreat and realizing, "Oh, I don't have to force my mind to stay on the object. I don't have to make the chatty mind stop. All I have to do is take care of the practice, and the practice will take care of me."

Soon I'd forget this insight and go back to my habitual doubt and struggle, only to again discover, "Oh, if I just take care of the practice, the practice will take care of me." I'm a slow learner.

As I experienced the practice working, I did develop more confidence in it and in myself. Some effort was needed to remember to pay attention and relax. But strain wasn't needed or helpful. The mind continued to wander, but I felt more patient with it—trusting that with gentle practice it would come around on its own.

Confidence and the accompanying patience are subtle signs of the second jhāna. Another sign is that we find ourselves smiling more, both on and off the meditation cushion.

Noble Silence

The most obvious sign of the second jhāna may be a change in attitude toward the mettā phrases: "May you be happy." "May you have ease." "May you be healthy."

At first, the phrases help the mind stay with sending mettā—they support the process and make it easier. But as the process deepens, the mettā flows more easily and freely on its own. The phrases begin to feel clumsy. Repeating them becomes more of a distraction than a support of meditation. The words feel awkward compared to the refinement of the feeling and the energy.

When I confessed to Bhante that the phrases were feeling thick and bulky, he smiled and said, "Good. Stop using them. Just send the mettā out silently."

I felt relieved.

"And you don't send mettā to yourself unless you need it, " he continued. "The flow is strong enough that you can just send it silently to your spiritual friend."

Bhante went on to say, "You are entering noble silence. When the Buddha spoke of noble silence, he wasn't referring to not speaking during retreats. It's fine to talk during training as long as you only speak about the dhamma and the practice. Students can learn a lot from each other if their speech is simple, mindful, and helpful.

"'Noble silence' refers to a naturally arising inner silence. Inner speech fades away. So continue to send out the feeling of mettā from your heart. But don't weight it down with phrases."

Simplicity

I didn't understand how simple these instructions were. I continued to use the phrases in each sitting until they felt awkward and then let them drop. When Bhante realized what I was doing, he gently corrected me. I was to always practice from noble silence. If my mind was hopelessly rambunctious, it was okay to use the phrases for a short period to help it settle. But I should keep the practice simple and always start with silent mettā rather than starting with phrases and trying to figure out when to switch.

By nurturing silence this way, I learned to drop into it more and more easily. When I couldn't, the Six Rs were always there to take care of the distractions and hindrances.

As I got the hang of it, I could see the wisdom of this approach. As I went on to other jhānas, my default practice would always be my leading edge–the practices associated with the highest jhāna I had been in. I didn't have to go through the complexity of figuring out which practice to use with my current mind state.

Adjusting the Practice

The qualities that characterize the second jhāna—confidence, silence, and patience—can also be found in the first, third, and other jhānas. They gradually deepen with practice. We may not recognize when they reach the second stage. It's not as if we are in a room called Jhāna One, unlock a door, walk through, and find ourselves in Jhāna Two. It's more like walking through a gradually rising meadow with no clear line between one end and the other.

We shouldn't worry about which jhāna we're in if we can help it. If we're working with an experienced teacher, she'll recognize our stage by our smiling, lightness, humor, amount of time we stay with the object of meditation, and ease with which we sit longer and longer.

The only adjustment to the practice in the second jhāna is noble silence. If we don't have a teacher to suggest when to drop the phrases, we can experiment. If we find the phrases are more a burden than a support and we're staying with the object of meditation for five minutes or more during our best sittings, we can drop the phrases for a few sittings. If this helps, then we continue without the phrases.

In the Buddha's Words

Let's take a look at what the Buddha actually said about the second jhāna. Picking up with verse 5 of the "Anupada Sutta: One by One As They Occurred" (*Majjhima Nikaya* 111), the Buddha speaks of his disciple, Sāriputta:

> *(5) Again, monks, with the stilling of thinking and examining thought, Sāriputta entered and abided in the second jhāna which has self-confidence and stillness of mind without thinking and examining thought, with joy and happiness born of collectedness.*
>
> *(6) And the states in the second jhāna—the self-confidence, the joy, the happiness, and the unification of mind; the contact, feeling, perception, formation, and mind; the enthusiasm, choice, energy, mindfulness, equanimity, and attention—these states were defined by him one by one as they occurred; known to him those states arose, known they were present, known they disap-*

peared. He understood thus: "So indeed, these states, not having been, come into being; having been, they vanish." Regarding those states, he abided unattracted, unrepelled, independent, detached, free, dissociated, with a mind rid of barriers. He understood: "There is an escape beyond this," and with the cultivation of that attainment, he confirmed that there is.

Notice that this description is quite similar to that of the first jhāna (see page 135). The cycle of joy, happiness, and "unification of mind" is still present, as are the khandhas ("the contact, feeling, perception, formation, and mind"). And Sāriputta views them all with the same detachment.

What's different is the self-confidence and the "stilling of thinking and examining thought." The mettā phrases are thoughts. So they feel awkward when thinking and examining thought is fading. There is thought in the second jhāna, but it's the kind that just notes what's going on without wandering into discursive ruminations, analyzing, and storytelling. The "unification of mind" hinted at in the first jhāna becomes a little deeper and steadier in the second.

The "Kāyagatasati Sutta: Mindfulness of the Body" (*Majjhima Nikaya* 119) verse 19 includes a metaphor for the deeper calm of the second jhāna. As you may recall, the first jhāna uses the metaphor of a small ball of bath powder. In the second jhāna, the metaphor is a much larger lake:

Just as though there were a lake whose waters welled up from below and it had no inflow from east, west, north, or south, and would not be replenished from time to time by showers of rain, then the cool fount of water welling up in the lake would make the cool water drench, steep, fill, and pervade the lake, so that there would be no part of the whole lake unpervaded by cool water; so too, a monk makes the joy and happiness born of collectedness drench, steep, fill, and pervade this body, so that there is no part of his whole body unpervaded by the joy and happiness born of collectedness.

For those living in a cooler northern climate, the metaphor of cool water may evoke mixed feelings. To those growing up in India where summer temperature may reach 120°F, the metaphor of pervading cool water is definitely soothing.

The soothing goes even deeper in the third jhāna, the topic of the next chapter.

14

Duck in the Waves: Third Jhāna

Bonnng...Bonnng... Bonnng. Bong. Bong. Bong, bong, bong, bongbong-bong. As the cadence of the gong picked up, several dozen dogs near and far joined in with yips, barks, and outright howls. My eyes opened. "Ah. It must be 4:00 a.m."

I was lying on my side, looking across a dark floor. In the dim light from the windows, I could make out cement walls.

My ribs felt bruised. They were an inch from the parquet floor. A cotton blanket and thin foam pad served as a mattress.

I rolled slowly onto my back. As the pressure and numbness came off my ribs, the pain grew intense. Then it faded.

I stared at the ceiling fan. This was a luxurious kuti (meditation hut) compared to the thatched hut I'd been in a month earlier. It was twelve feet square, with a fan, screens on the windows, and a sort of bathroom in the corner with a hose for a cold shower.

I closed my eyes. I was in no hurry to get up.

By four thirty in the morning I was up and dressed in my novice white pants and shirt. After turning the fan off, I heard chanting in the distance. There was an outdoor, screened area on the far side of the meditation hall, about seventy-five yards away. The monks had started their morning chanting.

I wandered out of my kuti, around the backside of the meditation hall, and sat on the back steps. There were monks' rooms upstairs above the meditation hall. A monk with a tattooed shoulder descended past me. "You can join us," he said, pointing to the rows of monks fifteen yards away. "Or, if you like, you can meditate upstairs. It's okay," he reassured me.

"Khòwp khun, kháp," I said to him in Thai ("Thank you kindly"). But I remained where I was on the stairs. I didn't intend to stay long.

By four forty-five I was back in my kuti. I knew the exact configuration of zafu and pillows that was most comfortable. I sat up straight with legs folded and hands on a small pillow on my lap. I relaxed, closed my eyes, and began meditating.

The meditation I used was different from what I'd learn from Bhante years later. It did not center on mettā or the jhānas. It centered on techniques developed by the revered Mahasi Sayadaw and passed down to Ajahn Tong and then to me. These included breath awareness, focusing on a series of specific spots on the body called "touching points," soft mental labeling to note each experience, and a lot of effort. But I had learned not to follow all the instructions literally.

During one of my first meditation interviews six weeks earlier, the monk concluded, "Work hard and diligently."

I said, "My teachers in America tell me I assert too much effort. They tell me to relax to come into balance."

"No," he said. "Right effort means putting strong effort into staying mindful and following the instructions."

So I went back to my room and followed all his instructions literally. In the next interview I told him the schedule I had set, how long I was sitting, and what I was doing in the sittings.

His eyes grew wide. "Go take a walk," he said. "Relax. Buy some ice cream. You're pushing too hard."

I had a flash of insight. He had been talking to me as if I were Thai. The Thai people are kind, relaxed, and mellow. They believe in sànùk: fun and ease. I couldn't imagine them meditating so hard. I was a Westerner used to stress and strain. To come into balance, I needed to be more Thai-like.

From then on, whenever I received instructions, I imagined how a Thai might engage them. I'd let go, relax, and adopt a kind, gentle, mellow Thai temperament. These were some of the attitudes in the Six Rs that I'd learn from Bhante several years later.

At four forty-five in the morning in Wat Chom Tong, I noticed my abdomen rise and fall with the breath. I widened my attention to take in my whole body sitting there. Then I narrowed my focus to a specific spot on my body: a "touching point." In the last five weeks I'd learned all 28 points.

With each shift of attention, I used a soft mental note: "rising" and "falling" for the breath, "sitting" for the whole body sitting, and "touching" for each touching point. Noting kept me honest and objective. "Rising, falling, sitting, touching, rising, falling, sitting, touching."

A dog barked. Like a rubber ball on an elastic band, my attention was yanked off the breath and landed on the sharp sound. I stayed with it. "Hearing." I knew the dog. He hung out about fifty feet from my kuti. He believed his job was to watch for terrorists. The dog was very suspicious, so he barked a lot.

I was tempted to picture the dog and what he was doing. But these were just mental constructs—thoughts. What I directly knew was hearing. So I labeled the actual experience: "hearing, hearing."

At the same time I noticed a feeling. I didn't like the dog barking and grabbing my attention. I noted: "disliking, disliking."

The dog stopped barking. My aversion hung around. I was tempted to push the uncomfortable feeling aside and go back to the breath. But the meditation instructions were to stay with a phenomenon until it faded or a significant amount of time had gone by. So I stayed with it. "Disliking. Aversion. Disliking."

In a few minutes the disliking faded. I looked for it, but it was gone. So I went back to "rising, falling, sitting, touching."

The dog barked again. "Hearing. Disliking. Disliking."

This time the aversion faded more quickly. Short barking spells recurred again and again. I just noticed hearing and disliking as they arose.

After ten minutes, the hearing continued to arise, but the disliking didn't come up anymore. In half an hour, even the hearing faded into the background. The barking was just part of the sounds of life around me: singing birds, chirping crickets, barking dogs, rustling wind. It no longer pulled my attention away from the breathing. Rising, falling, sitting, and touching were stronger than the sounds.

The dog no longer disturbed me. We call this "peace." I noticed the bark with greater clarity and precision than when I was averse to it, but it didn't perturb me. I was more serene.

Rising, falling, sitting, touching. Rising, falling, sitting, touching.

A thought flickered through my mind. It was five thirty in the morning. Thailand was fifteen hours ahead of California. Back home it was yesterday afternoon at two thirty. Erika, my wife, was at work dealing with her programs and organizational changes.

I was no longer aware of my breathing or my body. I was just thinking about Erika.

The meditation instructions were to not suppress or ignore anything. They were to be as mindful as possible of whatever was going on. What was going on was I was sitting in a kuti in a wat in Chom Tong in northern Thailand thinking about my wife. The content of my thoughts was not important. We love our thoughts and their content. But for spiritual training, the fact that I was thinking was more important than what I was thinking about. So I noted the process: "Thinking, thinking." This loosened the grip of the thoughts so that I noticed them more clearly.

Usually, it only took a few labels before the thoughts dissolved on their own. The thinking just stopped, often in mid-sentence. But this morning, the thinking faded slowly and reluctantly. There was more going on than just an idle thought. I was missing Erika. I felt lonely. So I labeled: "Missing her. Lonely. Lonely."

The temptation was to think about the feelings. But thoughts can go on forever. And what was driving my consciousness wasn't a thought. It was a feeling. I'd learned a trick in relating to feelings. They have body sensations with them. So I scanned my body. I noticed heaviness in my chest and fuzziness in my head. I noted: "Heavy heart. Fuzzy. Heavy heart." These feelings were uncomfortable. I didn't like them. "Heavy heart. Disliking. Lonely. Disliking."

The sensations were actually quite manageable. My heart softened and expanded. The disliking faded. A quiet aching remained for a while. "Aching. Poignancy. Aching."

Bonnng…Bonnng…Bonnng. Bong. Bong. Bong, bong, bong, bong-bongbong. It was 6:00 a.m.: time for breakfast.[27]

Equanimity

The hallmark of the third jhāna is equanimity (upekkhā).

Equanimity is not about quieting the noise around us or the noise inside. There can be inner peace amidst barking dogs and loneliness. Equanimity does not come from controlling our experience. It comes from how we relate to it.

One of my favorite poems captures this in an image of a duck. The poem was written by Donald C. Babcock and appeared in *The New Yorker Magazine* in the October 4, 1947 issue:

Now we are ready to look at something pretty special.
It is a duck riding the ocean a hundred feet beyond the surf.
No, it isn't a gull.
A gull always has a raucous touch about him.
This is some sort of duck, and he cuddles in the swells.

He isn't cold, and he is thinking things over.
There is a big heaving in the Atlantic,
And he is part of it.
He looks a bit like a mandarin, or the Lord Buddha meditating
under the Bo tree,
But he has hardly enough above the eyes to be a philosopher.
He has poise, however, which is what philosophers must have.
He can rest while the Atlantic heaves, because he rests in the Atlantic.
Probably he doesn't know how large the ocean is.
And neither do you.
But he realizes it.
And what does he do, I ask you? He sits down in it.
He reposes in the immediate as if it were infinity—which it is.
That is religion, and the duck has it.
He has made himself part of the boundless,
by easing himself into it just where it touches him.
I like the little duck.
He doesn't know much.
But he has religion.

There are several things I love about this poem. First, the Atlantic heaves. As far back as we can see in history there have been waves: war, disease, corruption, injustice, pain, suffering, dukkha in infinite variety. It's likely to continue through our lives. Rather than argue with the waves, the duck accepts the ocean as it is.

I also love that the poem is about an ordinary duck rather than some exotic bird. Too often peace and well-being are seen as characteristics of extraordinary beings. I find it comforting that a simple duck can realize the largeness of the ocean.

And I love that all the duck does is sit down. It's simple. It's not so easy to just sit and do nothing else physically, mentally, or emotionally. But when we can, we realize we are part of the boundless.

This is the essence of equanimity: being ordinary as we sit in life as it is.

Loss of Joy

As we move from the second to the third jhānas, joy and happiness fade away. Both of them can be sweet. But they have energy and a measure of tension in them. As we relax more deeply, we don't go through the cycle from joy to happiness to equanimity (pīti to sukha to upekkhā). Rather we go directly to equanimity.

Subjectively it can feel as if we are losing our meditation. We had become so familiar with upwelling of pīti and sukha. When this joy and happiness no longer arise, we may think our practice is regressing.

This can lead to some amusing exchanges:

A meditator comes in and says, "My practice is not going so well."

"How's that?"

"The joy is gone."

"How do you feel?"

"I'm fine. Kinda peaceful actually. But the joy is gone."

"Are there problems?"

"No. Well, I stepped on a nail this morning. There's a lot of pain. But it will heal and then I won't need this crutch much longer. No problem. Except the joy is gone."

I have a friend who has always had a lot of equanimity. When he started to meditate, he went through the first two jhānas quickly and settled into equanimity. He saw others around him meditating in joy and bliss and thought his practice was slow. In reality, they would catch up with him in a while.

Imperturbable

With the third jhāna, we begin to become imperturbable. The effect is different depending on whether we are practicing the stricter absorption jhānas or the gentler tranquility jhānas as described by the Buddha.

If we are practicing the absorption jhānas, the mind becomes one-pointed by adhering strongly to the object of meditation. If someone drops a garbage can on the concrete outside the window, the sound may break our concentration with a startle. It feels like being whacked by a wave of sound.

If we are practicing the tranquility jhānas and we move into the third jhāna, and someone drops a garbage can outside the window, we probably hear it clearly but aren't startled in the least. We feel the wave of sound gracefully flow through the body. Since there is very little gross tension, the energy wave has little to hit. It just passes on through.

Adjusting the Practice

The third jhāna is also characterized by a lessening of gross body sensations. The body feels lighter. Joy subsides. A sense of peacefulness settles in that makes it harder for sensations to disturb us. We become more like a simple duck content to rest in the waves that roll past.

These are signs that it may be helpful to adjust the practice—who we send mettā to and how we send it. A good teacher can help recognize when to shift. But if we don't have a teacher, we can experiment. Since the best times to adjust the practice may be toward the end of the third or the beginning of the fourth jhāna, I'll describe this in the next chapter, beginning on page 195.

In the Buddha's Words

Before we move on, let's look at how the Buddha described the third jhāna. Picking up at verse 7 of the "Anupada Sutta: One by One As They Occurred" (*Majjhima Nikaya* 111):

> *(7) Again, with the fading away as well of joy, Sāriputta abided in equanimity, mindful and fully aware, still feeling happiness with the body, he entered upon*

and abided in the third jhāna, on account of which noble ones announce: "He has a pleasant abiding who has equanimity and is mindful."

(8) And the states in the third jhāna—the equanimity, the happiness, the mindfulness, the full awareness, and the unification of mind; the contact, feeling, perception, formations, and mind; the enthusiasm, choice, energy, mindfulness, equanimity, and attention–these states were defined by him one by one as they occurred; known to him those states arose, known they were present, known they disappeared. He understood thus: "So indeed, these states, not having been, come into being; having been, they vanish." Regarding those states, he abided unattracted, unrepelled, independent, detached, free, dissociated, with a mind rid of barriers.

Notice the "fading away of joy"—it doesn't arise. Instead there is just equanimity that is mindful and aware. The equanimity may be felt as a balance of mind.

In the fourth jhāna, the feeling in the body will fade completely. But in the third it is still present though the body is lighter and more comfortable. This makes it easier to sit longer without any movement. In a retreat setting, we'd probably be sitting for over an hour.

The people around us may notice the smiling and ease ("He has pleasant abiding") that we carry into daily activities.

Verse 8 indicates that despite the equanimity (upekkhā), happiness (sukha), and mindfulness (sati), this is not an absorption state. The khandhas are still present: contact, feeling tone, perception, formations, and mind. The mind is not free from distractions. As long as we retain some contact with the object of meditation, we can let distractions float in the background. And when we become lost in thoughts or images, we use the Six Rs.

The "Kāyagatasati Sutta: Mindfulness of the Body" (*Majjhima Nikaya* 119) verse 20 includes a metaphor for a lotus drenched in equanimity (upekkhā):

Just as in a pond of blue or white or red lotuses, some lotuses that are born and grow in the water thrive immersed in the water without rising out of it, and cool water drenches, steeps, fills, and pervades them to their tips and their roots, so that there is no part of all those lotuses unpervaded by cool water;

so too, a monk allows the happiness without joy to drench, steep, fill, and pervade this body, so that there is no part of his whole body unpervaded by the happiness without joy.

15

Look Mom, No Hands: Fourth Jhāna

When I was in late childhood—big enough to take my own bath and small enough to stretch out in a tub, I liked to fill the tub with hot water and bubbles and play with toys. Then I'd stretch out and relax with arms floating in the bubbly water beside me. The water came up the sides of my head, but I floated high enough for my nose to draw air without water. My ears were below the water, giving the world a muffled sound.

After a while, I'd notice that my arms were missing: I couldn't feel them at all. I'd wiggle my fingers. Surprisingly, they worked just fine. With the slightest movement, I could feel them completely.

I became fascinated by the phenomenon and would try to "make my arms go away" again. It took a while. I'd float quietly in the water. With time, my hands, arms, and sometimes my legs would vanish from kinesthetic awareness. It was very peaceful.

"Look Mom, no hands," I mused quietly.

Arūpa

As we relax more deeply and clearly into the third jhāna, we may move into the fourth.

It's called *arūpa upekkhā*. In Pāli, *rūpa* means "body" and *arūpa* means "without body." "Upekkhā" means equanimity. So arūpa upekkhā means "equanimity without body." It sounds strange. But if you've ever floated in a bath or hot tub and lost perception of a hand, arm or leg, the experience is familiar.

If we sit in a chair or cushion in equanimity for long enough, we may experience the same phenomena without being wet.

If, as we relax, the mind goes dull or drifts off into fantasy, that's called "daydreaming." But if our awareness stays present and peaceful even as the body seems to fade, it's arūpa upekkhā—equanimity without body. It is considered an advanced stage of meditation. Congratulations!

When training with Bhante, my first entrances into the fourth jhāna were not graceful. I had been feeling intense joy—smiling so strongly I thought my face would break. Then suddenly it all stopped. I told Bhante it felt like a switch had been flipped. I'd be smiling to the point of tears. Then it all vanished. If I Six-R'd, the wave of joy would come up, then go silent.

I was sure I was doing something wrong—falling off the jhāna wagon. But Bhante said the feeling had cut off because I was losing contact with my body. It was a good sign.

I guess there are lots of ways to enter a jhāna.

The fourth jhāna is the first arūpa jhāna. Some people consider there to be only one arūpa jhāna with four sub-parts, realms, or bases: infinite space, infinite consciousness, nothingness, and neither perception nor non-perception.

Others people consider there to be five separate arūpa jhānas. They consider the four bases to be the fifth, sixth, seventh, and eight jhānas. I learned jhānas this way and find it simpler. So I'll use that language.

In the eighth jhāna and beyond, the senses can truly shut down—they stop functioning temporarily. In the fourth jhāna, the phenomenon is subtler. Various body parts fade from awareness.

Not Quite Arūpa

Forerunners to the loss of sensation may arise in earlier jhānas:

During my early years of retreats, I figured out how to sit for more than forty-five minutes or an hour. When I was relaxed in meditation for a long time, I sometimes perceived my body leaning at a forty-five degree angle. It was strange that gravity didn't pull it to the floor. Opening my eyes for a peek, I saw I was actually sitting erect. My internal kinesthetic sense had lost its bearing.

Shifts in kinesthetic accuracy may precede the complete loss of sensation. Other senses may fade as well. On one retreat in the high Sierra Mountains, a wind chime jingled outside the window. During the first day of the retreat, this annoyed me. A few days later, the annoying sound was gone. Then I noticed that the chimes were still there tinkling away but that they had faded from my awareness.

There was a road heading down the mountain a few hundred yards away. Trucks downshifted on the downgrade. The engines made sounds like huge mechanical flatulence right outside the window.

Later in the retreat, I could still hear the trucks, but they seemed far away. If I brought my full attention to them, I realized that the decibel level was the same. Now, psychologically, they were on the other side of the hill.

In the third jhāna, the body becomes so relaxed that sensory sensations are no longer disturbing. We are ducks riding the waves.

In the fourth jhāna, the body becomes so relaxed that sensations fade away until they stop registering—like floating in a hot tub of water, our hands or feet or other parts of the body are gone from awareness. Some meditators call this "ataxia" or "sensory ataxia," which is a neurological dysfunction. But the jhāna is not a dysfunction. The body has simply become so relaxed that it no longer generates signals. It is still able to function fully. Sometimes all we have to do is bring our attention to the "missing" body part and the sensation returns. Other times a bug may crawl up our arm and we find the arm is suddenly present.

Even knowing this, I sometimes wiggled my fingers just to make sure.

There are some reasons we may lose body sensation that have nothing to do with the fourth jhāna.

I've had chronic tightness in my shoulders for years. It's my favorite place to store tension; many people do. This tension can create what's called "body armoring," including a slight numbing. When a masseuse or physical therapist tries to loosen my shoulder muscles, she may have to hit them with the side of her hands or fists just to get sensation in there.

This is not arūpa. In the fourth jhāna, the parts of the body that fade from awareness are quite soft and relaxed.

Another phenomenon that is not arūpa is a body part "going to sleep." This is caused by sitting or lying in such a way that a nerve gets physically compressed and stops functioning, or an artery gets compressed, preventing nutrients to get to body cells. In either case, the nerves go a little haywire. They may send out erratic signals, causing a tingling sensation. Or they may go numb. When we try to move or put our weight on a foot that has "gone to sleep," it may not work properly for a few moments. My father once broke his toe when he got out of bed and fell over because his foot had gone to sleep.

Having a body part fall asleep for a few minutes is not dangerous as long as we don't try to use it in a critical way. But if it goes to sleep for several hours, it can cause nerve damage. This is why it tingles or aches, signaling us to move it around and get the circulation going.

But the fourth jhāna is different. The body becomes so relaxed that there are no signals. It is as if the body is gone. But if stimulated, the sensations are immediately present. There is no physical dysfunction.

The jhāna is called "arūpa" not because we *can't* sense the body, but because we *don't* sense some or all of it for longer and longer stretches of time.

Longer, Quieter

With this deep relaxation, we may find ourselves sitting easily for longer and longer stretches—an hour or more—while remaining fairly attentive.

Mind and body are deeply interconnected. As the mind relaxes, the body relaxes. And as the body relaxes and seems to fade, thinking may fade as well.

As we sit in deepening equanimity, we may not notice or care about these shifts. The mind becomes so sensitive that it notices subtler and subtler phenomena. So it may not feel that much quieter. The "noise" of gross phenomena is replaced by the "noise" of subtle phenomena.

We find it easier to see the rising and passing of these phenomena. We may notice subtle grasping or tightening (taṇhā) and relax before it generates a thought. We may notice a subtle feeling tone (vedanā) and release it before the grasping arises. The flow of Dependent Origination is becoming clearer and more obvious.

However, the mind still wobbles. It may drift. Hindrances arise (wanting, aversion, restlessness, sloth and torpor, or doubt). Yet now, it is easier to see them clearly and Six-R them without getting caught for so long.

Adjusting the Practice

The fourth jhāna is a time to alter whom we're sending mettā to and how we send it. If we're working with a good teacher, he or she will recognize when to make the change. Sometimes the change can be made late in the third jhāna. However, if we're clearly in the fourth jhāna with the fading of awareness of body parts, it's time.

There are two short-term practices that help make this transition. I think of them as "Removing the Barriers" and "Indiscriminate Mettā."

Removing the Barriers

To study the way is to study the self.
To study the self is to lose the self.
To lose the self is to be enlightened by all things.
To be enlightened by all things is to remove the barrier between self and other.

—Dōgen Zenji

Removing the barriers begins by sending mettā to many people. When my practice reached this stage, Bhante told me to not confine mettā to one spiritual friend but to send it to three or four. Then send it to several family members or friends who felt less special. Then send it to three or four neutral people–people I passed on the street or clerks in the store I knew but didn't feel one way or another about. And finally, send it to "enemies"—people I knew personally but wished I didn't because they got under my skin.

I was to send mettā to each person one at a time and stay with them until I could smile easily toward them and picture them smiling. Then I was to shift to another person. It wasn't necessary to send mettā to everyone I'd ever known—just the significant ones. I decided that if I wasn't sure if a person was significant or not, I'd send them mettā.

Doing this was particularly difficult with one relative. So I pictured him on his deathbed. I wasn't wishing him dead, just imagining what a gentle death might be like for him. I thought he'd have many regrets for how he'd lived. Seeing his difficulty touched compassion in me. As it flowed, I saw him resting more peacefully. The smile that arose wasn't a bright, happy smile. It was a quiet poignancy in which I truly wished him ease. That was enough.

All we need to do is get a toe in the door—find a way that allows the heart to flow naturally toward the person. Smile and see that person smile a little. Then move on to the next person.

All of us have difficult people in our lives. It may take a little longer with them. That's fine. It gives an opportunity to strengthen equanimity and well-being even with people who are not so easy. We don't have to fix the difficult relationships or work out all the issues—just find a way to soften the barriers enough to sincerely wish them well.

Even these can sometimes feel impossible. We may not be able to see them smile, may not want to see the smile, or may get caught up in what's wrong with them. If this happens, it is helpful to go back to a neutral person, build up a flow of mettā, and with this feeling go back to the difficult person.

Some people go through this practice in several hours. Some take longer. However long is fine and is good training.

Bhante told me to find him when I got through all of the categories of people. When I did, it was late in the evening and I didn't want to disturb him. I wasn't sleepy, so I went through the categories again. Ever-doubtful that I was doing it correctly, I decided to see if I could not only see the person smiling but see us laughing together as well. This took longer. But it was easier than I thought—even with George Bush and Dick Cheney. I got to the place where we were guffawing: "Isn't it silly how we'd gotten caught in our stuff."

After running through all the categories several times, I just sat sending it out to whomever popped into my mind, including animals.

Later I learned that it is not necessary to work with public figures. We don't really know who they are as people: all we know is a public caricature or their views of public issues. For the purpose of this practice, "enemies" are only people we know personally.

It's not necessary to take the practice as far as I did. We just need to find ways to soften the sense of barrier between others and ourselves.

Indiscriminate Mettā

The next morning when I reported to Bhante, he had me open the practice out even further. Rather than send the mettā in one direction, I was to send it in all six directions: in front, behind, to the left, to the right, above, and below. To get a feel for this, I could send mettā in each direction separately for a few minutes. But as I settled in, I was to send it in all directions at once.

I was also to send it to many beings at once. To get started in this, I could send it to various categories of beings: all males, all females, all four-footed creatures, all birds, all insects, all mammals, all fish, all sentient beings, all saints, all gods…whatever categories were meaningful to me. Or, if I preferred, I could just send it to all beings

I continued this for as long as I'd sent mettā to specific people. There was no rush.

However, as the practice got lighter and stronger, I began to feel the urge to send mettā to all beings all the time in all directions. The feeling came from a deep, still place. This became my base practice, as I'll describe in a moment.

Removing the barriers and indiscriminate mettā are rich practices in and of themselves. And they make sure our equanimity is deeply established and can be sent evenly to everyone and every kind of being.

Radiating from the Head

In the fourth jhāna, it may be hard to send mettā from the heart because the body is fading. So Bhante told me to send it from the head. This sounded strange. But I had felt pressure there—like two thumbs pressing into my hairline above the forehead. So it was easy to send it from that area. However, more often there is no body sensation, so we just send it from the top of the head.

Kindness and well-being flow from us genuinely and indiscriminately to all beings everywhere. This flow becomes the object of our meditation and our root practice. As before, as long as some of our attention is on this flow, we stay with it and leave distractions in the background.

When the mind drifts off and loses touch completely, we use the Six Rs. By now, the Six Rs may have rolled together into a smooth flow rather than six discrete steps. This is fine. The Six Rs truly are one flow. They are broken up into six just to make sure we do them completely and thoroughly. But at this phase of practice, they will naturally feel like one smooth process.

Nimitta

A common side effect of the fourth jhāna is luminosity. A subjective bright light sometimes emerges in our inner vision. It's not intense like a blazing sun, but softer and cooler, like a full moon on a clear night. It can be steady or fluid. Sometimes there are lines crossing where this spot appears. Other times not. It seems to draw our attention into it. In some traditions, the soft luminosity is called a "*nimitta*."

People who have a near-death experience often describe moving toward a light that feels like a loving presence. Depending on their belief systems, they may call it "God," "angels," "guiding spirits," "light," etc. Many report that it changes how they see their lives. I wonder—and this is speculation on my part—if that "white light of death" is the same phenomenon as a nimitta. I wonder if people who relax into death go into the fourth jhāna.

The fourth jhāna can be deeply healing and starts to shift how we see our lives. It can also be subtle.

A nimitta sometimes draws attention quite strongly. Because of this draw, it is sometimes used as an object of meditation, particularly in developing one-pointed concentration. In this case the spot may become large and stable.

The suttas also talk about kasiṇas (for example, "Mahāsakulidāyin Sutta," *Majjhima Nikaya* 77) that may be related to nimittas. Kasiṇas are disks of various colors that are used as objects of one-pointed concentration. They were used in Brahman (Hindu) practices and may have been added to the texts after the Buddha died.

One-pointed practices—whether kasiṇas, nimittas, or breath focus—can lead to deeply blissful states. However, they don't lead to insight or to seeing the flow of Dependent Origination that is key to waking up. Because of this, I have not been motivated to pursue them.

Nevertheless, some form of spontaneous nimitta is quite common in the fourth jhāna. If we experience one, we can take it as a sign of progress and encouragement to keep going. It's like climbing a mountain and coming to a beautiful, well-known waterfall. We know we've come a long way. There's no harm in enjoying the waterfall for a while. But it's not the mountaintop. Soon we want to continue the journey.

Continuing the journey means Six-R-ing the nimitta. It arises only because there has been a certain depth of relaxation. And it continues only because there is still a subtle tension that maintains the nimitta. By relaxing that tension, we move on up the path, and the nimitta fades.

Past Lives and Other Realms

The Buddha described his own awakening with reference to seeing past lives and visiting beings in non-Earth realms. In past lives he saw how he lived, what he had done, and the effects of his actions on subsequent births. In non-Earth realms he saw other beings, how they had lived, and the effects this had.[28] Seeing past lives and other realms can bring home the workings of karma. This is so helpful that the Buddha considered these practices worthwhile. But they should not be tried until we are established in the fourth jhāna.

I was curious enough to spend a good part of a retreat working under Bhante's guidance visiting hundreds of lifetimes and visiting several realms. In one life I saw myself half-crazed killing thousands of people with a sword. In another I smashed someone's head into a wall. After killing the person, I vowed never to let go of myself enough to risk doing such a thing again. Feeling this vow helped me understand some of the blockages that got in the way of letting go more deeply. I was able to relax that vow.

Most of what I saw was not so dramatic or disturbing. But all of us have done dreadful things. So it's important to be well-established in equanimity before engaging these practices. Equanimity is needed in order to see dispassionately and learn wisely.

Ultimately, I found myself more drawn to working with the jhānas than these practices. The Buddha said they could be helpful but weren't essential. So I did not stay with them long, and I don't feel confident enough to write about the practices in detail.

Even if we don't engage these practices, memories and images may appear anyway. They are different from "normal" images and imagination in that they can be unusually vivid if only for a split second. And they often start with seemingly irrelevant details. If we're stable in the fourth jhāna or higher and feel drawn to following them, we can observe them mindfully even if it's not part of our preferred practice.

Needless to say, some of us raised in Western scientific materialism may find concepts about other realms and past lives a bit incredulous. The art of working with these images is to neither hold onto nor push away our points of view and neither hold onto nor push away the images. In this way, whether or not the impressions are literally true or just metaphors, we can benefit from whatever insights arise, then Six-R the process and relax back into the moment.

In the Buddha's Words

Let's look at how the Buddha described the fourth jhāna. Picking up at verse 9 of the "Anupada Sutta: One by One As They Occurred" (*Majjhima Nikaya* 111):

> *(9) Again, monks, with the abandoning of pleasure and pain, and with the previous disappearance of joy and grief, Sāriputta entered upon and abided in the fourth jhāna, which has neither-pain-nor-pleasure and purity of mindfulness due to equanimity.*
>
> *(10) And the states in the fourth* jhāna*—the equanimity, the neither-painful-nor-pleasant feeling, the mental unconcern due to tranquility, the purity of mindfulness, and the unification of mind; the contact, feeling, perception, formations, and mind; the enthusiasm, choice, energy, mindfulness, equanimity, and attention—these states were defined by him one by one as they occurred; known to him those states arose, known they were present, known they disappeared. He understood thus: "So indeed, these states, not having been, come into being; having been, they vanish." Regarding those states, he abided unattracted, unrepelled, independent, detached, free, dissociated, with a mind rid of barriers. He understood: "There is an escape beyond this," and with the cultivation of that attainment, he confirmed that there is.*

Notice that equanimity ("disappearance of joy and grief") is deeper with the loss of body sensations ("neither-pain-nor-pleasure, mental unconcern due to tranquility," and "purity of mind"). The rest of verse 10 is the same as the description of earlier jhānas. There are still distractions, the khandhas, and lots of other things arising. There is no effort to get rid of these or to go into an absorption state. Rather, we just observe how they arise and pass: "not having been, coming into being; having been, they vanish." As we see the arising and passing more subtly, the flow of Dependent Origination becomes even clearer.

Manifold Lives

There are many suttas in which the Buddha talks about the practices of visiting past lives and other realms. Here is a typical passage from the "Kandaraka Sutta" (*Majjhima Nikaya* 51):

> *(23) Again, with the abandoning of pleasure and pain, and with the previous disappearance of joy and grief, he enters upon and abides in the fourth jhāna, which has neither-pain-nor-pleasure and purity of mindfulness due to equanimity.*
>
> *(24) When his collected mind is thus purified, bright, unblemished, rid of imperfection, malleable, wieldy, steady, and attained to imperturbability, he directs it to knowledge of the recollection of past lives. He recollects his manifold past lives, that is, one birth, two births, three births, four births, five births, ten births, twenty births, thirty births, forty births, fifty births, a hundred births, a thousand births, a hundred thousand births, many eons of world-contraction, many eons of world-expansion, many eons of world-contraction and expansion: "There I was so named, of such a clan, with such an appearance, such was my nutriment, such my experience of pleasure and pain, such my life-term; and passing away from there, I reappeared elsewhere; and there too I was so named, of such a clan, with such an appearance, such was my nutriment, such my experience of pleasure and pain, such my life-term; and passing away from there, I reappeared here." Thus with their aspects and particulars he recollects his manifold past lives.*
>
> *(25) When his collected mind is thus purified, bright, unblemished, rid of imperfection, malleable, wieldy, steady, and attained to imperturbability, he directs it to knowledge of the passing away and reappearance of beings. With the divine eye, which is purified and surpasses the human, he sees beings passing away and reappearing, inferior and superior, fair and ugly, fortunate and unfortunate. He understands how beings pass on according to their actions thus: "These worthy beings who were ill conducted in body, speech, and*

mind, revilers of noble ones, wrong in their views, giving effect to wrong view in their actions, on the dissolution of the body, after death, have reappeared in a state of deprivation, in a bad destination, even in hell; but these worthy beings who were well conducted in body, speech, and mind, not revilers of noble ones, right in their views, giving effect to right view in their actions, on the dissolution of the body, after death, have reappeared in a good destination, even in the heavenly world." Thus with the divine eye, which is purified and surpasses the human, he sees beings passing away and reappearing, inferior and superior, fair and ugly, fortunate and unfortunate, and he understands how beings pass on according to their actions.

Notice that verse 23 establishes the fourth jhāna as a prerequisite for viewing past lives and other realms. Verse 24 describes recollection of past lives and a very general description of the things the Buddha saw. Verse 25 describes how he used "the divine eye" (intuition) to see the effects of "ill conducted" and "well conducted" lives and how people reappeared in hell realms or heavenly realms depending upon how they had lived.

16

Space: Fifth Jhāna

When I was six years old, I liked to lie on the lawn and gaze at the sky. If I relaxed enough, the sky moved away toward infinity. It seemed to move even though I knew it wasn't. It was a very pleasant feeling.

"Hey, Ricky," I'd say to my big brother. "Ever see this neat thing—the sky moving away but not moving."

He'd look at his nutty little brother. "Get up," he'd say. "I'm the cowboy now. You're the Indian. Let's play."

I complied. He still thinks I'm his nutty little brother.

Looking back, I realize that this was a sign of the fifth jhāna. Traditionally it's called "the base of infinite space." But it's not "spacey" or fuzzy-headed. It can be quite clear. It's an expansive feeling available to children and adults alike.

After settling into the fourth jhāna, it can be tempting to try to hold onto the equanimity. But if instead we send it out in all directions, eventually the peacefulness spreads out even further into a vast spaciousness. It may be accompanied by the distinct sensations of things moving away without moving at all. But not always.

The experience may feel like sitting peacefully on a mountaintop gazing into a landscape several thousand feet below that spreads out to the horizon and meets the sky. Or it may be even vaster.

Before I had any understanding of the jhānas, I was meditating in a room in my attic in the middle of the night. With my eyes closed, it felt like I was looking at a black wall. Suddenly, the blackness changed. Visually it was the same, but it felt like all walls fell away. The floor and the earth beneath me were also gone. I was suspended in the universe looking into the emptiness. It was inspiring and a little scary—the ground had disappeared beneath me, and I was floating in a void. That bit of fear was enough to get rid of the spaciousness. As I relaxed and the vertigo faded, the expansiveness returned.

The base of infinite space is often described as feeling that space is boundless and center-less—that there are no edges or middle. It can be quietly exhilarating.

In this jhāna, gross sensations have faded. We sense little or nothing through the sense doors. Yet the mind-heart is quiet enough that subtle perceptions may be prominent. As we get used to them, they seem less special. We're left with a quiet feeling of expansiveness. Very little disturbs us.

At this time we can sit easily for an hour or two. The spaciousness may continue into walking meditation. We may remain in arūpa jhānas even as we move around our world in simple ways.

Since body sensations have faded, we continue to send mettā from the head. The quality of the mettā changes subtly. This shift is called compassion. It's said that the Buddha used to sit in the fifth jhāna and send compassion (karuṇā) out into the world.

But I confess that to me the term "compassion" was not helpful in describing this shift. It was very subtle. When I reflect on it, I notice a softness and ease—like cotton or very soft wool.

But the shift in texture may be too subtle for any labels. And our ease is probably too complete to care about descriptions. We are content to simply radiate well-being in all directions into infinity.

Adjusting the Practice

There are no adjustments to the practice needed at this stage. We continue sending out mettā or karuṇā or well-being in all directions. Adjustments take care of themselves.

We notice the arising and passing of phenomena more easily. Hindrances continue to arise, and we continue to Six-R them when they capture our attention completely. The flow of phenomena is slower and easier to see.

In the Buddha's Words

Returning to the "Anupada Sutta: One by One As They Occurred" (*Majjhima Nikaya* 111), we find the Buddha's description of the fifth jhāna a little sparser:

> *(11) Again, monks, with the complete surmounting of "gross" perceptions of form, with the disappearance of gross perceptions of sensory impact, aware that "space is infinite," Sāriputta entered upon and abided in the base of infinite space.*
>
> *(12) And the states in the base of infinite space—the perception of the base of infinite space and the unification of mind; the contact, feeling, perception, formations, and mind; the enthusiasm, choice, energy, mindfulness, equanimity, and attention—these states were defined by him one by one as they occurred; known to him those states arose, known they were present, known they disappeared. He understood thus: "So indeed, these states, not having been, come into being; having been, they vanish." Regarding those states, he abided unattracted, unrepelled, independent, detached, free, dissociated, with a mind rid of barriers. He understood: "There is an escape beyond this," and with the cultivation of that attainment, he confirmed that there is.*

In verse 11, Bhante uses the phrase "gross perception" rather than just "perception" to make it clear that we do continue to perceive things. This is affirmed in verse 12 when the Buddha explains that all the khandhas (contact, feeling, perception, formation, and mind) are still present. It's just that the perceptions are subtle.

And as with all jhānas and all insight meditation, it is important to continue to observe the flow of phenomena as they come into being and vanish.

The transitions from the fourth to the fifth to the sixth to the seventh jhānas are more of a subtle shift than abrupt discontinuity, more about nuance than drama. The fourth has spacious qualities that become more prominent in the fifth. And the fifth hints at a vastness of consciousness that becomes more prominent in the sixth jhāna, as we'll see in the next chapter.

17

Gaps: Sixth Jhāna

I knew the altitude of Caples Lake from a map and used it to calibrate the altimeter in my little GPS. Standing with my toes almost touching the water's edge, I entered "7802 feet" into the gadget. From here the trail would hug the edge of the lake for several miles. Then it would climb 800 feet up to Emigrant Lake higher in the Sierra Mountains. But the first leg of the hike would be level, easy hiking.

So I dropped the GPS into my shirt pocket, adjusted my daypack, headed out along the trail, and dropped into a walking meditation.

As I settled into the rhythm of walking, fragments of thoughts jumbled through my head: a debate about the identity of a soaring bird, snippets of conversations, people I'd see the next day, a scene from a TV show, fragments of a book I'd been reading, thoughts about my next sermon. None of them was pressing. Still, I wanted my mind to be serene and clear. I was annoyed at the mental chatter.

But I understood. A consultant had once told me that churches the size of mine are impossible to manage. This was comforting—it wasn't my fault that I rarely felt on top of all that was going on. Still, I tried. It made for long, hectic, multitasking days.

So when I had a day of hiking—a day clear of responsibilities—my mind would decompress by spewing thoughts. It was natural.

While I didn't like the tumble of thoughts, I didn't fight them either. I let my mind wander where it wanted. I didn't pay attention to the content. As I walked along the lake, I noted the energy in my mind—its mood and texture—and ignored the storylines, concepts, and images. I let the thinking float in the background. In the foreground, I quietly radiated joy. This was easy in the mountains.

Soon, the thoughts sputtered out. Like talking on a cell phone to somebody going out of range, the inner voice turned to static and then went silent. A moment later, another thought arose in the background, broke up, and sputtered out.

I was smiling deeply by now—so much that I didn't care if the thoughts sputtered on or disappeared. They were a natural release of tension. I felt tranquil.

Consciousness is Infinite

Thirty spokes share the wheel's hub;
It is the center hole that makes it useful.
Shape clay into a vessel;
It is the space within that makes it useful.
Cut doors and windows for a room;
It is the holes which make it useful.
Therefore profit comes from what is there;
Usefulness from what is not there.

—Lao Tzu

The sixth jhāna is characterized by holes in the flow of consciousness. They appear more easily in sitting meditation than hiking on a mountain trail. But once we get established, they can arise in many environments.

In Chapter 1, I described a retreat in a dude ranch outside of Jackson Hole, Wyoming (see page 19). I was doing walking meditation one morning as I walked from my cabin to the main hall. The ground flowed through my field of vision. Suddenly the steady flow broke into a series of still images—like separate frames of a movie. Normally, the frames pass so quickly that they blend together, giving the appearance of movement. But my mind was so relaxed and clear it saw each frame separately, causing the images to flash one at a time.

This phenomenon can happen at any sense door. And it can happen in the mind's eye as the flow of consciousness seems to sputter, flicker, or just fade away, leaving empty holes. In the space between thoughts, we don't fall asleep. The mind doesn't turn dull. It remains clear, present, and spacious.

The sixth jhāna is called "the base of infinite consciousness." In English this sounds grandiose. But it is merely a time when there are gaps in experience rather than a cluttered stream.

A similar phrase used in the suttas is "aware that consciousness is infinite." Consciousness—the space within which thought and experience arise—is indeed vast. Mind objects are just a small part. We begin to feel the larger "space" directly. It's so much larger than thought or sensory events.

In the sixth jhāna, we become aware of the content of our experience and the empty space within which it arises. This "emptiness" is subtle. But as the mind-heart become quiet, we can notice that is has its own changing texture and feel.

Three Characteristics

In the sixth jhāna, the "three characteristics" become more obvious. The three are dissatisfaction (dukkha), impermanence (anicca), and selflessness (anattā). We see on a microscopic level how thoughts and sensory-contact arise, flicker, and sputter out or fade away. Seeing how they come and go, it's obvious that holding onto them is unsatisfactory (dukkha) because none of them lasts (anicca). This happens by itself. There is no one doing it (anattā).

Space Odyssey

The subjective experience of this breaking up of consciousness can show itself in many different ways. In that retreat outside of Jackson Hole, one way was the flickering of the visual field as I walked. Another was the experience of swirling energy and light as I sat on my zafu.

I had received my first meditation instructions from Bhante just before going to Jackson Hole. But he wasn't there. I was trying to figure out how to practice in this style without being able to check in with him. But I knew that it was important to relax rather than fight against thoughts or other distractions. There was no need to struggle against hindrances—just soften the tension in them. As I did this, the tension turned into a little shot of joy. Rather than disliking distractions, I began to look forward to them because I knew that as I released them I'd get this mild euphoria.

As I became more adept at releasing thoughts, feelings, and images, I'd let the tension go before they fully formed. I'd notice them just start to arise, and I'd soften. I wasn't pushing them away, so there would be little swirls of residual energy. I just watched.

They were often so colorful as to seem psychedelic. They reminded me of a scene toward the end of the movie *2001: A Space Odyssey* as astronaut David Bowman approached a mysterious monolith floating in space around Jupiter. As he got closer, he realized it was not solid. It was a star gate that drew him in and shot him speeding through the universe faster than light. In the film, the sequence is filled with computer-animated strands of lights and turning shapes.

Sitting on my cushion, it was as if I was speeding through all these colorful strands of thoughts, feelings, and images that had not quite manifested. I was curious to see where they'd lead. But they just kept going and going. They didn't lead anywhere; they just went on and on and on. Finally I realized they could be infinite—there was no end to them. I relaxed a little more deeply, and they fell into a soft, warm nothingness.

At the time I had no idea what the experience was. Years later, talking to senior students, I realized it was similar to what they felt early in the sixth jhāna: "seeing" infinite strands of consciousness.

Stillness

Another sign of the sixth jhāna is a deepening stillness: a soft nothingness. The expansiveness of the fifth jhāna has subtle tension in it. As this relaxes, the expansion stops and we enter a more pervasive quiet. One student said it was like the quiet when the refrigerator compressor turns off. Before it quieted, he wasn't even aware of the humming in the background. But when it stopped, there was a deeper silence free of background noise.

When equanimity arose strongly in the third jhāna, it felt like a duck resting in the ocean swells. By the sixth jhāna, the waves seem much smaller—little wavelets lapping against a hull as we sail on without being pushed up or down, back or forth. Yet as the mind becomes quieter, it notices subtler phenomena and may not even realize how much subtler it has become.

Joy

In the sixth jhāna, we may sit easily without moving for a few hours and may stay with the object of meditation steadily for forty-five minutes or longer in our best sitting. The length of time we sit or stay with the object will vary from sitting to sitting. But the best sittings are longer than in earlier jhānas.

The well-being we've been radiating becomes subtler. It's said that the energy we send out shifts from compassion (karuṇā) to joy (mudita). Joy thus becomes the object of meditation. Usually these shifts are subtle—more like a different shade than a different color. And we're feeling so peaceful that we aren't concerned if the well-being we're sending out is compassion or joy. We just feel light in mind and body.

Picasso's Cow

On my first retreat with Bhante, I started at the beginning. In two weeks I went from the first jhāna up well into the seventh. But I passed through the sixth without knowing it. I wasn't trying to collect jhāna merit badges or get notches on my zafu. But I was curious about my progress and was looking for each stage. Still, I missed it.

When I began working on this book, I asked Bhante to describe the sixth jhāna for me. "I don't remember what it felt like when I first entered it," I said. "I remember the fifth and the seventh jhānas. But I passed through the sixth quickly without noticing."

Bhante said, "I remember very clearly when you were in it."

Hmmm. So I dug out my old journals. I've kept journals sporadically for years. On retreats I make brief notes about insights and experiences. I wanted to see if there was anything about the sixth.

And there it was. It was right there in my notes on that first retreat with Bhante. I didn't name it as such, but I described it in my notes from an interview with him:

Doug: "I have periods of deep peacefulness. Then a disturbance pulls me out. I've been trying to see these disturbances more clearly."

Bhante: "Your curiosity is inquiry."

Doug: "Yes, I know. I've always had a lot of curiosity."

Bhante: "And it can also indicate doubt."

Doug laughing: "Doubt has always been my favorite hindrance. It comes up often. It's ironic: I'm a minister. I'm supposed to have strong faith. I have doubt instead. But doubt is not such a bad thing for a Unitarian Universalist minister."

Bhante: "Why don't you take your inquiry and direct it to the equanimity rather than to the distractions? See what you see in the peacefulness."

Doug: "Hmmm. I never thought of doing that. That's a great idea. I'll give it a try."

Bhante: "Let me know what you find in those gaps. It's subtle, but you'll be able to see things in there."

With what I know now, when I read these old notes, it's clear I was describing the sixth jhāna. The "periods of deep peacefulness" were what Bhante called "gaps in consciousness." And Bhante suggested I examine these gaps—the periods of deep equanimity. This is standard advice for the sixth jhāna.

This exchange raises an important point about the jhānas in general. As we're first learning them, it's not helpful to be concerned about what jhāna we're in. It's helpful to have a teacher who understands, so they can adjust our practice as Bhante adjusted mine. But we may not know where we are until we become more familiar with the territory.

Jhānas can be hard to recognize for several reasons. The most obvious is that the qualities that define a jhāna are often not unique to that jhāna.

It is easier to sit longer in higher jhānas, but length of meditation is not a sign of a particular jhāna. The mind-heart become clearer, lighter, and more collected as meditation matures, but these aren't clear yardsticks for measuring specific jhānas.

Gaps in consciousness are a sign of the sixth jhāna. But before the sixth, consciousness is sometimes thick and sometimes thin. The gaps may not seem like anything new.

Clarity of the three characteristics is another sign of the sixth. But most of us know the three characteristics even if we don't put them together in a trio. We know suffering, impermanence, and selflessness. As the practice deepens, these become less intellectual and more of a direct moment-to-moment reality. But this deeper realization doesn't always arise as a flash.

And even if everything falls into place in an "oh wow" moment, the high fades. The bright realizations are memorable. But more often our clarity increases in small increments, not big jumps.

Radiating quiet joy—a lightness of body and mind—is another sign of the sixth. But these are part of many other states on and off the cushion.

Another problem in identifying jhānas is that we may think we are in one when we aren't. Some of the qualities of various jhānas have a unique texture and feel. But the words used to describe them may mean different things to different people. As Picasso pointed out, a picture of a cow is not a cow. The pictures we have in our mind may not point to the real experience.

Even if we recognize a jhāna correctly, we won't stay there consistently. For every "really good" sitting where everything comes together beautifully, there are several others where everything falls apart.

Rather than riding a jhāna elevator in one direction, mostly we find an ebb and flow, give and take, getting clear and getting foggy with only the general trend toward higher jhānas. Any given sitting may be elevated or not.

I offer these descriptions of the jhānas to indicate the general territory. How they come together in your maturing practice will be uniquely your own.

Adjusting the Practice

As in the fifth jhāna, there are no adjustments required to move into the sixth jhāna. It arises naturally from the fifth as the mind finds greater clarity and spaciousness.

In the sixth it is natural to notice the quality of the mind itself, including how much or how little energy is present. If there is too much energy, the mind gets restless and talkative. We need to relax. If the mind is too relaxed, the mind becomes sluggish and dreamlike. We need to bring in more energy. Fine-tuning these energies becomes important, especially in the seventh jhāna. We'll explore this more in the next chapter.

The one adjustment that helps when we are in the sixth jhāna is the one Bhante offered to me. As we notice holes in the flow of experience—times when the mind is exceptionally still—we can shift our attention to the holes themselves—the quiet or emptiness. Shifting awareness into these gaps helps move us into the seventh jhāna.

In the Buddha's Words

Let's look at the Buddha's description of the sixth jhāna. Picking up at verse 13 of the "Anupada Sutta: One by One As They Occurred" (*Majjhima Nikaya* 111):

(13) Again, monks, by completely surmounting the base of infinite space, aware that "consciousness is infinite," Sāriputta entered upon and abided in the base of infinite consciousness.

(14) And the states in the base of infinite consciousness—the perception of the base of infinite consciousness and the unification of mind; the contact, feeling, perception, formations, and mind; the enthusiasm, choice, energy, mindfulness, equanimity, and attention—these states were defined by him one by one as they occurred; known to him those states arose, known they were present, known they disappeared. He understood thus: "So indeed, these states, not having been, come into being; having been, they vanish." Regarding those states, he abided unattracted, unrepelled, independent, detached, free, dissociated, with a mind rid of barriers. He understood: "There is an escape beyond this," and with the cultivation of that attainment, he confirmed that there is.

Notice that even when we are aware that "consciousness is infinite," consciousness is not absorbed into a single object. There is still contact, feeling tone, perceptions, formations, and all the rest.

18

No Thing Left: Seventh Jhāna

"Thinking is a problem." Many years ago, I knew this wasn't the most enlightened attitude. But my mind had a mind of its own. I carefully explained to it how much more pleasant it would be if it just quieted down. My mind thought about that thought, echoed it in different ways, discussed strategies for dealing with it, or merrily rambled off in a hundred different directions, sometimes all at once. I knew I was supposed to be more gracious toward this mental proliferation. But in truth I felt that "thinking is a problem."

Then I got curious: what are thoughts really? Mostly I paid attention to the content of thoughts. Sometimes I paid attention to the mood of the thoughts—whether they were fast or slow, bouncy or serene, heavy or light. But I never actually explored the substance of thoughts.

Ice cream comes in ninety-eight flavors: chocolate, strawberry, vanilla, fudge ripple.... The flavors are analogous to the content of thought. Ice cream comes in different textures: creamy, icy, smooth, filled with chunks of fruit or nuts.... The texture is analogous to the mood of thought. But what is the ice cream itself? What is thought itself?

In meditation I had learned to hold my attention on the breath and let thinking fade into the background. I had developed the ability to suppress thinking for long stretches. This turned my mind into an iron lockbox—not much fun or comfort. But I had never explored the actual nature of thought itself.

This piqued my interest. I decided to investigate. By "investigate" I didn't mean "analyze"—analysis is just a collection of thoughts. I meant to observe thinking carefully to see its substance—what carried the content and the mood.

While on a retreat with John Travis in the early 2000s, I turned my awareness to the substance of thinking to see what I could discover.

The first thing I discovered was that all the thoughts had disappeared. Sneaky little guys! As soon as I turned mindfulness toward the thoughts themselves, they vanished. I watched and waited for them to return. Nothing. Then my attention began to drift. As soon as it went elsewhere, thoughts snuck out from behind a rock and started chatting. I brought my attention back to them. They were chattering too vigorously for me to see any one of them clearly. I held my attention on them, looking not at their content or mood but for their substance. They'd slide away before I could see their underlying nature.

For two years, my meditation project was trying to see the nature of thought—or at least to try to catch one forming so I could see where it came from and what it was made of. Sometimes when I was relatively still, they seemed like bubbles floating on a river and trying to emerge. I'd watch carefully for one to float up off the surface so I could see it fully. But if my attention remained on it, it melted back into the river and disappeared.

I came to appreciate two kinds of thought. I called them "primary" and "secondary." Secondary thoughts were thoughts triggered by other thoughts—sometimes long strings of associations. Most of my thoughts were secondary—reactions to previous thoughts. But every once in a while, there was a primary thought—one that seemed to arise out of nowhere and had nothing to do with anything else. I wondered if this was what the Buddha meant by the mind being like a sense organ that perceived thoughts the way the eye perceives light.

I also came to appreciate how I ordinarily identified with my thoughts. When they arose, it was as if I shrink-wrapped around them. I became them. They were "me, myself, and mine." But now I was stepping back. I was in the audience watching the thoughts move across the stage. "Me," the observer, was quieter and more peaceful.

Since I was curious about the thoughts, their existence was no longer a problem. I wanted to see them rather than get rid of them. Yet on retreats, I found myself sitting in the audience looking at a blank stage for longer and longer stretches. I became patient, watching and waiting for something to appear on stage. Forty-five minutes would pass with no action. Then my attention would drift to the exit sign or to the ceiling for a moment. When I came back to the stage, it was filled with actors. And if I quietly and openly watched them, they'd all disappear.

Sitting in the audience with nothing on the stage, I became aware of the observer—the "I" that was watching and waiting. This observer seemed less personal, more spacious, more relaxed, and faintly familiar—like someone I'd dreamed about once.

John told me that this observer was "pure consciousness." That seemed way too flattering. But he said, "No. When consciousness has no object, it turns back on itself. Consciousness observes consciousness. Awareness observes awareness. The observer observes the observer. It's not pure in the sense of pristine. It's pure in the sense of there being nothing in them but consciousness. You are seeing consciousness without external objects."

From this place of observation, the only thing I could see for sure about thoughts was that they had some tension. Compared to the quiet observer, they were tense. The empty stage was more peaceful than the thought-filled one. At first the tension seemed subtle. Eventually it seemed obvious.

There was nothing more that I could find in thought than this subtle tension. It was as if clear space tightened up slightly. That's what thought was.

I told John what I had observed. He didn't disagree with me.

Thoughts play such a dominant role in our lives and in the world, but they are all paper tigers. Underneath, they are nothing more than an expression of tension.

No Things

A few years later, I had my first interview with Bhante. The next evening I went to a small saṅgha in Davis, California, to hear him give a dhamma talk. As he explained Dependent Origination, he said, "And craving gives rise to clinging. Clinging always manifests as thinking—a kind of tightness." It all fell into place for me: he confirmed my observation about the essence of thought arising out of tension.

Shortly after that I began training with Bhante. As my equanimity deepened, it was still peppered with thoughts. I dusted off my old practice of observing thoughts from the audience. As before, they faded away. When I explained to Bhante my history with observing thoughts and having them relax and vanish, he said, "That's a good technique for entering the seventh jhāna."

The more common technique for entering the seventh jhāna is the one I mentioned in the last chapter. When gaps appear in the flow of consciousness, we move attention from the content and texture of the mind to these holes. We let awareness observe these empty spaces. It's as if we dive into equanimity and see what's there.

Another technique is to simply let awareness rest in equanimity.

The seventh jhāna is commonly called "the base of nothingness." I found this name confusing at first. It sounds like the mind goes into a void—nothingness. But there is actually a lot going on in the base of nothingness. It's just that there are no references to things outside the mind. It is "pure consciousness," not in the sense of being pristine and free of all tension. It is just that the content is no longer the boss's latest mishap, items on the grocery list, a conversation with our partner, concerns about a social justice issue, what we're having for dinner, or anything outside the mind itself. We may notice pushes and pulls, textures, movements…lots of stuff. But it's all about the present moment and the internal experience. It's all about our awareness of our consciousness.

Ordinary thought—that is, thought about stuff in the world—has faded. There are no external things in it. I call it "the base of no thing–ness." It's not that there is nothing. Just no things. I suspect that that is what the Buddha meant. He was talking about "no things" not "nothing."

Not only does the content shift, but the texture of thought changes as well. It's lighter and subtler. Thoughts become more of a dispassionate description of what's going on.

Several years ago I had an experience that is an analogy for the seventh jhāna. I had a severe concussion in a bicycle accident. It left my head spinning for months. The slightest motion made my head swirl as if I'd just rolled twenty feet down a hill. I was told the condition would correct itself but might take a while. In the meantime, I did what I could to keep my head perfectly still. So I spent the summer lying in a lawn chair in the backyard to keep motionless.

I was living in California, which has clear skies all summer. At least that's what I thought. Lying still, gazing up in the blue sky, I began to see an amazing number of birds. Many were tiny or far away, so faint that with a casual glance, I'd swear the sky was empty. Yet as I held still, I saw many subtle creatures I hadn't realized were there.

That's what the seventh jhāna is like. Initially what seems like empty space is actually populated by lots of subtle movement.

Six-R Everything

Once we're in the base of nothingness, the practice shifts in several ways. The most obvious is with the Six Rs.

Automatic

By this stage the Six Rs should be automatic—a deeply trained habit. They are not six separate movements. They are like a wave that rolls onto the beach. We can say that the wave moves landward, rises, crashes, spreads out on the sand, and slides back into the ocean as if those are six distinct phases. But in reality a wave is one continuous motion. Likewise, the Six Rs are not six processes but a single movement. It can happen very fast. We recognize a distraction and the mind releases, relaxes, lightens, and comes back in one quick flow. And it feels less like we are doing it and more like it just happens. It doesn't even feel personal, just something that does itself almost in the background.

Everything

So in this stage, it's important to Six-R everything. Up to now, we've Six-R'd only things that completely captured the mind's attention. If a distraction arose and we were still present with the object of meditation, we ignored the distraction rather than Six-R it.

In early stages there are too many distractions to Six-R everything. If we try, the Six R process creates too much activity and tension.

Now we Six-R everything, even if it's in the background. The Six Rs are so automatic that this should not disturb the mind's peacefulness. It just happens as soon as we recognize something.

Six-R-ing everything is important because starting with the seventh jhāna, we want to release even the subtlest tensions, not just the obvious ones.

Tune up

My only caveat is that it can be helpful to periodically bring the Six Rs in for a tune-up. Every several months or so, I'd realize that the Six-R process had drifted a little. I was using it to subtly push away distractions rather than just let them be as I released. Or I was coming back so quickly that I wasn't quite relaxing.

I've found it helpful now and then to slow down the Six Rs and carefully do each step to make sure they are all working properly. Then I let it go back on automatic.

Everywhere

And finally, it helps to Six-R throughout the day, not just in formal meditation. If we're living ordinary lives in the busy world, it is unrealistic to expect that we'll actually keep doing them continuously everywhere. But lightly holding the intention to do so helps the Six-R practice take hold in more places than we might expect.

This is enormously helpful because, in the end, the capacity to relax into a clear, dispassionate view of everything is what frees the mind.

Balancing Awakening Factors

Another practice that helps in the seventh jhāna is balancing the awakening factors (also known as "enlightenment factors"). In the last chapter I spoke of balancing energy and calm—too much energy and the mind gets restless, too much calm and it gets dull.

The Buddha talked of seven rather than just two enlightenment factors. There are three that energize—they are useful when the mind is too dull. There are three that calm—they are useful when the mind is restless. And there is one that helps balance both—it is helpful at all times.

By the seventh jhāna, it is possible to directly recognize all seven as distinctive. It's said that when all seven come into perfect balance even for a tiny fraction of a second, we wake up fully—hence the name "awakening factors."

It is helpful to recognize them. The energizing factors:

- Energy (viriya)
- Investigation of the dhamma (dhamma vicaya)—curiosity
- Joy (pīti)

The calming factors:

- Equanimity (upekkhā)
- Collectedness (samādhi)
- Tranquility (passaddhi)

The balancing factor:

- Mindfulness-heartfulness (sati)

Each of these energies has a different flavor. The words themselves connote different things to different people. So it's important to discover how we experience each and not rely too much on other people's descriptions.

One night on retreat, I didn't sleep well. During the 5:30 a.m. sitting, I was very sleepy—my mind was dull and dreamlike. Often, in this situation, I just go take a nap. But on this morning I decided to see if I could sit for a few hours.

I noticed that the dullness had a tinge of discouragement. So rather than bring in energy (viriya) to balance the mind, I brought in a little joy (pīti). The mind balanced out into a very clear state for a long time.

Then after breakfast, I took a nap.

Other times when my mind is lethargic, I might find that bringing in some curiosity (investigation—dhamma vicaya) helps most. I ask, "What's really going on right now?"

It took me longer to realize that curiosity is sometimes unproductive. If my mind is scattered and restless, I may be tempted to investigate more closely what's going on. But investigation (dhamma vicaya) is an energizing factor. It just makes the mind more restless.

With more faith in the awakening factors, I'm more apt to bring in more collectedness (stillness—samādhi) or tranquility (peacefulness—passaddhi) to the restless mind. It's surprising how helpful this is to calm and clear the mind.

The trick I learned with the awakening factors was to ignore the content of the mind. At this level of practice, we just attend to the energy levels. If those balance out, the practice takes care of itself.

And by the seventh jhāna, the adjustments are very small. Years ago when car engines were much simpler, I used to work on my cars. Carburetors have small adjustment screws. To get them set right, I'd turn it just a little and then let the car run for a few moments. It takes a while for the new setting to take full effect. It's very easy to set them too far in one direction, then overcompensate and turn them back too far the other.

Adjusting awakening factors feels like this. If I need more joy, I bring in a very small amount and then wait several minutes to see how the mind responds. The response is rarely immediate. It takes a while.

It's amazing that very small adjustments can have big effects. So be patient and gentle. Balancing the awakening factors is fine-tuning.

Being Equanimity

The objects of meditation shift slightly from one jhāna to the next. In the fifth, the energy being sent is said to be compassion. In the sixth it's joy. In the seventh it's equanimity. In talking to other meditators, most find the shift very clear in some jhānas but not in others. But which shift is clear and which is not varies from meditator to meditator.

For me, the shifts in the fifth and sixth jhānas were so subtle at first that I didn't notice them. But the shift in the seventh was very clear. So if we notice a shift in quality, that's fine. If not, it's not a problem.

However, in the seventh there is a shift not only in the quality of the energy but also in how it's being sent.

In one interview, I told Bhante that sending out the energy of equanimity was feeling more and more like a "doing," something that was a chore rather than a natural flow. It was an effort to keep pushing it out.

He said, "Don't send it out anymore. Just be it. Be mettā. Be upekkhā."

This was a relief. Rather than send energy out, I noticed it radiate. I was no longer the doer. It just happened on its own. If I was out of the jhāna, I might send out equanimity for just a moment, but soon, it just broadcast itself. My job was just to stay out of the way.

Dependent Origination

While I was first working with the seventh jhāna, every time I went for an interview with Bhante, he asked me what I was experiencing. I might say, "The mind dropped into stillness. I just hung out watching it. Then it started to wobble."

"What happened before it wobbled?" he'd ask.

"Nothing," I said. "It was just still and then it wobbled."

"No," he said, "something happened before it wobbled. You need more mindfulness."

So I'd go back to my kuti, balance the awakening factors, become very still, and watch some more, trying to stay relaxed and attentive to see what happened before the wobble.

Eventually I saw it. I won't tell you what it was. Bhante doesn't like people to know beforehand. He'd rather have them discover for themselves. I honor his wisdom in this.

The point is that by the seventh jhāna, the links of Dependent Origination become clearer and clearer. They are no longer conceptual. They don't resemble neat arrows on a flow chart. They are tangible events that flow from one to the next.

There are several ways to attend to Dependent Origination. One is to ask the question, "What comes next?" and watch to see what arises. Another way is to ask Bhante's question: "What came before?"

Remember, the Buddha said that insight into Dependent Origination (paticcasamuppāda) is the key to the dhamma and the key to awakening. In the seventh jhāna, the movements of paticcasamuppāda become easier to see directly. The Buddha recommended looking for the flow of Dependent Origination by looking "upstream" rather than "downstream": seeing what events give rise to a phenomenon. If we're dealing with clinging, we try to see the craving (taṇhā) that gives rise to the clinging, and relax the craving. If we are dealing with craving, we try to see the feeling tone (vedanā) that gives rise to the craving. In every case, we're looking for the source of our experience and Six-R-ing that source.

During one retreat, I became vividly aware of how every single distraction that came to mind was related to some event in the past where I had held on to some tension. Some of the past events were just hours old, like a comment someone made that annoyed me and that I hadn't Six-R'd. Others came out of old wounds or unfulfilled longings from long ago that had sat tightly inside me for years—a jilted love affair, a job application that was rejected, the cutting remark of a parent. It was time to Six-R them.

With this growing sense of anattā (selflessness), even these hindrances looked impersonal. They simply arose out of past causes and conditions. They were helpful in revealing where I needed to release and relax. It was important to Six-R everything.

Seeing hindrances and Dependent Origination can be disturbing. At one point I felt I was seeing the roots of the struggling that permeated my life. I thought, "Do I have to Six-R this? How will I survive without struggle? Tension has run my life. Will I remember how to brush my teeth?" Again, it's important to Six-R everything, including fear. And it's helpful to keep a sense of humor.

In the eighth jhāna, hindrances and paticcasamuppāda become even starker and less personal. We'll look at this in the next chapter.

In the Buddha's Words

But before turning to the eighth jhāna, let's look at the Buddha's description of the seventh. Picking up at verse 15 of the "Anupada Sutta: One by One As They Occurred" (*Majjhima Nikaya* 111):

(15) Again, monks, by completely surmounting the base of infinite consciousness, aware that "there is nothing," Sāriputta entered upon and abided in the base of nothingness.

(16) And the states in the base of nothingness—the perception of the base of nothingness and the unification of mind; the contact, feeling tone, perception, formations, and mind; the enthusiasm, choice, energy, mindfulness, equanimity, and attention—these states were defined by him one by one as they occurred; known to him those states arose, known they were present, known they disappeared. He understood thus: "So indeed, these states, not having been, come into being; having been, they vanish." Regarding those states, he abided unattracted, unrepelled, independent, detached, free, dissociated, with a mind rid of barriers. He understood: "There is an escape beyond this," and with the cultivation of that attainment, he confirmed that there is.

Note that as before, there is still feeling in the body if there is contact. There are still the five aggregates (contact, feeling tone, perception, formations, and mind). Even in this deep stage of meditation, the mind is not in one-pointed absorption. It's important to have the wider, clear awareness that allows for insights that can free us. It's also important to remain dispassionate about the whole process.

19

Preperception Perception: Eighth Jhāna

I like the log kuti at Dhamma Sukha Meditation Center. It's small and has eight sides and two large glass doors. I moved a portable air conditioner into it. On hot July days I could sit inside away from of the heat, humidity, and insects and still have a view of the surrounding woods. The tin roof collected more heat than the air conditioner could manage. By midafternoons the temperature rose into the mid-80s. But the AC took moisture out of the air. With a fan blowing on me, it was quite comfortable, even luxurious compared to Southeast Asia.

I spent a few weeks in that kuti in July of 2009. I wanted to get into the eighth *jhāna*. I told Bhante, "*I* can't get into the eighth," with an emphasis on "I."

He laughed and said, "You're right. Identifying with any I or desire blocks the eighth. All you can do is let it happen when it's ready."

So I tried to not identify with my identity. I wanted not to want what I wanted. As you can imagine, it wasn't happening. I was comfortably into the seventh jhāna. Still, the eighth eluded me.

Then one afternoon, I could barely get into any jhāna. If you looked into my kuti, you'd have seen me looking as serene as a Buddha. But if you looked inside my head, you'd have seen a swarm of butterflies.

After an hour, I took the butterflies for a walk. Maybe walking meditation would release the restlessness.

Yet when I sat again, I began daydreaming. I took a deep breath, came back to the present, and drifted off into nah-nah-noo-noo land. I gave up, relaxed, and let my mind drift into fantasyland.

After fifteen minutes, a shudder ran through me and brought me back into the present. "I wonder what that…" Before the thought was fully formed, a blast of joy rose through me leaving soft stillness in its wake.

Then it happened again. And again: every time a thought began to form, a flash of joy wiped it away.

Joy has a lot of energy (and some tension), so I tried to balance it with samādhi (collectedness) and upekkhā (equanimity). However, the effort to invoke these triggered another upwelling of joy.

I relaxed and tried to observe the surges as they arose.

I felt goose bumps on my feet. Then on my ankles. Then the hairs on my leg stood on end. Slowly the wave moved up my legs, through my abdomen, trunk, and neck and out the top of my head. It left me smiling, peaceful, and clear.

The more mindful I was, the slower and stronger the waves were and the longer the gaps between them.

After a half hour, a tidal wave started forming. It seemed like a mass of repressed joy. "No resistance," I told myself. My face smiled intensely. There was joy. There were lights of every color. I cried. My body shook. The energy grew until my teeth rattled and tears ran freely down my cheeks.

Then it evaporated. I dropped into a deep stillness. My mind shrank to a tiny point—empty space with a small light in the distance. I was suspended for thirty or forty minutes. Maybe it was an hour. No seeing, no hearing, not the subtlest ripple—just hanging out in soft nothingness.

Eventually my mind drifted and I came back into my normal consciousness.

Staying Out of the Way

That evening Bhante asked how my practice was going. I described what I could.

He nodded and said, "Now your practice will get really interesting. But I don't think there is much more I can teach you. Your mind is starting to untangle itself. It knows more than you or I." He was silent for a minute. Then he looked at me and said, "The only thing I can tell you is, 'Stay out of the way.'"

"What about distracting thoughts?" I asked. "Should I release them and relax as before?"

"No," he said. "The Six Rs should be automatic by now. Just stay out of the way. Take all you've learned about meditation in the past thirty-five years and forget it. This is different. Don't do anything."

Meditating with effort was difficult. But meditating without effort seemed nearly impossible. Nearly.

Over the next few days I tried staying out of the way. If my mind went off into thought, I did nothing about it. Very quickly, the thoughts rose in a crescendo, popped, and left behind an intelligent-compassionate-stillness. If the mind started to drift into dull drowsiness, I'd let it drift. Very soon, a luminous energy arose out of nowhere and brought alert, loving clarity. It was fascinating watching how skillfully, intelligently, and kindly it straightened itself out if I could just stay out of the way.

This was my introduction to the eighth jhāna. I hope it's easier for other people.

Paradox

The eighth jhāna is fascinating and filled with mystery and contradiction. It's the last stage of the Buddha's path, but not the end—that is nirodha (cessation) and nibbāna (extinguishing). It is the most non-intuitive in that it makes the least sense, and yet cultivating intuition is a key to finding our way through it. Just as the seventh jhāna is based in nothingness even though there is a lot going on, the eighth is based in non-perception though there is a lot that can be perceived. Its very name is a triple contradiction. It's not perception; yet it's not non-perception; it's neither perception nor non-perception.

I began calling it "preperception perception" because in the flow of Dependent Origination, it "sees" things before "seeing" (contact) arises. So precontact or preperception could be called "perceiving things that can't be perceived in the normal way." In normal perception the nervous system amplifies seeing, hearing, tasting, touching, smelling, and thinking. Yet the eighth jhāna perceives things without the nervous system. That sounds impossible. But it's real.

Often when I tried to describe to Bhante what I had experienced, I fell mute. It seemed so clear until I tried to find words. But not always. Sometimes our conversations were quite fluid and illuminating. One time another experienced meditator was listening in on the conversation. Afterward she said, "I have no idea what you two were talking about."

I laughed because I didn't know what we were talking about either. It made sense to me nonetheless.

As these paradoxes imply, language and concepts are too coarse to describe the eighth jhāna.

In this chapter I want to talk about the eighth jhāna. I'll use language and concepts because they are the only tools we have. But bear in mind that the actual experience lies a little beyond what can be spoken. I suspect there are many others who have experienced some of these phenomena without knowing what they were. I hope this chapter helps.

Neither Perception nor Non-Perception

I'll start with the awkward name for this jhāna and where it comes from. In the suttas it's called "the base of neither perception nor non-perception."

As the mind gets quieter and more relaxed, we see that forming memories requires effort. The effort is so subtle and automatic that we don't ordinarily notice this little bit of tension. But as the mind becomes serene and subtle, it is obvious. And it's possible to relax this tension enough that the memory never forms.

We may have experienced this in the lower jhānas. A thought began to arise, we relaxed, the thought disintegrated, and in a few moments we couldn't remember what it was. It's like a dream we remember having but can't recall its content. Perhaps if we put some effort into it, we could pull it back. But we're more interested in relaxing than straining, so it's gone.

Then we notice the same thing about perception. Sensory information comes in through sight, sound, touch, taste, or smell. We compare the sensation to a vast catalog of experiences to see if we have a name for it. If we find one, we recognize the sensation. We literally "re-cognize" it or "re-think" it. We place a label on it. If we have no match in our memory, we don't recognize it.

Perception involves memory and effort. The effort is so subtle and automatic that we ordinarily don't notice. But if we relax enough and stay mindful, we can see that bit of tension and release it before the perception process is complete. Hence, no perception and no memory.

It may feel like looking through a pair of high-powered binoculars into a thick fog. We know we are seeing and sensing but don't know what. We aren't asleep, but we aren't perceiving or remembering. Hence it's called neither perception nor non-perception.

Outside of Buddhism, it has been alluded to with other terms. In the latter half of the fourteenth century, an anonymous Christian mystic wrote a guide to contemplative prayer called *The Cloud of Unknowing*.[29] He described a state where we are caught between the "cloud of unknowing above" and the "cloud of forgetting below." His descriptions sound like the Buddhist eighth jhāna even if couched in terms of late medieval Christianity.

Self-Lite

Another characteristic of the eighth jhāna is the self lightening up, disappearing, or breaking apart.

Lightening up is probably familiar from the relaxation of the lower jhānas. Indeed, we experience it all the time even without meditation. When we are angry, depressed, or frightened, our sense of self feels thick, dense, and opaque. When we are mellow, loving, or expansive, our sense of self feels light and transparent or it vanishes.

Years ago I was fascinated by this fluctuating sense of self and tried to track down the sensation itself. Sitting in meditation I found it in the middle of the head. I suspect most Westerners can find their sense of self in the center of the head a little below eye level. From here we seem to look "down" on the rest of our body, "up" to the top of our head, and "out" to the rest of the world.

As I explored this sensation, it seemed like nothing more than tightness. It's denser than the tension of memory or perception and easier to see. So I relaxed it, and the sense of self thinned out and vanished. Just like that. I looked for it and the effort of looking recreated it. If I relaxed again, it vanished. It was like playing peek-a-boo.

Another way the self disappears requires more stillness. I never saw this until I was steadily in the seventh jhāna. As described in Chapter 6 (see page 97), one morning I was just watching the movements of the mind—sensations, pulls, movements of energy, subtle vibrations. I noticed "I" watching. There was an observer and something observed. This watching requires a little tension—"standing back" so I could see from a little "distance."

I began to relax this tension. Subjectively, the distance between the observer and the observed got smaller and smaller until they fused. Rather than being a subject (me) and object (the movements of the mind), there was just a flow of experience uninterrupted by any sense of self.

Loss of Cohesion

In both of these kinds of experiences, the self remains coherent. It stays together even as it lightens up or vanishes. There are times when the various aspects of the self remain, but the "glue" that holds them all together disappears.

Once when I was meditating, a very vivid image arose. I "saw" before me my knee that had been operated on, my first kiss as a teenager, my pet raccoon from childhood, the bent car fender from a minor crash, my wife Erika, the cesarean birth of our second son, and thousands of other images. They were all floating in space, disconnected. All were aspects of my self suspended with nothing holding them together.

More recently I reported to Bhante a similar meditation though the imagery was different: "There was a giant ball. Images slid across it so quickly I could only make out a few of them: the face of a woman, an old desk, an ocean beach, a dog I once knew, a mountain forest. There were thousands of pictures flashing by. They had something to do with my life but had nothing else in common. They weren't like frames in a motion picture with each closely related to the next. There was no theme holding them together.

"Am I going crazy?" I asked.

Bhante just smiled.

I didn't think I was crazy, but the images seemed weird. They reminded me of a schizophrenic man who used to talk with me at a church I served. He was smart and was curious to know how "normal" minds worked. He asked how I knew what to pay attention to in various situations. He couldn't figure out what was important and what was irrelevant. I realized that his life was like the tape recording of a conversation in a restaurant. Listening to the recording, it's hard to separate the words from the background noise. Yet in the restaurant itself, we have no trouble filtering out the background. We do it so effortlessly that we don't even know we do it. Yet this man was not able to filter out anything without a great deal of effort.

I came to appreciate that "normal" consciousness filters out most stimuli and focuses on a few relevant items. It weaves these few together into a coherent story. It's an amazing capacity.

In the eighth jhāna, these "normal" mechanisms of perception and memory relax. The filtering doesn't work the same. Sensations and thoughts become disjointed.

I suspect it's similar to sleep. There are parts of the brain that help us create a sense of time and location—integrate our experience into a coherent storyline. When we go to sleep, those brain centers go off-line. In dreams we may jump back and forth in time or jump from one location to another. Just last night I had a dream in which I was looking around at the world. Then I was looking down at the top of my head and seeing a curious bald spot. Then I was looking out of my eyes again.

If we remember our dreams, these shifts in time, location, and perspective may seem a little crazy. But in the dream itself, they seem perfectly normal because those integrative functions of the brain aren't operating.

I suspect that in the eighth jhāna, these integrative areas of the brain have relaxed: they don't fully function. I remember asking Bhante, "Is it possible to be awake and dreaming at the same time?"

He nodded and said, "Oh yes."

Later I found out that most people going in and out of the eighth jhāna ask this question. As normal memory and perception "go to sleep," what little perception we have left is less filtered and less integrated. This creates a dreamlike quality where our sense of self and the world loses cohesion.

I told Bhante, "I feel like I tried to hold a garage sale. I took everything out of the house and sorted them on card tables on the front lawn. Everything that was 'me' was organized neatly and on display. Then a horde of shoppers came through. They didn't buy much, but they messed everything up, knocked over the tables, stirred things around, and left. Now as I pick my way through the piles of stuff on the lawn, many things are broken. Most of the stuff I can't even recognize. And I don't understand why I ever wanted any of it."

It is normal in the eighth jhāna for the sense of self as well as the sense of the world to lose its cohesiveness. It sounds a little scary from the perspective of everyday consciousness. But in the experience itself, it feels perfectly normal.

Flying below the Radar

Another aspect of the eighth jhāna is the ability to perceive things that fly below the radar of normal perception. I discovered this as I tried to pull my awareness as close to the present as possible. Let me explain.

Normal perception is never in the moment. As we read the words on this page or look at our hand or listen to the birds outside, everything we see and hear is in the past. There is a split-second delay between the time when the light or sound strikes the body and the time we become aware of them. There are so many neurons between our sense organs and the prefrontal cortex that turn these signals into perception that events slide into the immediate past before we are aware of them.

Knowing this, I sat in meditation trying to get as close to the present as I could—letting go of each perception so I could get closer to the most recent one.

As I got closer to the present, it felt as if there were thousands and thousands of perceptions coming at me. It was like standing on the prairie as a herd of horses ran toward and around me. The individual "horses" were like balls of energy shooting by so fast it was hard to see them.

This experience was so faint that I almost didn't share it with Bhante. But when I did, I said, "The balls of energy weren't yet anything specific. They could potentially become a thought or feeling or part of my body or anything. They were like stem cells: they were something in and of themselves. But they had yet to become anything specific. I tried to see where they came from. They seemed to arise out of nothing."

He looked at me for a moment and said, "You are seeing formations, the first link in Dependent Origination."

I was a little taken aback. "How is that possible?" I asked. "Formations happen before contact or perception."

"Oh, it's very possible," he said. "We can perceive these links. It's just not the normal kind of perception. The texts have descriptions of it just like what you saw."

"I just thought it was all my imagination," I said. "It was so faint I almost ignored it. Yet you say the suttas map all this out. That's amazing that someone could make sense of this."

"The Buddha was an amazing map maker," Bhante said.

Perception at this level reveals a world that looks nothing like the everyday world we're used to. It's like a mural I saw by the artist Christian Moeller. It is "painted" by shadows. Thousands of narrow shelves stick a few inches away from the wall and create shadows. Where the shelves are cut away, there are no shadows. The artist used light and dark to create portraits.

When I stood a hundred feet away, I saw a face. From thirty feet away, I saw parts of the face and the individual boards creating the shadows. Up close, all I could see were boards. There was no way to tell they were part

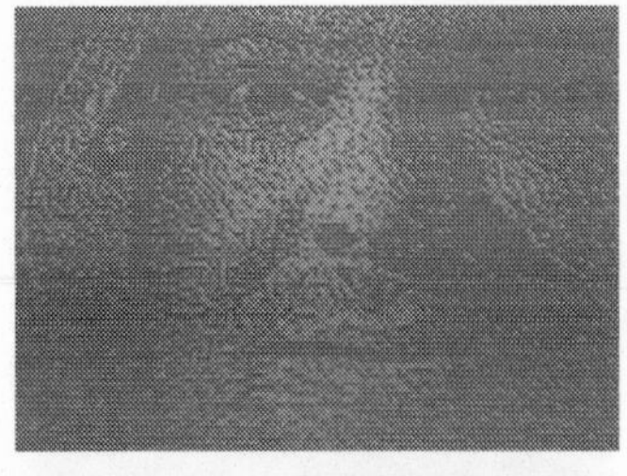

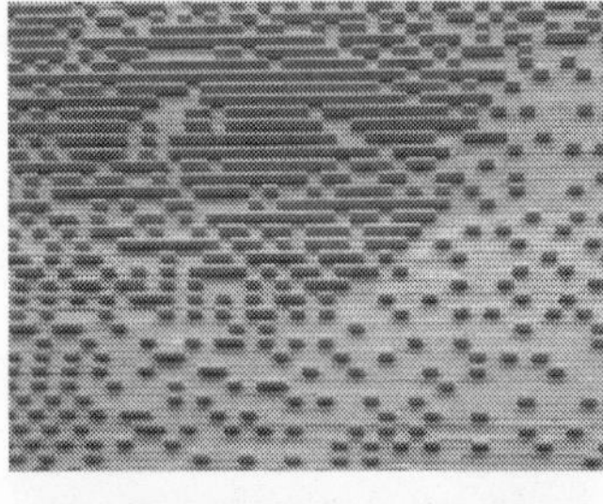

of a larger portrait. Up close was a different world from the image seen from afar.

Preperception perception is like this. We see the microscopic ingredients of ordinary perception, but it's a different world.

What may not be clear from the metaphor of looking at Christian Moeller's mural close up is how fascinating the close-up can be.

I lent my wife my camera once. It fell apart in her hands. It wasn't her fault—the camera was old and she just happened to be the one holding it when it fell into pieces. But she felt bad about it. So for my birthday, she bought me a camera with a stronger zoom and higher resolution.

I took the new camera with me on my next walk along the American River near our home. I took several close-up pictures of thistles that were going to seed.

Later, when I put the pictures on my computer and enlarged them, I felt like I was looking into another dimension. It was beautiful, strange, and fascinating.

Preperception is strange, beautiful, and fascinating.

Recognizing the Eighth

Let's summarize using two questions: How can we recognize the eighth jhāna? How can we work with it most skillfully?

We'll start with ways of recognizing the eighth jhāna.

Difficulty Knowing Where We Are

As we have seen, as normal perception and memory shut down, there are other very interesting ways of perceiving. Since they are less familiar and very subtle, it's hard to know if we actually perceive something or are just making it up. And since the mind is deeply relaxed, it is easy to mistake the eighth jhāna for sleepiness or torpor. Conversely, if we really want to be in the eighth, it is possible to mistake torpor for the eighth. One way to sort this out is to bring in more mindfulness.

Nevertheless, the most common report is, "It's a fog. I don't know what's going on. I think stuff is happening, but I can't tell what."

Loss of Spaciousness

The mind can narrow into a kind of tunnel vision, shrink to a tiny point, or "wink out" completely. The spaciousness of earlier jhānas is gone.

Unusual Perceptions

As subtler perception becomes noticeable, we might see colors of light or circular patterns. But not everyone does.

Images may flash through our awareness that are different from normal thought or imagination. The mind has to be deeply relaxed for these to arise in the first place. However, the images can be so vivid they startle us and disturb the relaxation. This can happen in a tiny fraction of a second, leaving us wondering if we saw something or not.

I'm convinced that some of these impressions are from other lifetimes or other realms because they are beyond anything I could make up. But that's just an opinion—and in the eighth, we take opinions lightly.

Far Away

Seeing the affairs of this life as far away and barely relevant is another hallmark. The relaxation of self-identity strengthens a sense of multiple lives. I often feel like I'm seeing less in terms of one life and more in terms of many. Whether or not this is literally true, the affairs and dramas of this life feel less real, while trans-lifetime qualities like kindness and compassion seem more real.

Longer Sittings

Sitting comfortably for longer and longer stretches is another indication of the eighth jhāna. The attention may drift very little.

Navigating the Fog

How do we work with the eighth? Navigating this fog is tricky. Binoculars are not useful. Here are a few suggestions I've found helpful:

Get out of the way

Bhante's advice was helpful. Our sense of self is too dense and clumsy for the subtleties of the eighth jhāna. So we can relax any tension in the head, forget anything we know about meditation or the dhamma, and get out of the way.

If we have a lot of faith, this is easy. If we have a lot of doubt, it's not. I have a lot of doubt—it's my favorite hindrance; confidence doesn't come easily for me. Over time I saw that nothing I tried worked in the eighth jhāna. This left me with no other alternative but to get out of the way.

One of my worries was that if I got out of the way, old conditioned habits would fill the vacuum. To ease this concern, I sometimes waited until I was in the seventh jhāna before vacating completely.

Six-R

Subtle hindrances still arise in the eighth, so the Six Rs remain helpful. By now they should work automatically. They can be used on anything that pulls the mind's attention.

Since there are subtle tensions below normal awareness, it helps to Six-R before we are conscious of tightness. This may sound impossible: "How do we release something we haven't seen yet?" But I've found that the intention to intuitively release before I feel a tension actually works.

Cultivate Intuition

As I mentioned earlier, if we remain in the eight jhāna rather than slipping into nirodha or nibbāna, then, like most people, we still have residual hindrances and holding. These blockages can be so subtle that external teachers are less and less able to see them. Our own inner wisdom is more intimate and a better guide. It's helpful to cultivate what's called "wisdom's eye" or intuition to help navigate the subtle terrain.

Balancing

A friend once took me up in his single engine plane. After we were at a safe altitude, he asked, "Would you like to take the wheel?"

"Yes," I said. "What do I do?"

"Just keep the plane flying level," he said.

I found this almost impossible. If the nose of the plane pointed up slightly, the plane would gradually rise and slow down. If I tried to lower the nose to compensate, it invariably went down too much. So I'd pull the nose up and it would rise too much again. The result was that my "level flight" was a series of waves as the nose gently rose and fell.

My friend laughed and assured me that level flight was very difficult. "If you try to make a correction, you'll overcompensate every time," he said. "So put your hands on the wheel and don't try to do anything. If the nose rises, just think 'down' without moving. If the nose lowers, think 'up' without moving."

I tried this and found it worked. The plane leveled out if I just paid attention without trying to do anything.

In the seventh jhāna it is important to keep balancing the enlightenment factors. If there is too much energy or restlessness, we bring in stabilizing factors like tranquility or samādhi. If the mind is groggy or drowsy, we bring in energizing factors like joy or energy.

In the eighth jhāna we may need to continue this balancing. However, the process of evaluating our state and deciding which factors to bring in is too crude. It's like level flying—the effort to compensate can disturb the subtlety of the jhāna. In the eighth, "balancing" means simply inviting the mind to balance itself–and getting out of the way.

Noticing Dependent Origination

The Buddha said that understanding Dependent Origination is the key to the dhamma and to awakening. As we move in and out of the eighth jhāna, Dependent Origination becomes clearer and starker—less theoretical and more the obvious way energies flow. And Dependent Origination itself seems empty—there is nothing driving it. It's just a mechanical process like the laws of physics. Since perceptions in the eighth jhāna can be so fleeting and dreamlike, it helps to reflect, like Sāriputta did, on what we've seen after we come out of it. This helps the wisdom we've gained deepen and free us.

Winking Out

Finally, one phenomenon that arises in the eighth jhāna is what I affectionately call "winking out." It's a momentary blackout. It's helpful to know how to work with these. We don't see them coming but may suddenly notice that we were "gone" for a moment. At these times, it's especially important to reflect back on what happened. There may be tension inside those blackouts. In the suttas they are called "taints." It's valuable to release anything we can remember afterward. This helps the mind release the tension subliminally the next time it happens.

As we come back from winking out, Dependent Origination is even clearer. It helps to take a moment to reflect on this immediately afterward.

I'll speak more about winking out in the next chapter as I speak about what comes after the base of neither perception nor non-perception.

In the Buddha's Words

Now let's look at how the Buddha described the eighth jhāna. Picking up at verse 17 of the "Anupada Sutta: One by One As They Occurred" (*Majjhima Nikaya* 111):

> *(17) Again, monks, by completely surmounting the base of nothingness, Sāriputta entered upon and abided in the base of neither perception nor non-perception.*
>
> *(18) He emerged mindful from that attainment. Having done so, he contemplated the states that had passed, ceased, and changed thus: "So indeed, these states, not having been, come into being; having been, they vanish." Regarding those states, he abided unattracted, unrepelled, independent, detached, free, dissociated, with a mind rid of barriers.*

There are several things to note in this short passage:

1. Unlike descriptions of earlier jhānas, this does not mention "contact, feeling, perception, formations, and mind; the enthusiasm, choice, energy, mindfulness, equanimity, and attention." Normal perception has vanished.

2. There is a new phrase, "*He emerged mindful from that attainment.*" Unlike the earlier stages, he was not totally aware that he was in the jhāna until he came out of it.

3. After he came out, he "*contemplated the states that had passed.*" As faint and relaxed as the states were, there was still tension. Otherwise he would have gone into nibbāna. So he reflected on what had happened and released the tension in it: "*Regarding those states, he abided unattracted, unrepelled, independent, detached, free, dissociated, with a mind rid of barriers.*"

4. And as before, there is reference to the arising and passing (the second and third Noble Truths) that accompany each link of Dependent Origination: "*these states, not having been, come into being; having been, they vanish.*"

20

Winking Out: Nirodha and Nibbāna

Adyshanti is a spiritual teacher who trained in the Zen tradition. Someone once asked him, "How do I know if I'm enlightened?" He answered, "If you have to ask the question, you're not there."

This makes sense to me. In the full light of enlightenment, we see things as they are. Before enlightenment, we can be confused. We can think we are enlightened when we aren't. But I don't think we can be enlightened and not know it. If we have to ask the question, we aren't there.

So I'm confident I am not fully enlightened.

This creates a dilemma. Nibbāna is part of the journey laid out by the Buddha. It should be part of this book. But I'm reluctant to talk about things I don't know directly. If I had extended experiences of moving in and out of nibbāna, I might write that it is beyond words and concepts, so I can't say anything. But for me, that's a dodge. Until I've had lengthy experience, I don't have the authority to say there is nothing to say.

Do you see the problem?

Nevertheless, I've had flashes, glimpses and even long stretches of things that go beyond all we've considered so far. They may be beyond the eighth jhāna and stretch through cessation (nirodha) into nibbāna. Or they may be glimpses of something else.

I suspect many people have had similar glimpses of voidness. They are so difficult to get a handle on that we may ignore them and miss their true value.

In this chapter I'd like to share glimpses I've had. Then I'll speculate about full awakening in the West. And I'll close with some reflections on motivations to seek nibbāna.

Ceasing and Arising

When I was training in Thailand, every ten days I entered a phase called "determination." They gave me a sign to put on the door of my kuti that said "determination" in Thai. They brought me meals in little round tins so I wouldn't have to leave my kuti. I was to stop sleeping and to alternate between sitting and walking meditation around the clock. I continued this for two, three or sometimes four days in a row.

When I entered this phase for the first time, the monk guiding me asked, "Do you have moments of blanking out for an instant?"

"No," I assured him. "I don't think so."

"Well," he said, "I'd like you to watch for them. Keep a count of how many occur."

I took this as a warning to stay mindful and not let my attention drift. So I tried very hard. The next time I saw him I reported, "I've had none."

He looked at me for a moment and said, "Continue. Keep a count if you have any."

The next day I reported, "None." He looked concerned. "I wonder what's getting in the way."

"Getting in the way?" I asked. "I thought you wanted me to prevent them. So I stay very vigilant."

"No. You misunderstand," he said. "We expect them. We call them 'ceasing and arising'—moments when we lose contact with the conventional world (ceasing) and quickly reconnect (arising). Subjectively it feels like blacking out for a fraction of a second. Perhaps you're trying too hard—straining to stay in contact with the sensory world. So relax."

I did. And when I saw him next I reported "ceasing and arising" as often as eight or nine times an hour.

He looked pleased. I was skeptical. I suspected I'd just nodded off for a second—nothing romantic or mystical about falling asleep on a cushion.

Winking Out

Years later I experienced a similar phenomenon under very different circumstances. Bhante did not want sleep deprivation. "If you're tired, rest," he told me simply. He wanted the mind fresh, relaxed, and alert.

As I moved into the higher jhānas, I noticed that remembering something took effort, as I mentioned in the last chapter. But in the inner quiet, I could feel a slight tightening. I released it.

This brought me into a gray zone where I sensed something was happening but didn't see or remember quite what: neither perception nor non-perception.

In this gray zone I sometimes "winked out." It was as if someone quickly flipped the light switch off and on. I couldn't see it coming. I couldn't see it when it was there. But I could notice coming out of it. And I was never groggy or sleepy. It didn't feel like nodding off—it was quite different from sleep.

Bhante said that after the experience, I was to reflect back on what had been going on during the blackout and Six-R it. At times I could recall images—sometimes vivid images. Other times there was nothing—total void.

Peaceful Cessation

Back in Thailand, the determination phase did not end with ceasing and arising or winking out. After the first day of sleeplessness, Ajahn Tong told me to "notice longer stretches when you black out. Time them." He called these "peaceful cessation."

His instructions were perplexing. How could I keep track of time when I was unconscious? I'd seen people practicing what they called cessation. When they came back, they yawned, stretched, and rubbed their eyes.

"Peaceful cessation?" I thought. "Yea right. Give me a break. They're falling asleep. This is hokey." I didn't want to have anything to do with it. "Get me outta here."

But Wat Chom Tong is a long way from home. Having invested all that time and energy to fly to the other side of the planet and hang out with a Buddhist superstar, I thought I should at least give it a try—give it as sincere an effort as I could muster.

So I made a low table from a board and positioned it next to my zafu. I placed a clock, candle, piece of paper, and pen on the table. While meditating, I could open my eyes and, with the minimal effort, record the time on the paper. Then, if I blacked out, I could figure out how long it had been.

Though I set this up, I was still skeptical of the whole project.

During the first day of meditation without sleep, I was tired. But the second day, the fatigue left. My body felt light. My physical energy was low, but my mind was alert and clear and my mood was serene.

Early one morning I sat down for my next sitting. I looked at the clock and wrote "3:10 a.m." I closed my eyes in meditation. After a month of fairly continuous practice, my mind didn't drift. I was relaxed and present with the subtle flow of phenomena. And if something began to appear, I noticed the first split second and released it.

After five minutes, I half opened an eye. The clock said "4:37."

Huh? 4:37? Subjectively it felt like five minutes. I had lost over an hour. Had I fallen asleep and not known it?

Ordinarily when we wake from sleep, the mind is groggy. There may be after-traces of dreams or a sense of the passage of time. But I was not the least bit groggy before or after. There was no sense of time passage. It was like I'd time-warped ahead over an hour.

I hadn't wandered off into daydreams, fantasies, or random associations. In fact, there were no thoughts at all. My mind was luminous: exceptionally clear, fully present, deeply relaxed, minutely aware of the pushes and pulls of the subtle flow of experience, flooded with a quiet joy.

Later that day, Ajahn Tong and another monk questioned me and concluded it was peaceful cessation.

Nuts

I experienced these blackouts or "peaceful cessations" in other ways. Coming out of it felt like coming out from under anesthesia in that I didn't know where I was for a few moments. At first all I saw were colors, shapes, and textures. These assembled themselves into objects: floor, wall, table, fan. These objects came together into a room. Then I remembered I was in a kuti in Thailand. Then I remembered feelings I had about being there.

All the time my mind was incredibly clear and quietly joyful. Even the dark room seemed bright.

Later on, I'd start to reflect on how wonderful the experience felt and what it meant. One thought led to another. One feeling triggered another. The clarity faded. Within a few hours, I was racing over hundreds of topics, thoughts, fears, aspirations, worries, dreams, and fantasies in dizzying confusion. I wrote in my journal, "My mind checked half the books out of the Library of Congress and is reading them all at once. I must be nuts."

My mind was picking fights with old enemies, worrying, obsessing. I couldn't stop it. My consciousness was like a herd of stampeding buffalo raising such a cloud of mental dust that I couldn't make out individual thoughts, just a rumbling mass.

It was discouraging. "Oh well. So much for enlightenment." I smiled at my pretentions, relaxed, and went back to simple mindfulness. Things gradually calmed down.

Why?

I asked Ajahn Tong why we did this practice. What was the point? What use was it?

He smiled almost imperceptibly and began to talk about cooking a particular Thai vegetable. "The stem is the only edible part. So you hold the base of the stem with one hand, circle the fingers of your other hand just above the base, and pull the plant through your encircling fingers. The fingers strip all the leaves off the plant in one motion.

"The stem is your core purity. The leaves are impurities. Peaceful cessation strips the impurities away, exposing your true nature unobstructed. That total stillness and openness is nibbāna. It feels like blacking out."

Then he added, "It is mundane nibbāna because there are still impurities in you. They are just turned off. Eventually, they wake up and sprout new leaves. These new leaves are the thoughts and feeling racing through you. You feel like a beginning meditator again.

"So you clear those leaves. You keep doing this over and over until the leaves no longer grow. Then you are pure and liberated, and no more disturbances grow.

"Maybe it takes a few months, or a few years, or a few hundred lifetimes. Who can know?"

Insights

Ceasing and arising, peaceful cessation, winking out, and cessation (nirodha) are far from the ordinary daily experience of walking down the street or playing Frisbee with a child. But as we go in and out of these extraordinary stages, deep insights arise more easily.

Less dramatic insights arise at all levels of this practice. After all, this style of meditation, vipassanā, means "clear insight into the nature of things." So let's consider the experience of insight itself.

Insight is different from figuring something out. Figuring out involves thinking, and thinking involves tension. Insight involves perception, and perception becomes clearer as the mind-heart relaxes. What Ajahn Tong called "impurities" are just various forms of tension. As the mind-heart quiets, thought-patter gets out of the way and we "see" more deeply. Realizations may come to us "out of the blue."

As we follow the Buddha's map, the first insights may relate more to our personal psychology. In the last chapter I mentioned seeing how deeply I was identified with struggling. I feared that if I stopped struggling, I might evaporate out of existence.

Another time I realized that most of my thoughts were explanations. I saw that part of the motivation behind explaining was trying to make myself feel special. Trying to feel special was a cover for feeling defective. I also saw that in order to move into cessation, I had to be free of wanting to be anything special.

Some insights hit me so intensely that they would unfold for an hour or more. I would "four-R" them: recognize, release, relax and re-smile. I would not bring my attention back to mettā as long as the insight was unfolding and not repeating itself.

But most insights simply dropped in fully formed in an instant.

Anyone who has meditated for a significant length of time probably has had insights into the workings of their own psychology.

Visions

In the upper jhānas, personal insights tend to give way to wider realizations about how life works. The Buddha taught the jhānas to create conditions that would give rise to this kind of "knowledge and vision of things as they are" (*yathā bhūtañā nadassana*).

As we approach nibbāna and cessation, thought is gone, and ordinary perception starts breaking down. It has not ceased completely. This is a time ripe for purer and clearer insights. When these are intense, they seem more like visions than insights.

I woke in the middle of the night on one retreat. My mind was deeply relaxed, yet I was wide-awake. I could see the darkened room around me. Hanging in space in the middle of the room were vivid images. They weren't hallucinations, because I knew they were from my mind, not from external reality. It was as if I was awake but still dreaming and knew I was dreaming.

The images were bright and luminous. I knew that if I wiggled my finger or if my mind flickered, they would vanish. But I was peaceful and very still.

The image was of a vast mountain range covered with snow. The snow flowed down one mountain then up the next. The image was not from my current lifetime, this world, or even this universe. It felt like a memory. And it was incredibly beautiful.

The scene shrank and moved away to be replaced by another: a forest, equally non-earthly and breathtaking. It seemed to be a memory from a world far away.

This image shrank and moved away to be replaced by another and another and another. They moved past more and more quickly until dozens flashed in each moment.

Then I was outside all of them—suspended in the middle of thousands of universes. And I could see my mind-stream. It wasn't really me. It was just a flow of energy that had passed from one lifetime to another, carrying with it impressions of past events and lessons learned. It appeared as a translucent stream of blue energy that came from impossibly far away.

I knew that I (or that energy) had incarnated countless times. I knew that all of us have memory traces from millions of lifetimes in hundreds of thousands of universes.

The universes have been expanding and contracting, beginning and ending, for countless trillions of years. Existence truly has no beginning. It just is. And our consciousness has flowed through countless lives in countless universes.

My current life was less than a footnote on a footnote. All my struggles and dramas were insignificant compared to the breathtaking expanse of time and existence. Whether anybody remembered me, valued me, despised me, or treated me well or poorly in this lifetime didn't matter. This life was less than a flash of a lightning bug.

I knew all this. In this lifetime I've had lots of doubts—I can question anything. But I had absolutely no doubt about anything in that vision. I simply knew it was all true.

I also knew that the state I was in that allowed me to see so clearly was temporary. The slightest movement of my littlest toe would create enough physical sensation to pull me out of the vision. But my physical body was far away. I felt no urge to move. Still, knowing it wouldn't last, I asked what would be most helpful to remember when I re-entered my current life.

I saw that kindness was more important than anything else. What I actually said or did mattered little as long as it was guided by kindness. Over the span of thousands upon thousands of lifetimes, kindness is the force that has the most potential for making any difference—in seeing things as they are and moving one toward freedom.

Knowing that my confidence in this simple truth would fade, I made vows. I don't remember the words if indeed there were words at all. They had to do with letting kindness guide my life and following that vision even when I consciously forgot it.

After about twenty or thirty minutes, my eyes moved a little. It was as if I took a tiny step back. I could still see the vision but was looking at it rather than living inside it. Maybe it was just a crazy idea. Who can know? My capacity to doubt and question was returning. The vision was still powerful, but I was moving toward my normal state.

Years later, that vision and those vows are still alive in me. I can feel their texture. The importance of kindness lives in me though it often floats in the background.

They feel like the old Pac-Man computer game where a little creature moves around the screen gobbling up everything it encounters. That vision moves quietly around inside me, reminding me of kindness, of this life being a footnote on a footnote, and of the vastness of time and consciousness. I don't live that vision or those vows fully. I forget them at times. But like a Pac-Man, they continue to move through me, gobbling up self-identities, releasing old tensions, and releasing the pull the world has on me.

How long until my self-identity collapses completely? As Ajahn Tong would say, "Who can know?" Maybe a few months. Maybe a few years. Maybe a few hundred lifetimes. In the span of existence, not so long.

Higher Path

In Chapter 4, when talking about the "higher path" of Dependent Origination (paticcasamuppāda) (see pages 65–68), we saw that tranquility (passaddhi) and collectedness (samādhi) set the stage for the "knowledge and vision of things as they are" (yathā bhūtañā nadassana). This knowledge and vision leads to disenchantment (nibbida), which leads to dispassion (virāga), which sets the stage for liberation (vimutti) followed by "knowledge of destruction of taints" or fruition (magga phala).

The Higher Path	
English	*Pāli*
Suffering, Dissatisfaction	Dukkha
Faith	Saddhā
Gladness, Relief	Pāmojja
Joy	Pīti
Tranquility	Passaddhi
Happiness	Sukha
Collectedness	Samādhi
Knowledge and Vision of Things as They Are	Yathā Bhūtañā Nadassana
Disenchantment	Nibbida
Dispassion	Virāga
Liberation	Vimutti
Knowledge of Destruction of Taints	Magga Phala

These terms can sound abstract. But as we move into the eighth jhāna or nirodha, we'll have times of seeing and knowing. How they manifest will vary depending on our lives, mind-streams, and conditioning. But in these deep states of ease, the unconditioned and the universal cannot help but leak into our awareness. This leakage can feel faint and dreamlike. It can feel overpowering. And it can be both at once.

It helps to share these experiences with someone who has touched some of the same territory. It helps not to dismiss them simply because they seem so extraordinary. And it helps to know that they may be just as they seem.

Waking Up in the West

Freedom's just another word for nothin' left to lose.
—Kris Kristofferson

What implications do ceasing and arising, peaceful cessation, winking out, ordinary insights, or powerful visions have for entering nibbāna? Nibbāna is nothing, absolutely nothing. With perception and memory turned off, there is no experience whatsoever. The Buddha called it imponderable.

But what we're interested in is how to get "into" nibbāna. Once we're in the eighth jhāna and have flickers of cessation, how do we take that last step?

I suspect that there may be differences in how Easterners and Westerners approach this last step—what it looks like and what helps or doesn't help.

Most of the practices we have in the West came from Eastern teachers. It may help to tweak them to account for cultural differences. So I'd like to reflect on waking up in the West. Having not fully awakened myself, all I can do is speculate. But these speculations may be helpful.

To be clear, I don't think there are essential differences between Easterners and Westerners. The human mind and heart are the human mind and heart—no differences from one culture to another. But how enlightenment appears as we approach it may be affected by cultural conditioning.

Imagine one person spending her entire life surrounded by yellow. When she sees orange, she'll be aware of how red it looks. Compared to yellow, orange looks red.

Imagine another person growing up surrounded by red. When he sees orange, he'll be aware of how yellow it looks. Compared to red, orange looks yellow.

Orange is still orange. But different backgrounds will make different people aware of different aspects of it. This will be reflected in what they say and how they experience it.

As the average Easterner approaches full awakening, the practices and cues that are most helpful may be a little different from the ones most helpful to the average Westerner. One may need to keep one eye out for red, the other for yellow.

I have only anecdotal evidence of this. But the evidence comes from people who know more than I.

Inquisitiveness

One clue about the difference in how awakening manifests in the East and the West came from Ajahn Tong and the way he treated Westerners.

He taught in the Thai forest tradition that included daily interviews with each student. The interviews were formal: I'd enter his interview kuti, bow three times, approach, bow three more times, repeat the *yana* (meditation knowledge) he'd asked me to invoke, and describe anything significant I'd experienced in the previous twenty-four hours. He'd comment and maybe fine-tune my practice. I'd bow three times and leave.

The total interview could take only a few minutes. But with as many as fifty or sixty students, I could wait a long time for my turn.

Most of Ajahn Tong's students were Asian. There were a few of us Westerners. But no matter how early we arrived for an interview, we were always last. Asians who arrived late were scooted in before us.

This bothered me—it seemed arbitrary and prejudicial. So I spoke with a senior monk. He said the reasons were practical. Asians tended to be brief and listen without comment to what Ajahn Tong said. Westerners tended to be elaborate and ask questions. After Ajahn spoke, they'd ask more questions.

The monk assured me that Ajahn Tong enjoyed the questions—he found Western inquisitiveness refreshing. But it made for longer interviews. Having the shorter interviews first meant that fewer people had to wait a long time.

Most of the Asian meditators had a devotional temperament. Their faith was strong. Most of the Westerners I met (including me) had an inquisitive temperament. We'd learned to question authority and find out for ourselves.

This colored our attitude toward teachers and toward awakening. One temperament was not better than the other. Faith was not better than inquisitiveness. They were just different perspectives.

Getting It

Tsoknyi Rinpoche also noted these differences. He's a Tibetan teacher who spends a few months each year teaching in North America. When he met with a group of senior Western dharma teachers, one asked him the difference between his Tibetan and Western students. He said, "Westerners come to realization much more quickly than Tibetans."

This was surprising. Considering the depth of spiritual tradition in Tibet and its reputation for producing teachers of the caliber of the Dalai Lama, it was perplexing.

But Tsoknyi said he found Western students to have intelligent, probing minds. When given teachings, they "got it" relatively quickly.

"However," he said, "Westerners don't stabilize in these realizations. They go home and say, 'Did I really experience that? I wonder. Maybe I'm fooling myself. Oh well, let's see what's on TV.'

"Tibetans are slower to get it. But once they realize something, it sticks. They don't lose it."

Self-Esteem

Another cultural difference may be self-esteem.

Asian masters coming to America have been blown away by the amount of self-hatred they see in the average American. We take it so much for granted that we don't even recognize it. In one often-quoted conversation with the Dalai Lama, some Western psychologists spent an hour trying to explain to him what low self-esteem was. From the Dalai Lama's perspective, feeling arises because of past conditions. He had a hard time understanding how someone would take them so personally that they became part of his or her self-identity.

In the West, the monotheistic religions talk of original sin. Even those who don't believe in original sin may still have a cultural remnant: an inner critic.

In the East, the predominant model says we are creatures of light—original goodness. Impurities get into us and mess up our lives. But our core is not bad. Impurities can be removed to reveal our true Buddha nature.

People with a hypertensive inner critic—or even a gentler inner nag—may need slightly different practices than people who start with a fundamental trust in their goodness.

Hanging on the Edge

Bhante Vimalaramsi has been one of my teachers for a number of years. On the way to the airport shuttle after a retreat, I said, "I've always had a lot of doubt. As I go home, do you have any advice as to how to work with it?"

"I've told you most of what I know," he said. "But I've always had a lot of faith. I don't have much personal experience with doubt. I may not be the best to guide you through it."

He had guided me easily into the seventh jhāna. It had taken me longer to relax, let go, and move into the eighth. But once I was there, it was easy enough to return to it. He said, "My job is done. I've taught you all I can. Now it's up to you and your intuition to move into nibbāna."

I continued to do retreats with him. It helped to talk about my practice and experience with someone who knew the terrain better than I, even if I had to find my own way through it.

Nibbāna had still eluded me. Toward the end of one retreat, I went to him feeling discouraged. "You are right on the upper edge of the eighth," he told me. "For my Asian students, once I get them to the eighth, they slide over into nibbāna on their own. But not my Western students—none of them has actually entered."

I found this comforting. He had helped me in so many ways. The fact that I hadn't moved fully into nirodha and nibbāna may have had more to do with what I had in common with Westerners than anything that was more uniquely me. And the fact that Bhante, despite growing up in the West, had always had a lot of faith while Westerners often had little is another clue.

Easing Awake

Two years after that conversation with Bhante, I and several other of his Western students have slid off the map into nibbāna to varying degrees. But the question remains: why do the same techniques take longer in some cultures? What implications does this have for awakening in the West?

Reflecting on the observations of Ajahn Tong, Tsoknyi Rinpoche, Bhante, and others and letting them settle in with my own experience with the eighth jhāna and winking out, don't lead to new ideas, practices, or perspectives or to a precise conclusion. They lead to something akin to a mood or gentle attitude toward waking up. Part of this mood is kindness and self-forgiveness. And part of it is the paradox of going to sleep and staying awake at the same time.

I'll speak about each of these moods. Then I'll close this chapter with a journal entry about motivation, selflessness, and heart. It speaks to the mood itself.

Self-Forgiveness

Given the prevalence of low self-esteem and self-doubt in the West, self-forgiveness is a good tool to have available. Particularly when we feel stuck, discouraged, or frustrated, forgiveness may be helpful.

Self-forgiveness can seem counterintuitive: selflessness (anattā) is a key realization. Doesn't self-forgiveness just reinforce the sense of self we're trying to get rid of?

Actually, no. Selflessness arises out of feeling good about ourselves. Trying to transcend low-esteem creates a dark, hidden sense of self. It creates repression and tension, not dispassion and selflessness.

As I mentioned while describing the forgiveness meditation (see page 170), when I was having difficulty getting into the eighth jhāna, forgiving myself for not being there was very helpful. And I've seen it help people trying get into the first jhāna. When we seem to be stuck and not able to make progress, it may be that we're taking ourselves too seriously. Our inner critics may be getting overexcited. Forgiving ourselves may be a way of lightening up.

Self-forgiveness, taking ourselves lightly, and having a sense of humor go hand in hand with anattā.

Go to Sleep and Leap

In the last chapter I described how Bhante told me to forget everything I had learned about meditation and cultivate "wisdom's eye" (intuition). The eighth jhāna is so subtle that the nuances of intuition may be the most useful tool in fine-tuning the practice.

So when I'm unclear as to what to do, I close my eyes in meditation and silently ask, "What would be helpful now?" I drop into stillness and wait to see if guidance arises.

One afternoon, three phrases arose one at a time over the course of a two-and-a-half-hour meditation. Together the phrases were "Go to sleep with your eyes open and leap."

Let me unpack these.

"Go to sleep" was the first guidance to arise. It was surprising. This whole enlightenment project is about waking up, not going to sleep. But going to sleep is not something we can do. When I lie in bed at night, if I try too hard to put myself to sleep, the effort keeps me awake. If I worry about being able to go to sleep, the worry keeps me from going to sleep. Falling asleep is not something we do, it's something we allow. Perhaps we relax gracefully and let sleep overcome us. Perhaps we are so exhausted that our resistance wears down and it takes us over. But it is not something we can control. The best we can do is get out of the way and let it happen.

And waking up in the morning is not something we do either. It just happens on its own.

So when Tsoknyi Rinpoche talked about his Western students "getting it" easily and then sliding out of the realization, he may have been referring to the overly inquisitive mind that can't relax enough to let the realization settle in. This may be what's happening with Bhante's Western students. If we can allow our curious doubts to go to sleep, we might wake up.

The phrase "go to sleep" also refers to the sense of self. The Western, hyper-developed sense of self needs to take a deep rest. For me this can be very specific—noticing that holding in the center of the head a little below the level of the eyes and allowing it to relax. When I do, self-sense fades.

"Going to sleep" also means letting go of all attempts to get anywhere, realize anything, or accomplish any goal. It means allowing that hypertensive nag of an inner critic to go to bed. I give up on enlightenment and just soften into a comforting nothingness.

"...with eyes open..." was the second phrase to emerge. This was to clarify that "going to sleep" didn't mean shutting off awareness. It was just letting that sense of self go: forgiving it, forgiving myself, and letting it go.

"...with eyes open..." also was a reference to a game I invented. I lay in bed one evening on retreat wondering if I should go to sleep or get up and meditate a little longer. I decided to try both at once.

I strive so easily and habitually that I often don't notice the tension it produces. Even on retreat where I'm trying to mellow out, I'm still trying. So going to bed at night, I often give myself a treat. I take a break from "meditating." I lie in bed with my eyes open and see if I can remain aware of the visual field at the same time that I fall asleep. I'm better at doing one or the other than I am at doing both at once.

If I can do both, after a few minutes I begin to see pseudo-hallucinations. In the dim light of the darkened room, the shadows start to form repetitive patterns. If I focus on what I'm seeing, they disappear. But if I stay relaxed, they form and reform and start to move. If I continue to relax, bright lines appear around some shapes. And if I continue to relax without falling unconscious, vivid images flash out of nowhere.

It's entertaining.

The trick to getting these effects is to allow the body, emotions, and mind to get as relaxed as if I'm in a deep sleep and at the same time remain awake—literally with my eyes open. Awareness itself also has to be deeply relaxed. It's not looking for anything. It is just dispassionately receiving.

I've played this game on retreats for years. I've not thought much of it. I've taken it to be hypnagogia, a transition state between waking and sleeping. Researchers have known about it for years without associating it with meditation. My mother even talked with me about it when I was little.

But the guidance was to use this state during meditation—to allow myself to go to the threshold of sleep while remaining aware. Since I don't have a devotional temperament, this game helps me practice surrendering and trusting.

" …and leap" was the last phrase to emerge. This was guidance to follow intuition even when it seemed confusing or doubtful.

When I "went to sleep with my eyes open," sometimes my mind seemed to daydream in the background or slip into blackness or have other perceptions that I wasn't sure were helpful. I wondered, "Can I trust this?"

"Leap" meant, "Yes, Trust it. Go for it." "Leap" was an antidote to the doubt and self-distrust noted by many teachers in Westerners. When guidance arises, follow it even if it feels like walking off a cliff. As long as it's about meditation, the worst that can happen is nothing—I'll just sit a little longer.

It Takes a Lot of Heart to Destroy Your Self

In the end, moving into nibbāna is so subtle that it has less to do with specific guidance and more to do with mood—a balancing of awakening factors. In the West with our stress on individualism and habits of being so hard on ourselves, the mood needs to be both selfless and heartful.

It also helps to look deeply at our motivation to engage these practices. Are we trying to improve ourselves as if we need improving? Are we trying to get somewhere as if there is somewhere to get?

I suspect that deep down our motives may be purer than we realize. It's not a matter of cultivating "better" motives—that's just more self-improvement. It's about seeing what motives are beneath our social and personal conditioning.

So I close with a journal entry about selflessness, heart, moods, and motives:

> *My eyes open. I gaze around the dark kuti where I'd been sleeping. Outside the window, the sky has turned from black to predawn deep gray. Inside, the*

clock says "4:30." I'm wide-awake. I pull on my clothes and slip out the door quietly so as not to disturb my roommate.

Outside, the moon is full and bright on the western horizon. Moisture hangs in the cool mountain air. Cicada and crickets are loud. A dog barks a half mile away. The world is lovely and precious. Life is lovely and precious.

I've always loved being up in the hours before dawn. Some people are night people—they come alive in the late evening. Some are morning people. I guess I'm a pre-morning person. I always have been. Even as a teenager, if I had a lot of homework, I'd go to bed early and get up at two or three o'clock in the morning to do my studies.

I don't think our spirit—our life force—ever sleeps. But at night, our worries and fears, our aspirations and ambitions slumber. Except for occasional dreams, our egos and sense of self relax. The collective human psyche is tranquil. The ether feels silky and smooth.

In the wee hours of the night, nobody asks me to be anything. There is no place I have to go, nothing I have to be. I can be nobody and it's just fine. The "Doug" that I try to be fades into irrelevance.

Outside my kuti, I smile gently as I walk up the little hill to the main building. I climb the outside stairs that lead up to a second-story deck. I often like to meditate in a library off that deck. But instead, I walk to the railing and gaze across the moonlit Ozark Mountain woodland.

Ralph Waldo Emerson once wrote, "Standing on the bare ground—my head bathed by the blithe air and uplifted into infinite space—all mean egotism vanishes. I become a transparent eyeball. I am nothing; I see all; the currents of the Universal Being circulate through me; I am part or parcel of God."

Years ago when I first came across this passage in his essay on nature, I

pictured that transparent eyeball suspended in the air like a damp volleyball, with the optic nerve and blood vessels dangling behind it. It's an awkward and grotesque image. I wondered, "What is he talking about?"

So as I sat with the image and the other words—transparent, egotism vanishes, being nothing, seeing all, currents of the universal flowing through…, I thought, "Emerson was a far-out dude. He was describing the experience of selflessness. He was a Yankee mystic."

Ralph Waldo Emerson died on April 27, 1882. I was born on April 27, 1948. The anniversary of his death and the anniversary of my birth are the same. I'd like to think I'm a reincarnation of Ralph Waldo Emerson. I don't believe it for a moment, but I like to think it. He's my Unitarian hero. I'd like to be like him when I grow up.

Even more, I'd love to sit in the blithe mountain air and have a quiet conversation: "Waldo" (he preferred to be called "Waldo" rather than "Ralph"), "Waldo, can you tell me more about what you experienced when you wrote about being transparent? Can I tell you a few things I've experienced and hear what you think about them?"

But he's not here. I can't speak with him. So I sit on the top step, open my journal in the dim moonlight, and begin to write:

It takes a lot of heart to destroy ourselves—to witness the mind and consciousness dissolving into infinite space, to become a transparent nothing who is part and parcel of everything.

It can't be done with will power. That would be relatively easy. Will is the bastion of the opaque self. It can be done with relaxation and letting go. Surrender is the bastion of the heart.

It's not glorious. Glory is the realm of the ego.

And it doesn't make us anybody special. It just makes us a nobody, another critter in the forest at one with all the other critters.

But at some point, what else is there to do?

Looking out into the larger world, we have many urgent problems: the species extinction rate has skyrocketed; we're burning through the earth's resources one and a half times faster than she can replace them; our economic system is a Rube Goldberg contraption barely held together with chicken wire; and our political system is seizing up in gridlock.

When we look around at the human collective, it's clear that we're going through a transformation. There are so many of us that we all live in each other's backyards. Disparate cultures that used to be far distant are now sitting in each other's laps. Television, cell phones, the Internet, and other technologies link us more intimately than ever.

Any transformation holds both promise and peril. But the greatest perils we face are not natural disasters. They are manmade disasters that grow out of a hyper-developed sense of self: The ecological crisis comes from too much emphasis on "what I want now" and not enough on what's sustainable. Political gridlock is too many childish egos—like Nero playing his lyre as Rome burns. Economic crisis is rooted in greed.

And a self-centered search for spiritual well-being is like a mountain trail that peters out at high altitudes. The highest fulfillment is only possible with selflessness. It's a paradox: to find the greatest happiness for ourselves, we have to get rid of ourselves. Not easy.

Yet selflessness arises easily and naturally as the human spirit matures. Selflessness won't solve all the specific problems we face in this time of transition. But it provides an environment within which urgently needed remedies are easier to find.

It takes a lot of heart to destroy one's self. But at some point, what else is there to do?

Try to be less, not more.

—Ramana Maharshi

21

Buddha's Map

We shall not cease from exploration
And the end of all exploring
Will be to arrive where we started
And know the place for the first time.

—T.S. Eliot

The GPS on the dashboard of my car has several settings. The "off-road" mode computes the most direct route from where I am to my destination. If I could fly, it would be the fastest route—a straight line. But since I'm not a bird and can't leap over buildings, cliffs, forests, and rivers, it's usually not a practical route.

The second mode computes the shortest "on-road" route. It confines itself to drivable roads and finds the most direct course. If I were on foot or on a bicycle, it might even be the fastest route. But in a car, it might not be the fastest, because it makes no distinction between an eight-miles-per-hour alleyway and a sixty-five-miles-per-hour highway bypass.

The third mode computes the fastest route by using the time it takes to drive a specific road rather than just its length. Since most cars are more fuel efficient when driving steadily at higher speeds than starting and stopping at slower speeds, the fastest route often is the most energy efficient.

I leave my GPS set to the "fastest route" mode.

At the beginning of this book, I used the ancient metaphor of a mountain for the spiritual journey as a way to say that there are many paths to the summit but that not all paths go all the way to the top. It's also true that among the paths that reach the peak, some are faster and more efficient.

I'm a little hesitant to use the metaphors of speed and distance for spiritual development. I remember hearing Larry Rosenberg, the guiding teacher at Cambridge Insight Meditation Center, say, "Most people are trying to get from A to Z. In this practice we're trying to get from A to A." There is nowhere to go. As T. S. Eliot put it, we're trying to "arrive where we started and know the place for the first time."

And yet we engage spiritual practice in hopes of getting somewhere. Maybe the "somewhere" is a mountain peak, or maybe it's merely "here." But whatever the metaphor, given the choice, I'd rather get there (or get here) using the fastest GPS setting.

When I began to understand more clearly what the Buddha actually said about meditation in the earliest suttas and, with Bhante's help, follow those instructions, my meditation gained speed and distance. I got further in the next few years than I had in nearly thirty years of previous practice. I've gone further than I imagined possible.

When I say this, some people respond, "Well, you've been meditating a long time. You're building on all those years of practice." Perhaps subvocally they're also saying, "And I've been practicing just a few years, so I won't get the same results as you."

I have no doubt that my current practice is built on all I've learned over the years. I'm grateful for that. Nevertheless, I've seen people with very little meditation experience and even less understanding engage this way of meditating and move very quickly to get just as far. They used a faster, more efficient GPS setting to avoid all the slow alleys and windy one-lane roads I've wandered down.

Another comment I hear when I describe the teachings of the earliest suttas is, "Yes, I've heard that and practice the same way." Perhaps subvocally they're also saying, "So I don't have anything new to learn from what you're describing."

Maybe that's true. And maybe not.

There is nothing I learned from Bhante that I had not learned somewhere before or practiced to some degree. What I learned from him was not a specific technique but a precise way of integrating certain techniques.

When I first met Bhante, it was as if I had a large garage. Over the years I had filled it with automobile parts, enough to build a wonderful car. I also had fragments of instructions on how to attach the water pump to the engine block and the driveshaft to the transmission. But I didn't have a complete manual to guide me in putting the whole thing together. So I didn't actually have a car, just a bunch of parts strewn around. He showed me how to put them together.

As I look around that garage now, I see that I not only had all I needed, but I also had parts that I didn't need: snow plows, bicycle pedals, airplane propellers, etc. that are superfluous to a car and are best set aside.

In this book I've attempted to transcribe the full manual for building a well-tuned practice. To describe various insights and techniques, I've drawn from my experiences in different traditions. Some of those traditions have ingredients I've set aside. I included the experiences anyway if they shined light on an aspect of the early sutta practice. After all, they started from the same source, the original teachings of the Buddha.

My hope is to build bridges between various practices and the one I'm advocating. If you have a practice that serves you well and gives you what you need, that's great. But if your practice has plateaued, is grinding along, or leaves you far from awakening, perhaps there is something in the early suttas that can enliven it. Perhaps.

Though I freely and gratefully honor all I've gained from different approaches to the dhamma, there are ways my practice has changed since I started training with Bhante Vimalaramsi. Some of the changes are small and subtle, but the effect has been dramatic.

At the risk of overusing the metaphor, the color of the paint or the kind of hubcaps has no effect on how smoothly that car runs. On the other hand, the wrong gas filter, a tiny difference in the sparkplug gap, or a little oil leak can make the difference between a car that hums along and one that chugs, sputters, and stalls out.

In this chapter I'd like to review the essential elements in the Buddha's dhamma practice as I have come to understand them. This chapter is a CliffsNotes digest of five essential ingredients: (1) relaxation, (2) middle way, (3) stages, (4) Dependent Origination, and (5) everyday relevance.

Ease and Relaxation

Ease and relaxation may be the most important aspect of this practice for most Westerners.

I saw this in my very first retreat with Ruth Dennison. Even though she had significant physical pain, there was a sense of ease about her. It was encouraging to see. But it was a few years before I had a clue as to how to cultivate that ease other than scold myself, "Lighten up!"

In those years, the term "samādhi" was most often rendered into English as "concentration." On one retreat, Joseph Goldstein described two kinds of concentration. As best as I can remember, he called them "sustained concentration" and "returning concentration."

Sustained concentration is the quality of mind that stays solidly on the object of meditation. It's what most meditators aspired to at that time.

Returning concentration was gentler. It didn't try to stick to the object of meditation. It merely noticed when attention wandered from and returned to the object.

Joseph said it was very difficult to cultivate sustained concentration—so difficult that it wasn't worth trying. It was wiser and easier to remember to return to the object. Practicing returning concentration cultivated sustained concentration. It developed both types.

Hearing this encouraged me to relax and not strain so hard to stay one-pointed.

Several years later, Corrado Pensa was the first teacher I heard talk at length about the word "samādhi" itself. He translated it as "calm abiding," a settled, steady, and gentle attention.

The Tibetan Yongey Mingyur Rinpoche had a specific practice of relaxing. He called it "dropping." Rather than trying to quiet the mind, we let all thinking drop into silence for a second or two.

Larry Rosenberg talked about "effort without strain."

The more I think about the various teachers I've had, the more I remember them talking about relaxing, softening, and balancing effort and ease. Many used the metaphor of the strings of a musical instrument being not too tight or too loose.

Yet it wasn't until training with Bhante that I understood the precise meaning of relaxing in the early suttas. This meaning shapes specific practices as well as the general approach to the Buddha's Dhamma.

The specific meaning is found in a phrase repeated in the suttas: "tranquilize the formations." In Pāli, the key words are pas'sambaya ("tranquilize," "bring tranquility to," or "relax") and saṅkhāra ("formations," "that which has been formed," or "that which is held together"). The phrase explicitly does not counsel us to get rid of, push aside, or repress the distractions, concepts, diversions, or other things that capture the mind's attention. We merely soften the tension (taṇhā) in them. We relax any holding.

In this way, relaxing is not just a state to cultivate—a noun. It's a practice to engage—a verb. It is engaged in concert with other verbs. Bhante describes these relationships as the Six Rs: Recognize, Release, Relax, Re-Smile, Return, Repeat.

When a distraction arises, the first step is to do nothing about it other than see it or *Recognize* it on its own terms. The second step is to *Release* it or let it be. It's only then that we *Relax* any mental, emotional, or physical holding (taṇhā). And to emphasize the relaxation, the fourth step is to smile or bring up some light mood. In this way, relaxation is not just general mellowing out. It's a precise step in the flow of the Six Rs.

Furthermore, it's done every time the mind wanders. This is very important! Easing isn't a loose standard to measure the quality of the meditation every once in a while. It's something done over and over and over until it becomes a powerful, automated habit. With practice it becomes so deeply ingrained that it continues even in the eighth jhāna and beyond when ordinary perception has faded and the sense of a self is evaporating.

Bhante also encourages relaxation in the more general sense. In fact, he insists upon it. He wants his students to smile all the time. "This is a smiling meditation," he says. It's hard to smile and stay tight at the same time. Whenever I felt stuck, he asked if I was trying too hard. (Usually I was.) He encourages people to laugh, take themselves lightly, and have fun while meditating.

While relaxation has a role to play in almost every Buddhist practice, it is central in the early suttas. After all, taṇhā is the Second Noble Truth: the source of all suffering is an instinctual tightening. So we relax, "tranquilize the formations," or "bring tranquility into whatever is being held together."

Middle Way, Integration, and the Larger Whole

Probably the first thing I learned about Buddhism was that it was a middle way. Unlike many religions that hold to an extreme, Buddhism seeks balance between opposing qualities.

As I learned more, I found Buddhist practice wasn't simply balancing qualities. It was integrating them until we discovered a larger whole that includes them both. It's like balancing the colors yellow and red. At first we swirl paints together, creating intertwined spirals of yellow and red. As we continue to mix them, the swirls integrate into a larger whole, the color orange that contains yellow and red but is neither.

Ease and Effort

For example, in deep practice, ease and effort are integrated into a larger whole. If relaxation and ease were the only qualities we had to cultivate, then we could all take a long nap and become enlightened. But the practice integrates ease and effort to help us drop into the nothingness of cessation rather than the nothingness of sleep.

I've emphasized ease because most Westerners usually bring enough effort with them. But as the practice matures, it's important to balance ease and effort, relaxing and paying attention.

Most teachers I've known acknowledge this need for balance. One of the most interesting strategies for balancing was the method used by Ajahn Tong in Thailand (see pages 248 to 252).

The senior monks around Ajahn Tong emphasized effort, diligence, and working hard. They wanted me to spend the same number of minutes in walking meditation that I spent in sitting meditation: if I sat meditating for sixty minutes I was supposed to do walking meditation for sixty minutes. As an overzealous Westerner, I didn't find this strictness helpful.

As I entered the advanced practice, Ajahn Tong asked me to meditate continually for several days at a stretch—no sleep. At first this made me tense from striving and groggy from sleepiness. After eighteen hours, my mind was sluggish and I found it harder to maintain strenuous effort. I lost the will to keep pushing so hard: I kept going but stopped straining.

After twenty-five to thirty hours, my mind became clear and precise. My physical energy was low so I still couldn't push even if I wanted to. Yet I was surprisingly alert. My mind felt relaxed and sharp.

In this state I began to "wink out"—I had short moments of blacking out which Ajahn Tong called "ceasing and arising." And after longer continuous practice, I had longer stretches of loss of perception and memory that he called "peaceful cessation" or "mundane nibbāna." At first I thought I was falling asleep. But the clarity, brilliance, and precision of mind going in and out of peaceful cessation suggested something other than ordinary sleep.

Looking back, I suspect the practice was blending great effort with the deep relaxation of sleep deprivation. When these came into balance, the experience was profound.

Yet the tremendous effort to get into those states left residual tension which, a few hours later, sent my mind into a firestorm of thinking. Ajahn Tong understood and expected this. He advised me to re-enter the practice over and over until there were no more "impurities" (residual tensions).

Both Ajahn Tong and Bhante Vimalaramsi teach balance. A key difference is that Bhante not only balances the various factors, but he also integrates them from the very beginning. It's not a matter of building up tremendous effort and then balancing it with ease. They are both cultivated as different aspects of a unified process, the Six Rs.

In the Six Rs, explicit effort comes in the last two Rs: Return and Repeat. After seeing, releasing, softening, and lightening up, we use a light and clear intention to bring awareness back to the primary object of meditation. And since all Six Rs are used anytime the mind wanders, relaxation and effort are practiced together and often. As the Six Rs roll together into one process, they are integrated into an awareness that is attentive and relaxed, clear and spacious, mindful and easy.

I found that both Ajahn Tong's and Bhante Vimalaramsi's approaches had powerful effects. But Bhante's was easier on my body, easier to use outside a monastic setting, more stable, less prone to confusion caused by going through a translator, and set to a faster GPS setting.

I've learned from the earliest sutta practice that the middle way is found not so much by balancing but by integrating effort and ease into a quality of mind-heart that is larger than either one alone.

Mettā Passaddhi Vipassanā

The Buddha said that insight into the nature of experience is key to awakening. The word "insight" (vipassanā) is connected with many Theravadan practices. But it's easy for a strict insight practice to become dry. It's also easy for a mettā practice to lose some clear seeing. So early sutta practice doesn't separate vipassanā (insight) from mettā (loving kindness) or tranquility (passaddhi). They're done at the same time.

When insight and tranquility are practiced together, the primary object of attention is a light, uplifted state: kindness, joy, compassion, peace, etc. In this way, it is a mettā or passaddhi practice.

However, when the mind wanders, the practice shifts to insight: seeing where the mind went by using the Recognize step of the Six Rs. This cultivates insight into how the mind's attention moves. The last of the Six Rs Returns to broadcasting uplifted states.

In this way mettā, passaddhi, and vipassanā are part of the same integrated process.

One-Pointed and Choiceless

The process also integrates techniques used for one-pointed concentration and techniques for choiceless awareness. By integrating them, it is neither one-pointed nor choiceless. It is a middle way between them both. It's a larger whole that contains them both.

Choiceless awareness emphasizes not controlling the mind's attention and just allowing it to go where it will, as we stay mindful of its travels. One-pointed practices emphasize keeping the mind's attention on one object (and thus increasing collectedness and decreasing insight). One of the most effective ways to cultivate one-pointedness is to remember to return to the primary object when the mind wanders.

The Six Rs use both. Like choiceless awareness, the Recognize step notices where the mind has gone without judging or pulling back. There is some wisdom in why the attention went there, so we see where it is. This cultivates insight.

Unlike choiceless awareness practice, we don't let the mind's attention wander in free association from one object to another. After recognizing where attention went, we release it, relax, smile, and return to the primary object—sending out mettā.

Unlike one-pointed techniques, the Return is preceded by Recognition and insight.

The combined effect is cultivating a mind that is clear, bright, relaxed, and insightful—not as separate qualities but as an integrated whole.

Jhāna Wars

They say the world is vexed with us on account of our wicked writings. I trust it will recover its composure.

—Ralph Waldo Emerson (writing to his brother)

Over the years I've heard many teachers speak about the development of meditation. But Bhante's roadmap was more detailed than any I had heard.

The map includes jhānas or markers to know where we are and how to practice most effectively from that place. Following that roadmap makes the journey much faster than I had previously imagined. The word "jhāna" means "stage" or "stage of meditation." These are described throughout the early suttas. It's impossible to read the suttas thoroughly and avoid the jhānas.

I did my first serious study of the suttas under Bhante. After a number of years, to broaden my scope, I joined a dhamma study group in my hometown of Sacramento. In the first meeting there was a discussion of the "jhāna wars" in the Buddhist community. There are a variety of ways to understand the jhānas. On the one hand are strict, Burmese-style absorption jhānas. On the other hand are "softer" jhānas that allow more space for insight to arise.

I thought, "Oops. Am I on the front line of this skirmish? I have found the 'softer' tranquility jhānas very helpful. I have an opinion on this. Can I get noncombatant status?"

In the suttas, the jhānas are not described as one-pointed absorption. They are described as the stage-by-stage cultivation of qualities that bring the mind-heart into a deeper integration and wholeness. Each jhāna is an ingredient for the next. Each gives power to the one that follows. It's a bootstrapping process.

It's not until the eighth jhāna that perception begins to shut down. The stricter absorption jhānas have perception shutting down in the first jhāna. This interpretation is not found in the suttas.

This leaves me in the "soft jhāna" camp, if there is such a thing. But there are beings clearer than I advocating opinions in both "camps." So I'll merely describe my experience and go back to my cushion rather than go off to war.

Dependent Origination and Cessation

Another essential ingredient is Dependent Origination (paticcasamuppāda). The Buddha said that anyone who understands paticcasamuppāda understands the Dhamma and anyone who understands the Dhamma understands paticcasamuppāda. So a crucial element of any practice based on his teaching should include techniques which give insight into Dependent Origination.

Dependent Origination says that everything arises from something subtler than itself. The Buddha said that we become wiser as we can see these links. By relaxing the cause giving rise to an event, the event ceases. So the first step is to see the origin of the event. The second step is to relax the tension (taṇhā) in it.

Seeing the links of Dependent Origination is superficially similar to seeing the links between thoughts of free association. Yet below the surface, it is very different.

I was daydreaming in a hammock one afternoon. I caught myself in the middle of an idle thought and wondered, "Where did that come from? How come I'm thinking about my kindergarten teacher?" I traced my thoughts backward:

- The memory of my kindergarten teacher arose from thinking about my last day in kindergarten when I wore my superman cape to school and forgot it in my locker.
- The memory of the locker arose from thinking about padlocks.
- The image of a padlock arose from remembering a newspaper story about how the raccoons at the Houston zoo used to play with the padlocks on their cages. One day they opened the lock on a big cage and released about fifty fellow raccoons.
- I'd been thinking about the cage break because I'd been remembering Amy, my childhood pet raccoon.
- I'd been thinking about Amy because I'd been remembering climbing the trees in my backyard with her.
- I'd remembered those trees because I was looking at the tree leaves above me as I lay in the hammock.

Since childhood I've been fascinated by how far the mind can wander in a string of associations.

Tracing the links of Dependent Origination is a little like this, but not really. In this example, one thought led to another thought, which led to another thought. Each thought was still a thought even if the content was different.

Such idle meandering does not generate wisdom. Any of us who has ever wandered off in idle daydreaming can attest that it can be relaxing but doesn't make us wiser.

Tracing the links of Dependent Origination is different. To trace the links, I would not go into the content of the thought. I'd just notice that I was daydreaming. Then I'd notice that the thoughts arose from a single thought about leaves. That the single thought arose from gently honing in on a pleasant feeling. And the pleasant feeling arose from seeing the leaves in the sunlight above me.

To couch this sequence in traditional terms: a habitual thought pattern (bhava) had been triggered by a single thought (clinging or upādāna), which had been triggered by honing in (craving or tightening or taṇhā), which had been triggered by a pleasant feeling (vedanā), which had been triggered by seeing the leaves (contact or phassa).

However, it is neither necessary nor helpful to analyze experience and make it conform to these particular labels. What is helpful is just noticing each event arising from a different and subtler kind of event. As we notice the subtler event, see the tension (taṇhā) within it, and relax that tension, the mind becomes more peaceful and perceptive.

Free-associating in daydreams leads to mental proliferation. Relaxing the subtler and subtler links of Dependent Origination leads to mental calming.

Meditating in a way that quiets the mind and sees Dependent Origination is simpler to do than to explain. All we have to do is notice what gives rise to an experience and relax the tension in it.

Bhante was always asking me, "So, what happened before that?" When I answered, he'd ask, "And what happened before that?" And he'd keep going until I could not remember what came before. This sensitized me to the subtlest events I could recall. In my next sitting, I'd be more alert to noticing what came before these events and the subtle tension in them.

With this, my awareness became subtler and clearer and calmer until I was seeing events that were subtler than I had ever seen before.

Practicing this way, we eventually see events that arise out of nothing. If we can trace them back into a true nothing, we go into cessation and nibbāna.

Buddha versus Buddhaghosa

Theravadan Buddhist practices as taught in the West and much of Asia rely heavily on the *Visuddhimagga*, or *The Path of Purification*, as a core text explaining the Buddha's teaching. Buddhaghosa composed the *Visuddhimagga* in Sri Lanka around 430 CE.

In his younger years, Buddhaghosa had mastered the Vedic scriptures. These are the foundation of Brahmanism (Hinduism). He had traveled far and wide debating finer points of the Vedas.

Before Siddhārtha Gautama became a Buddha, he had been deeply educated in the Vedic texts. In his quest for enlightenment, he used Brahman meditation practices. He mastered them more than anyone else in his lifetime. Though they nearly killed him, he found they did not bring him to full realization.

So when he sat down under the Bodhi Tree, he modified and adapted his practices. His new practices worked. He woke up and became a Buddha. Over the next forty years, he taught these new practices to thousands of people.

The old Brahman practices did not simply disappear. Not everyone became a Buddhist. Many sincere seekers continued the earlier practices.

In the generations after the Buddha's lifetime, many people who self-identified as Buddhist had different understandings of what the Buddha taught. Some of the old Brahman practices leaked back into various Buddhist communities. By the time of Buddhaghosa a millennia after the Buddha, there were eighteen different schools of Buddhism.

Buddhaghosa, in writing the *Visuddhimagga*, was attempting to find the common elements in the eighteen schools and bring them back together. Notice that his primary motivation was to find common ground rather than necessarily finding what the Buddha actually taught.

Buddhaghosa was a scholar more than a meditator. He had more training in disputation than in meditation. He knew the Vedic scriptures more thoroughly than the early Buddhist texts. Many of the refinements in the Buddha's insights are difficult to put into words, particularly by someone who may not have experienced those insights directly.

Buddhaghosa's *Visuddhimagga* was a monumental achievement. There is much in it of great value. But in the area of meditation practice, it reflects the blending of the Buddha's teachings with older Brahman techniques more than a true exposition of what the Buddha taught.

If we look at earlier texts such as the *Majjhima Nikaya* and the *Saṃyutta Nikaya*, we find the simpler, more integrated, less striving approaches I've tried to describe in this book. If some of these seem different from what you've learned from other teachers (including Theravadan teachers), it may be because they or their teachers have relied more on Buddhaghosa and the *Visuddhimagga* or the *Abhidhamma* than the earlier texts that are truer to the Buddha's actual teaching.

Of course, the proof is in the pudding. As the Buddha put it, "be a lamp unto yourself." Trust your own direct experience. Try out these practices and see if they work for you. That's all that really counts.

Everywhere and Every Day

The last essential ingredient to this practice is how it can be used every moment of our day. This is not an ingredient added to the practice but a byproduct of it. It's relatively easy to take this practice off the meditation cushion and into everyday life.

Sitting meditation, walking meditation, and meditation retreats are a wonderful way to strengthen the practice. Ultimately, however, the Dhamma is about how we live in our daily lives. I can't remember a Buddhist teacher saying otherwise. What's important is not becoming a good meditator, but meeting life with more wisdom and heart.

I've found this style of meditating to be the easiest to take into daily life. I find it easier, for example, to walk down the street radiating tranquility (passaddhi) than walking down the street concentrating on the breath. And the Six Rs are helpful in any situation. If I'm in the middle of a verbal fight, I can notice the tightness in me and use the Six Rs to soften. If I don't want to soften, I can Six-R that resistance.

I'm not claiming I use the practice all the time. I get lost and caught a thousand times a day. But it's relatively easy to slip back into it when I want to. And when I don't want to, I can always smile, relax, and ask myself if I'm taking myself too seriously.

Invariably, I am.

Epilogue

I wake up at four thirty in the morning seeing more clearly than ever the nature of the predicament I'm in as I approach cessation. I get out my journal and begin to write these words.

It feels like I'm standing in a doorway with my hands on the doorframe as I look into blackness. There is nothing, not even a floor, on the other side. That is cessation. To go through, all I have to do is let go of the doorframe and fall through. But when I try, my hands are glued to the frame. The very attempt to let go strengthens the glue.

I'm reminded of an episode in the original *Star Trek* TV shows. The series featured Captain Kirk, a human, and his first officer Mr. Spock, who was half human and half Vulcan. Vulcans used mental discipline to augment their intellect and suppress their emotions.

In one episode, Kirk and Spock got caught in an alien force field. It formed an energy barrier around them. When they were relaxed, the field grew weak and transparent. If they pushed against it, it got a little stronger. If they threw themselves against it, it became dense and powerful. The more they fought it, the stronger it got.

Finally they realized that their prison was only as strong as their effort to be free of it. If they just saw that they were free, they could move out without effort. If there was any doubt in their mind—even a flicker of concern—that was enough to feed the force field.

Kirk couldn't get out. He intellectually understood that they were free, but he still wanted to get away from the alien apparatus. He thought he would be a little freer "over there." That hedging was enough to keep him trapped. Spock, with his greater internal discipline, could see that they were free and harbored no doubts. He simply walked out while Kirk remained trapped.

I'm in Kirk's predicament. But rather than a sticky door frame or alien force field, here's I how I think it works:

"Wisdom's eye" is a phrase the Buddha used to indicate the knowing faculty in its purest state. It is awareness without any thought or mental constructs.

When I experience this knowingness directly, it feels more intimate and closer to my essence than thought itself. Knowingness is part of everything I know or perceive. Knowingness mixes with thought to create the experience of seeing, hearing, touch…any perception. For example, to see a tree, wisdom's eye perceives something. Then we compare that to a mental catalog until we come up with a match: "Oh, that's a tree." So perception has subtle but vital thought as part of it. Knowingness precedes the thought and precedes the perception.

When the mind is still enough, we can actually know this subtle process directly.

In ordinary consciousness, the first link of Dependent Origination that we experience is ordinary perception—knowingness mixed lightly with thought. This perception may give rise to pleasantness or unpleasantness. This may give rise to desire, aversion, or fuzziness. If this craving persists, it gives rise to normal thought. If thinking persists, it gives rise to our habitual tendencies, emotions, thought constructs, story lines, and all the rest. At this point, there is very little knowingness left. There is mostly thoughts and emotions that give rise to mental, verbal, and physical actions.

Wisdom's eye or pure cognition is part of normal consciousness. But in normal consciousness, it is jerked around a thousand times a second—pointed in one direction or another by our thoughts, conditioning, and habit patterns. Normally, wisdom's eye is moved around so fast that it can only notice superficially. That's why normal perception is so unrefined—it moves too quickly to know clearly.

One awakening strategy is to forcibly hold wisdom's eye still—to concentrate on one object and one object only. This strategy creates absorption states of one-pointedness.

These states can feel quite wonderful and create "oh wow" experiences from seeing so clearly and deeply. But the knowingness sees only one thing, so it doesn't cultivate the wisdom the Buddha encouraged.

And since it takes massive energy to hold the eye of wisdom still, it can't go through the door into cessation. The eye becomes too massive to fit through the door, if you will. To take this final step, it has to relax all the energy and control that have been cultivated so diligently.

The strategy of awakening that the Buddha favored is to relax all control of the knowing faculty—and through this to let all thinking dissolve. This lets the eye of wisdom find its natural state. It will find a stillness that is inherent in it rather than one forced upon it. This natural stillness is more fluid. Awareness may rest on something for a long time, but still shift its gaze easily and naturally. This creates a relaxed, clear awareness.

Now, here's the kicker.

As intimate as wisdom's eye is, as much as it is central to everything we experience, it is not who we are. We create our sense of self out of thought, habit, memories, tendencies...but not out of pure knowingness. Knowingness exists only in the present moment. It knows nothing of history or future. It only knows this very instant.

So to get through that door into cessation and *nibbāna*, we have to let go of everything that is self, everything that we have an ounce of control over, including trying to direct our attention.

I think this is why my mind can feel so clear when I wake up in the morning after a good night's sleep. To go to sleep is to let go of all attempts to control consciousness. When I awake, if I've had enough rest and am not clinging to sleep, my mind is relaxed.

So the trick of awakening fully is to "go to sleep" in the sense of relaxing all control, all thought, all sense of self, everything we think we are and, at the same time, stay awake and stay connected to knowingness.

Simple! But it's the hardest thing to do because "I" can't do it. Kirk couldn't get himself out of the force field. "I" can't let go of the doorframe. The letting go has to be deeper than "I."

And for me, there is one more kicker.

I love insight. I like to collect insights, think about them, be stimulated by them, be inspired by them, and share them with others. As a minister, I've made a career out of collecting and sharing insights.

But insights are complex perceptions—they have lots of thoughts and images woven through them.

Insights arise out of knowingness—they start with wisdom's eye. But they don't become full-fledged insights until they've been cloaked in thought. The cloaking can become so thick and heavy that the original knowing gets lost. And they can get so thick they can't get through the door.

As I travel the Buddha's path of awakening, I love to stop and examine every interesting rock, tree, or panoramic view along the way. At higher altitude, there are so many interesting things to see—so many insights to be had.

To really wake up, I have to give up insights. This doesn't mean suppressing them or throwing them away. It means releasing knowing when it arises and moving on. It means not stopping and translating knowingness into insights.

I even have to let go of the thoughts that arose in writing these words.

So I stop writing and look at my watch. It is five fifteen. Outside my meditation kuti, the overcast of the evening before has cleared. The sky is deep black and filled with stars.

I put away my writing and put on warm clothes to walk the quarter mile down the hill from my kuti to the farmhouse that holds the dhamma hall at Dhamma Sukha. As I approach the farmhouse, Isis, a petite gray, orange, and white cat, runs up the path to meet me as she does every morning. I pick her up and hold her against my chest. Her warmth presses against mine as I walk. She looks intently into the darkness. I stroke her. She starts to purr.

At the door, I set her down. This morning she goes inside with me.

At five thirty, I and the other meditators take the three refuges—in the Buddha, the dhamma, and the saṅgha—as we do every morning. And we take the eight training precepts. Then I close my eyes to meditate.

Isis jumps into my lap, curls up, and starts to purr.

My mind doesn't settle as easily as she. I think about how my journal entry might make a good chapter in this book. I think about changes to words and phrases.

I recognize what my mind is doing. I release it—just let the thoughts do their own thing. I relax. My breath shudders. My shoulders drop an inch. I hadn't realized they were tight. My back softens. A deep smile arises out of nowhere. I almost laugh.

In the Buddha's time, monks meditated in huts more often than in dhamma halls and more often sitting at the base of trees than in huts. The Buddha ended a number of talks with a simple encouragement: "There are these roots of trees, these meditation huts."

Appendices

Appendix A
Dhamma Sukha

If you'd like to explore the jhānas, The Dhamma Sukha Meditation Center is a place where you can train under a master. Bhante Vimalaramsi is a blend of Asia and America. He's Caucasian and grew up in America, and he trained and taught in Southeast Asia for many years. He's an ordained, robed Buddhist monk living within the traditional 227 precepts. And his home base is in the center of the United States in the Missouri Ozarks.

He has a deep understanding of the development of the jhānas. He's a bit of a character—and likes it. He doesn't fit the stereotypical image of a Buddhist monk that you'll find in popular literature. I've had occasional disagreements with him about politics and the larger social order. Still, he's remarkably imperturbable. And when it comes to the dhamma and the Buddha's teaching about meditation, his understanding is both exquisite and practical.

He has a special gift for recognizing where someone is in his or her unfolding practice. And his advice and guidance in shaping an individual's practice is precise and effective.

I have the deepest gratitude for his teachings and his patience with me. I've learned a tremendous amount from him.

He teaches in the Asian Thai forest tradition. This means that much of the practice is done on your own with daily interviews and dhamma talks in the evening. A typical day starts at five in the morning and includes the following:

5:30 a.m.—group sitting that begins with taking the traditional three refuges and eight precepts. Even in this group sitting, people follow their own rhythm in shifting from sitting to walking meditation depending on the needs of their practice.

7:00 a.m.—breakfast

8:00 a.m.—work period

9:00 a.m.—individual sitting and walking practice

11:00 a.m.—the midday meal, which is the major meal of the day. There are no meals or solid food taken after that meal (unless there are medical needs).

Noon—rest. Bhante wants people to rest for an hour.

1:00 p.m.—individual practice

6:00 p.m.—dhamma talk and questions. All dhamma talks are sutta-based.

8:00 p.m.—individual practice

10:00 p.m. (or later)—evening rest

There is at least one individual interview each day. If there are a lot of students at the center, these may be scheduled. If not, he is available as needed. If there has been no interview during the day, he'll check with you about your practice before the dhamma talk.

Dhamma Sukha calls itself a meditation center, but it is more of a monastery—a living community with a number of people in permanent residence. It is tucked deep into the Missouri Ozark Mountains.

Students wishing to train make arrangements to come when it is convenient for them. As of 2013, Bhante is in residence typically from late May to early October. Since the instructions are individualized for each student, you can begin a retreat at any time. There is no need for everybody to start at the same time or end at the same time.

Accommodations are a bit rustic compared to some of the more expensive meditation centers. They feel more like an American version of an Asian style. I find them comfortable, and I appreciate living a little closer to the land. During the several years I've been going there, they've air conditioned all the kutis and built a large new dhamma hall, kitchen, dining hall, library, and balcony.

For more information about Dhamma Sukha, retreats Bhante is leading elsewhere, information about web-based retreats, guidance, and more, you can find them here:

Dhamma Sukha Meditation Center and
Anathapindika's Park Complex
8218 County Road 204,
Annapolis, MO 63620
Phone: 573-546-1214
Web: http://www.dhammasukha.org

Appendix B

No-Frills Instructions

This appendix offers a no-frills summary of the meditation instructions. The fuller version is found in relevant sections of this book.

Preparation

The best preparation for meditation is to smile whenever you think of it. This helps calm and open the mind-heart.

Spiritual Friend

Before starting this practice, choose a spiritual friend. A spiritual friend is someone who is alive and someone for whom it is relatively easy for you to wish the best. Your friend should not be a partner or an adolescent daughter or son. You may have much love for him or her. But those relationships can be complicated. For meditation purposes, it is best to choose a simpler relationship. For similar reasons it is best to choose someone of the gender you are least likely to have sexual feelings toward.

A few examples of good spiritual friends include a teacher who has your best interest at heart, an aunt, uncle, or grandparent who always looks out for you, or a kind friend you can always trust.

Once you have settled on a spiritual friend, you will stay with them throughout the early phases of your practice. It is unhelpful to switch spiritual friends from sitting to sitting.

Seclusion

Find a place to meditate that is relatively secluded: quiet, no phones, no interruptions, and comfortable seating. The perfect location is not possible, but it helps to do what is reasonable to be comfortable and quiet.

Posture

Posture ultimately is unimportant. There is nothing better about sitting with crossed legs versus sitting on a chair. So sit in a posture that is relatively comfortable. Once you settle into meditation, it is best to not move. The urge to move should be Six-R'd. When you have to move, it is better to get up and do walking meditation than to wiggle around and try to continue sitting.

Mettā Phrases

To generate mettā, begin with simple phrases: "May I be happy." "May I have ease." "May I feel joy." "May I feel safe." "May I be comfortable." "May I know kindness." Any uplifted state is fine. The phrases are used to "prime the pump"—to generate some feeling of uplift. Once the feeling arises, it becomes the primary object of meditation. Seventy-five percent of your attention goes to this feeling. Twenty percent goes to the person to whom you are sending mettā. And five percent—a very small amount—goes to the actual phrases.

Say a phrase silently no more than once per breath. If the feeling of mettā or uplift is strong, use a phrase less often. Repeating the phrases mechanically or quickly is of little value. Choose wording that works for you so that you can say the phrases sincerely.

Six Rs

Thoughts, sounds, physical sensations, and other distractions will arise. If some of your attention remains with the feeling of loving kindness or with your spiritual friend, just ignore the distractions. They are not a problem. Don't be concerned about them.

However, when a distraction completely hijacks your attention, use the Six Rs: Recognize (see and know where your attention went), Release (let the distraction be there without holding onto it or pushing it away), Relax (soften the body, emotions, and mind), Re-Smile (bring in an uplifted state; if none feels natural, then raise the corners of the mouth in a half smile), Return (bring this relaxed and uplifted consciousness back to the object of meditation), and Repeat (know that it is normal and natural to use the Six Rs many times in the course of a sitting).

First Jhāna—Joy

To begin, sit comfortably in your secluded space and send mettā (or any uplifted feeling) to yourself. Do this sincerely. If you are unhappy, this wish that you feel happiness can still be very sincere. That's all that matters.

Send this well-wishing to yourself for about ten minutes. Then send it to your spiritual friend for the remainder of the sitting.

It is best to sit for at least a half hour. More is better if you can do so without strain.

At some point, a feeling of genuine joy will arise. It may be very short in duration, or it may linger for a longer time. This feeling quiets into happiness. Happiness quiets into peaceful equanimity. Equanimity can be very subtle so it tends to fade.

This cycle of joy to happiness to equanimity is a sign of the first jhāna. The cycle may pass through and fade very quickly. That's fine. With patience, it will return. Meanwhile, know that you are making progress.

It is not necessary that you know what jhāna you are in. Some people may not recognize them even when they are in them because words do not adequately describe the actual experience: the jhāna may not feel exactly as you expect it to feel.

The only thing that is important is sending mettā or well-wishing, and Six-R-ing distractions. Everything else will take care of itself.

Second Jhāna—Confidence

With practice, the cycle from joy to happiness to equanimity lasts longer. Perhaps the happiness or equanimity lingers for a while without fading. Distracting thoughts arise less often and less insistently. It becomes easier to Six R. You may notice a confidence that the practice really works.

These are signs of the second jhāna. It is not a distinct break from the first. Rather it is a deepening of joy, happiness, equanimity, and confidence and a lessening of distractions. There are still plenty of distractions. They just are not as powerful.

You may find that the phrases begin to feel coarse or awkward: the well-wishing flows naturally, and the phrases seem less helpful. If so, it's okay to drop the phrases. You still have the person and the feeling of the phrases in the mind-heart: you continue to send out mettā to them, but do so in inner silence. This is called "noble silence."

Some people find at this stage that sending mettā to themselves first and then remembering when to switch to a spiritual friend seems to keep the practice from going deeper. In the second jhāna, it is okay to just send out the loving kindness to your spiritual friend. You will be included in the feeling just by sending it out. You don't have to keep purposely sending it to yourself for the first ten minutes.

However, if you sense that it would be of value or uplifting to spend some time sending it to yourself, that is fine as well.

Third Jhāna—*Peace*

As your meditation deepens, joy arises less often or may not arise at all. Rather than go through the cycle from joy to happiness to equanimity, you find there is just equanimity. The feeling is strong and tangible rather than elusive as it was in the beginning. It is not uncommon for meditators to think there is something wrong with their practice because there is less joy. For other meditators, joy shifts from a bright and relatively coarse feeling to a broad, pervasive sense of peace.

You find you naturally want to sit longer and that there are longer stretches without distractions—or at least without distractions strong enough to capture your attention.

These are all signs of the third jhāna.

Again, the shifts from the first to the second to the third jhāna are not distinct. Often there is no sudden shift of energy or feeling—just a steady deepening. If you are working with a meditation teacher, she or he may not hint at what jhāna you are in even as he or she adjusts instructions.

Worrying about which jhāna you are in is not helpful. Just take care of the practice, and the practice will take care of you.

Fourth Jhāna—Fading of the Body

As you continue to relax attentively, your body becomes so tranquil that physical sensations fade. At first it may just be in one area of your body—perhaps you notice no sensations in your hands. If you move them slightly or direct your attention toward them, you feel them. Similarly, sounds may fade into the distance. Perhaps you don't notice them at all unless you think about them. Or perhaps they do not disappear but seem far away. They have less capacity to disturb you.

Meanwhile you are sitting for longer stretches. And during your best sitting, you are staying with your object of meditation without drifting for longer periods of time.

You are in the fourth jhāna. According to the early Buddhist texts, you have become an advanced meditator.

There are a number of shifts in the practice with this jhāna. Your equanimity is so powerful that your teacher (if you have one) is less concerned with you wondering about which jhāna you are in. She or he may speak more openly about the jhānas.

Since the body tends to fade from awareness, it becomes difficult to send mettā out from the heart because you have so little physical sensation. You may find yourself sending it more from the head or the crown of the head. Or your teacher may invite you to try that.

Your teacher may also invite you to use several different practices. The first is to send mettā or well-wishing to a different spiritual friend. You do this until you can see them smiling. Then you shift to another friend.

When you've done this for several people, you may be invited to send it to any significant person in your life, including some difficult people for whom it is less easy or natural to send happiness, ease, or comfort. You may be invited to send it to each person until you see them smiling.

When you have done this for all the significant people in your life, you may be invited to send well-wishing to all beings in all six directions. At first it helps to get a feel for the directions by doing one direction at a time: in front, behind, to the left, to the right, above, and below. After you have a good sense of the six directions, you send out well-being to all beings in all directions all at once.

When you can do this, your equanimity is indeed well established. From here on, you continue to send out kindness, joy, well-being, and uplift in all directions and to all beings.

Fifth Jhāna—Spaciousness

Some of the traditions refer to only four jhānas with the fourth having four different "bases." I find it simpler to just refer to the bases as the fifth, sixth, seventh, and eighth jhāna.

In the fifth jhāna, a vast feeling of spaciousness arises. It's called "the base of infinite space" and is described as a circle whose center is everywhere and circumference is nowhere. It feels as if it continues to expand though it is already infinite. You send out spaciousness in all directions.

Sixth Jhāna—Holes

As you relax into spaciousness, there are moments when there seems to be nothing going on—there are gaps in your awareness. These may be periods of deep stillness, or blinks when everything stops for a fraction of a second. Your consciousness is so relaxed that none of this is disturbing. It feels natural. You are seeing consciousness itself arise and fade.

This is the sixth jhāna.

Seventh Jhāna—No Things

When your awareness goes into these gaps, you find yourself in the seventh jhāna. Here you experience longer stretches where awareness remains on the object of meditation—sending out equanimity, spaciousness, peace, and well-being. The distractions that do arise have nothing to do with anything outside the mind itself. You may notice pushes and pulls, various kinds of energies, moments of peace, and moments of restlessness.

But there are no thoughts about what's for dinner or how to make the next tuition payment. "Outside" references have faded.

At this stage your awareness is very refined and subtle. It may not seem so because there are still many disturbances. But they are all internal. The seventh jhāna is traditionally called "the base of nothingness." There is nothing going on related to the "outside" world, but there is a lot going on inside.

In the seventh it is particularly helpful to pay some attention to the seven awakening factors. If one seems to be weak, you can gently ask that it be strengthened to bring the mind into balance. The seven include three energizing factors (joy, investigation, and energy), three calming factors (tranquility, collectedness, and equanimity), and mindfulness.

The seventh is also the place to Six-R everything, even if the distraction has not completely captured your attention. In earlier stages, it is not wise to attempt this, because there are so many coarse distractions that Six-R-ing everything generates restlessness from doing too much. But in the seventh jhāna, you have enough peace that it helps to Six R things that have not completely captured your consciousness. And by now, the Six Rs should be automated: they are a deeply conditioned habit done with little effort.

Be sure that ease, well-being, or mettā continues to flow out from you in all directions. It may flow on its own without effort—this is fine. But you don't want it to stop.

Eighth Jhāna—Loss of Ordinary Perception

It is difficult to describe the highest jhāna because the mind-heart are so relaxed that ordinary perception and consciousness fade. It takes a small amount of tension to remember what you experienced a moment ago. It takes a tiny bit of tension to just perceive what is going on now. So as consciousness relaxes deeply and subtly, normal perception fades. You enter the realm called "neither perception nor non-perception."

In this jhāna it is common for meditators to not be clear where they are. They may wonder if they can be both asleep and awake at the same time because it feels like falling asleep while remaining aware.

In the eighth jhāna, you cease all meditative effort except to Six-R anything that arises. Otherwise, you simply get out of the way and let the mind itself run the show.

If your progress seems to get stuck, you can ask intuitively what adjustments might help and follow that guidance. But do this sparingly.

There will be moments where everything is gone. You won't notice them until you come out of them. I call these "winking out"—short moments of gently blacking out. My Thai teacher called them "peaceful cessation." There are differences in the traditions and amongst teachers about when these periods of winking out are just part of neither perception nor non-perception, when they are true cessation (nirodha), and when they are nibbāna (nirvana).

In practical terms, what you call them is not important. When you come out of one, reflect for a moment on what was going on during the winking out. Sometimes you'll recall a lot or a little. In these cases, Six-R what you recall even though it has passed. Other times, reflecting on what happened feels like looking into a black emptiness. In these cases, just continue on.

When the winking out is true cessation or nibbāna, when you come out, the flow of Dependent Origination will be clearer than ever. Just notice this. Sometimes pervading joy can be very intense even while it is serene.

Beyond the Jhānas

Once you are established in the eighth jhāna, the instructions stay the same up until full awakening. You will go into short and then longer periods of nibbāna followed by clearer and clearer seeing of Dependent Origination. These will help you move up through the various stages of enlightenment until you reach full liberation.

Exploration of these higher insights and awakening is beyond the scope of this book. But I can suggest a few things that may help:

- *Do nothing, Six-R everything.* Six-R even the slightest of perceptions. Otherwise do nothing.
- *Stay out of the way.* Soften any sense of self that arises.

- *Set an intention to awaken, but seek only clarity and acceptance.* Dispassion naturally grows in the eighth jhāna. You are not trying to get anywhere anymore. You just want to see clearly what is and to be accepting and trusting of things as they are.
- *Put your faith in the Buddha, the Dhamma, and the Saṅgha.* That is to say, put your faith in the truth of how things are, in your inherent enlightened nature, and in the collective wisdom of those who have walked this path ahead of us.
- *Let go.*

Appendix C
Meditation Games

We are not a perfect expression of any ideal. Ideals are too simple. We are perfect expressions of what we are. The path to freedom is discovering what we are and allowing it to flow forth. This is unique in each of us.

The jhāna instructions work well in the early stages of practice. They have plenty of room within them for our uniqueness. But in the upper stages, what's left in each of us is more and more unique. The meditation instructions may be shaped by our intuition to better fit our particular meditative needs.

The practices below are meditative games—varieties of sànùk—that I have found helpful as well as engaging over the years. I mentioned some of these earlier in the book. Others are new. I collected them here to have them in one place. Which ones are helpful for you will depend on your inclinations, blind spots, gifts, and patterns. I offer them only as games to try out and use if helpful. Many of them have to do with finding ease in the midst of struggle.

Some of these games can be used at almost any stage of meditation practice, including at the beginning. Those are listed earlier. Others are easier to play in the higher jhānas when there is greater ease and stillness. Those are listed later. This ranking is far from precise. I invite you to play with them and use the ones you find helpful.

Remember, whatever your stage of practice, meditation works better when it's fun.

Car Watching

During my second retreat many years ago, Jack Kornfield described this game:

Imagine you are standing beside a freeway. Thoughts are whizzing by like cars on a road. If you try to see each one coming and going, you'll get dizzy turning your head to follow them. Instead, imagine gazing across the highway. Notice when a car / thought whizzes by without turning your attention to follow it. Just let it speed through your awareness and go on its merry way. Where it came from or where it goes is not a concern. Just notice the moment and let it go.

Interstellar Travel

When you're relaxed and at ease, close your eyes. Imagine you're a multidimensional being who just arrived on Earth via a cosmic radiance. Your body did not travel through time and space, just your consciousness. You've never had a body or a personality before. You've just arrived inside a specimen of the human species. The sensations are altogether new to you. Notice what arises.

You play interstellar travel by just being with sensations and thoughts as if they are completely new to you.

Beyond Mind-Body

If you enjoy interstellar travel, you might want to try version two. You play the game as before, but take it one step further. Rather than just notice what arises in this strange wonderful body, notice and then set it aside.

For example, you experience sounds and smells. Notice them…Then set them aside.

What else is there? Thoughts and emotions…Again, notice and look further.

Sensations: touch, kinesthetic feelings, light patterns. Notice these and move on…

Gently shift your awareness away from anything that seems to arise from the five senses or thought. …There's an energy that remains. Be with that. Don't interpret. Don't translate the sense into thought. Feel it on its own terms, direct and simple…

You may sense something essential in you that has nothing to do with instincts, reflexes, or inhibitions—something that has nothing to do with the body, personality, or conditioning. What is it?

Don't Fight Reality

The teacher Byron Katie says, "If we fight reality, we lose—but only a hundred percent of the time."

The truth is that reality doesn't care what we like or don't like. It is what it is regardless of our opinions and preferences. And yet we all have opinions and preferences. Despite our best intentions, we all fight reality at times. It's a losing battle.

So in this game, notice any resistance in you. If your mind is busy and you wish it were quiet, can you just relax and let it be busy without fighting it or indulging it? If you are sleepy and wish you had more energy, rather than try to create more energy, can you just let the sleepiness be sleepiness without indulging or fighting it? Just see it as it is as clearly as you can. If you are restless and wish you weren't, can you just relax into restlessness?

Notice any difficulty—or resistance to reality—and let the feeling of difficulty be a feeling of difficulty or the feeling of resistance be a feeling of resistance. Let reality as it is be as it is. Remember, your opinions and preferences don't count. What is true is all that counts. So be with what's true. Don't fight reality. Enjoy it.

Resistance Is Futile

Another version of "Don't fight reality" is a quote from Star Trek. A powerful collective of people called the Borg used to say, "Resistance is futile," meaning, "We are so powerful that any attempt to resist us will come to naught, so you might as well give in now."

Any time something comes up in meditation that you don't like and wish you could get rid of, just remind yourself lightheartedly, "Resistance is futile."

DROPS

Bhante has an acronym that I find helpful. It is "DROPS," which stands for "Don't resist or push. Soften." When you find yourself struggling, use it to remind yourself that rather than harden against something, try softening.

Here We Are

When the mind is particularly jumbled and hard to sort out, the phrase "Here we are," can serve as a reminder not to try to sort or figure things out. Instead, just drop everything but the present moment. "Here we are" says, "Let's just look at what's here in this present and let everything else go." It playfully invokes mindfulness.

What's Happening Right Now?

"What's happening right now?" is similar to "Here we are." But since it's a question, it tends to evoke inquiry more than mindfulness. (Both inquiry and mindfulness are awakening factors.)

Dropping

The Tibetan teacher Yongey Mingur Rinpoche sat before a large group of meditators with one of his arms raised. He said, "When I drop my arm, let all your thinking drop away."

I watched him intently. As he let gravity pull his arm down onto a cushion, I let my thinking drop as well. He was right. My mind went completely silent. Within a second or two, thoughts started right back up. But for that short moment, there was natural stillness.

When I'm sitting in meditation trying to figure out which technique to use to straighten out my inner jumble, dropping all my thoughts for a moment has been a way to "clean the slate" and simply start afresh. Dropping is a way to simply let go of things without figuring them out.

Thought Theater

Imagine sitting in a theater looking at a stage. The actors are your thoughts. See how they move across the stage. Some move smoothly, others in rapid jerks like a squirrel; some move quickly, others meander; some dress primly, others dress slovenly. Sometimes the stage is empty and you just wait for them to make an appearance. If so, don't rush them. Just observe the empty stage.

Thought Bubbles

A variation of Thought Theater is seeing thoughts as bubbles floating down a stream. It is not until the bubble opens that you know the content. Can you see thought before you know what it's about?

Suspending Doubt

Doubt is one of my more enthusiastic hindrances. I find it not so helpful to try to force doubt to leave or to suppress it. As with most hindrances, force of will is not an effective tool.

But I find I can sometimes bargain with doubt: "I'm only suspending you for a short while. I'll be right back. Give yourself a little vacation, a well-deserved rest. And I promise I won't make any big decisions without you. We'll just have a little fun and see what it might be like without you. But I love you and will be back shortly."

Nobody

Without a sense of self, there are no hindrances. Yet the sense of self can be quite persistent. Perhaps this is why hindrances can be persistent.

In the game of Nobody, try to locate that sense of self as a physical sensation—a kind of tightness—and relax it. Many people will find that it resides in the middle of the head, a little below the eyes. But wherever you find it, once you feel it as a physical sensation, try to relax the tension in it. See what happens. The sense may simply fade: self becomes nobody.

Nobody has no hindrance. Nobody is free of problems. Nobody is pervaded with tranquility. Nobody is very wise. Nobody is free.

What Happened Before?

In the flow of causation in Dependent Origination, everything has a cause. This game is noticing the "upstream" events. To play it, just notice what's in your mind now and what came before that arose.

The trick is to not analyze the current contents of your mind or even try to remember what came before. Instead, see if these earlier events are still subtly present. If you are in the midst of a thought, the tension that gave rise to it is probably still there. The preference that gave rise to the tension is probably still present.

This game is to simply see if the subtler forerunners of your current mind state are still here. And if so, see if you can relax them.

Neural Network

Most if not all that goes through our mind-hearts has some neurophysiological correlates. Repeated thoughts or feelings will grow new dendrites and make new neural connections. So if there is any free-floating tension in the mind, it can stimulate these neural patterns and give rise to the experience of the return of a thought or feeling.

This game notes the neural network when an old thought or feeling returns. It's as if you're saying, "Ah, it's no big surprise that this is showing up. It's just something wired in my brain." This helps to see the mental event objectively. Rather than struggle against it, you just relax and let it be. By not reinforcing it, it will fade in time.

Go to Sleep. With Your Eyes Open. Leap.

These three phrases guided me for several years. They first came to me when I asked intuition to help my practice. "Go to sleep" means letting my sense of self fall asleep, take a rest, or go on an extended vacation. "With your eyes open" is a reminder that while I let the body go into the deep rest of sleep, I let the mind stay awake. "Leap" says that even though I may doubt my intuition or instincts, it may be best to take a leap and follow them anyway to see where they lead.

Song

It is not unusual for song lyrics, instrumental music, or a repetitive jingle to arise in the mind. On long retreats, some meditators feel these as intrusions that are impossible to get rid of. They can be very annoying. Of course, trying to get rid of them puts more energy into them. We may be able to stop them for a few moments. But, when we relax, they may sneak back in. If we try to be tolerant and make ourselves let them be there, we're ignoring our irritation. The song or phrase continues.

So make a game of it. In the Song game, we let the song be the object of meditation. We truly welcome it. We relax and open to it. In doing so, we try to perceive the actual "sounds" in our minds as clearly as we can.

When I first started playing this game, I was surprised that when I let my full attention rest on a song, the melody slowed or stopped completely. There would be just one note left—perhaps the first note or syllable of a phrase. I began to see that the very act of perceiving shaped and formed a single sound into a phrase or an entire piece. And I could see that when I fought the song, I was actually creating my own adversary in the struggle against it.

If I just relaxed with no agenda other than seeing what arose, there was nothing but a single sound. Sometimes that sound was just the sound of my breathing. Other times it was more purely mental.

As I just watched, there was usually a little holding or tightness somewhere around that sound. If I relaxed, the sound tended to fade. But in the process, I could still see a lingering preference to have or not have the sound. If I relaxed that preference, I was left with a deeper stillness. If I let my mind ramble a little, then the sound would start up again. If I relaxed the rambling, there was only silence.

Playing this game takes advantage of the flow of events in Dependent Origination. I can see contact leading to feeling tone, leading to preferences, leading to clinging, leading to habitual tendency (the song or melody). The game of song turns a hindrance (aversion to melodies or jingles) into a tool for cultivating wisdom (seeing the flow of Dependent Origination).

Elusive Present

In this game, I try to bring my awareness as close to the present moment as I can. The present is elusive. When light, sound, or other sensory information strikes the eye, ear, or other sense organ, nerve impulses are sent to the brain. Inside the brain, they are relayed to the cerebral cortex to be deciphered. It is only after they have been analyzed that I become conscious of the sensory experience. It takes a sizable fraction of a second for all this to happen. So by the time I become aware of a sight or a sound, the event itself is at least a fraction of a second into the past.

If I notice a sound and tell myself a story like, "Oh, that car sounds like its muffler is shot," by the time I'm done telling myself about it, several seconds have gone by.

If I simply say to myself, "Oh, that's a car sound," I'm closer to the present, but still lagging a second or so into the past.

If I let go of the sound before I even label it, I'm only a fraction of a second into the past. But it's still in the past.

If my mind is tense or busy, it takes a little longer.

The game of Elusive Present is to see how close I can bring awareness to the present, knowing that I'll never get there completely. To play it well, I have to relax and let go of thoughts, stories, labels, and even perception itself.

Word Generator

This game is to watch words as they arise in the mind space. The trick is to see them not just for their content but to see them as mind objects. The intent of this game is not to see a stream of words but to see individual words as events. Perceived clearly, they seem to arise out of nowhere, like globs of water flowing out a hole in the sky.

In the flow of Dependent Origination, words don't arise until clinging (upādāna) and habitual tendencies (bhava) arise. So if I can see the words arising, I look to see any tension (taṇhā) around them. Invariably there is some, though it may be subtle. If I relax that tension, the flow of words slows or stops.

If I notice the feeling tone (vedanā) and relax it, the mind usually becomes silent of words.

A variant of this game is to watch for mental labels—moments of perception—and see them arise. These labels may arise without words but flow into words very quickly unless I'm deeply relaxed. It can be interesting to see the difference between the actual experience of hearing and the label put on it, or between the sight of purple and the label "purple."

Pseudo-Hallucination

When I go to bed in the evening on a retreat, I often play pseudo-hallucination for a while. This game works best when the room is dark, but not completely black such as is common at night with the lights out but with a little illumination coming from outside.

To play this game, I try to fall asleep with my eyes open and engaged. I let my body relax as if I'm dropping into slumber, but keep my eyes aware. I relax all the tension in my eyes yet remain mindful of the visual field. The temptation is to either close my eyes and fall completely asleep, or be more intentionally alert to the visual field and thus bring in tension.

If I can both deeply relax and stay visually conscious, after five or ten minutes (or less) the visual field starts to form into patterns. If I remain relaxed and conscious, bright psychedelic glows start to appear around some visual impressions. And if I remain relaxed and conscious even longer, I may see brief, tachistoscopic images that seem to be from other worlds or other times. They are quite vivid and often a little startling. The slight startle makes them disappear.

I call these "pseudo hallucinations" because a true hallucination is an image we confuse with conventional reality. What we "see" we believe to be concretely present. But I know that these images are a product of either the visual system or the mind itself. I never believe what I see is literally present.

Still, it's difficult to know what actually causes these. And I don't know if other people experience them. But late at night on retreats, my mind is too relaxed to worry about such things. I simply enjoy the entertainment.

And the skill of relaxing completely while remaining mindful is highly useful in meditation or life even when it's not a game.

Blackout

Several years ago while sitting in the seventh jhāna and trying to figure out how to get into the eighth, I tried to relax completely and stay aware. Suddenly the visual field blacked out. I had not been paying much attention to the visual field at the time. I was just relaxing. But I was vaguely aware that with my eyes closed in the daylight, a glow of light still came through my eyelids. Suddenly it was gone. The blackness was total.

The effect was startling. With that startle, the visual field came back instantly.

This phenomenon occurred several more times in the next several sittings. Gradually I became used to it enough that when the visual field blacked out, I didn't startle. The blackness remained black. Then I gradually brought in an ounce of tension and the visual field returned.

Over the next few days, it became a game to see if I could relax enough so that I visually blacked out. In subsequent retreats, when my mind was deeply at rest, I found I could play blackout.

I've wondered if blackout is a phenomenon associated with the eighth jhāna except that there is just one sense door that shuts down while others remain partially intact. But to play the game, I have to be so deep in meditation that I'm not curious enough to figure it out.

So it remains a game that I don't fully understand. And that's okay.

Do Nothing, Allow Everything

Going into the eighth jhāna, it is important to get yourself out of the way. The phrase "do nothing, allow everything" can be a reminder to just relax and be with things as they are.

Other Games

If you have games that are useful for you in meditation and you are willing to share them, I'd love to hear about them. You can send them to games@dougkraft.com. Thanks.

Appendix D
Translation Notes

In the early 1960s, the engineering firm where my father worked got a large set of engineering specifications from Germany. A computer translated them into English. The English version made references to water goats. What was a water goat? Finally, a bilingual engineer read the originals. He told them, "'Water goat' was supposed to be 'hydraulic ram.'"

When the Ford Motor Company marketed their Pinto in Brazil, sales were terrible. Then someone told them that "pinto" was Brazilian slang for "small penis." Ford renamed the car "Corcel"—Portuguese for "horse." Sales took off.

When Pepsi started advertising in China, they used their slogan, "Come alive with the Pepsi generation." Unfortunately, their translation came out meaning "Pepsi brings your ancestors back from the dead."

Frank Purdue's chicken created the slogan "It takes a tough man to make a tender chicken." When translated into Spanish it became "It takes an aroused man to make a chicken affectionate."

When Parker Pen marketed ballpoint pens in Mexico City, their advertising campaign adopted the phrase, "It won't leak in your pocket and embarrass you." It was rendered in Spanish as, "It won't leak in your pocket and make you pregnant."

Translating from one language to another is fraught with difficulty.

The earliest recordings of Siddhārtha Gautama's talks were written in the Pāli language. This book is written in English. There are words in Pāli that have no good English equivalent. A Pāli speaker and an English speaker can experience the same things, but they may speak and think about them differently. There may be no word-for-word translations from one language to the other.

Mistranslations of "hydraulic ram," "pinto," and "generation" are relatively easy to sort out compared to the nuances of consciousness and the subtleties of awareness.

One of the first Pāli words I learned was "samādhi." I was told it meant "concentration." When the mind is restless and jumping around like a squirrel on caffeine, samādhi is a remedy.

This made sense to me. To concentrate means to use a lot of energy and effort, like a conductor leading an orchestra or a chess master calculating his next move. When my mind was out of control, concentration might wrestle it to the ground and get it to sit still and shut up. Yet results were discouraging. My mind either became more restless or locked up like an iron box.

Years later I discovered that samādhi is a calming factor, not an energizing factor. It is described as the quality of a mother's attention as she gazes upon her sleeping child. I had completely misunderstood the Buddha's intention because of the difficulties of translating "samādhi" into English.

In Chapter 1, I talked about samādhi in more depth and unpacked what it really means.

Another word that bedeviled me was "saṅkhāra" which is often translated as "formations." It is the second "link" in Dependent Origination. As such, it refers to phenomena that fall below the radar of ordinary perception. It's so subtle that only a very calm and clear mind-heart has a chance of noticing it. But it is key to awakening.

Saṅkhāra is also the fourth of the five aggregates. As such, it refers to phenomena that are so obvious they can be seen with ordinary awareness.

In chapters 3 and 4, we saw that the phenomena saṅkhāra refer to have no English equivalent. Yet what it refers to is important on the meditative path.

In the English-speaking world, perhaps the word used most in connection with meditation is "mindfulness." I typed it into Google and got over sixteen million references.

"Mindfulness" came into widespread use as a translation of the Pāli term "sati." But "sati" doesn't distinguish between mind and heart the way English does. To translate sati as "mindful" loses half of its meaning. It could be translated as "mindfulness-heartfulness" or "holding something fully in your mind and in your heart."

Translations are even more complicated because of how the Buddha himself used language. He spoke to goat herders and milkmaids as well as scholars and monks. He assumed that his listeners might understand words differently depending on their backgrounds and levels of education. So he didn't speak using strict, scholarly language. A strict scholarly understanding of Pāli doesn't always help us understand his intent.

He spoke in a loose, colloquial style, seeking to evoke meaning rather than proscribing erudite descriptions. Like a poet, he took words that commonly meant one thing and stretched them to mean something else.

All these implications and subtleties are impossible to capture in a readable translation.

One way I could have avoided these difficulties was to avoid Pāli terms altogether. Since all of us, regardless of the languages we know, can experience what the Buddha taught, we can describe the practices and experiences without using Pāli. Direct experience is not the problem—it's the solution. This approach influenced this book.

However, avoiding Pāli had drawbacks. People who had been exposed to Buddhist terminology might have already internalized misconceptions, such as my misunderstandings of "samādhi" and "sati." The quickest way to clarify these issues was to explore the Pāli terms themselves.

It was tempting to not translate crucial terms but to leave them in their original Pāli. This, however, would have made the writing unduly esoteric for those who didn't know Pāli. It would have made the reading cumbersome.

I tried to manage these challenges by including both the English and the Pāli terms together. I gave the closest English meaning in a particular context. Including the Pāli term was meant to alert you that the English was only a rough approximation.

I also included a glossary at the end.

Despite all the problems of translation, I found it fun and illuminating to dig into some of the etymology and nuances of Pāli terms. I hope you found it useful as well.

When quoting suttas directly, I used Bhante Vimalaramsi's rendering. Scholars have done good technical translations of the suttas but may not have understood the words in the context of deep meditative experience. Or they may have been influenced by the commentaries of later writers whose understanding drifted from the Buddha's original intention. Bhante Vimalaramsi consulted many scholars in his interpretation of the text but ultimately used language that was closer to the actual experience than to scholarly understandings. This, I think, was what the Buddha intended.

Notes

1 For example, see the "Anupada Sutta," *Majjhima Nikaya* 111

2 For short instructions, see page 28. For fuller instructions, see the chapters in the "Path" section beginning on page 135.

3 In chapter 17, "Gaps: Sixth Jhāna" (starting on page 209), we'll come back to this experience when we explore "the base of infinite consciousness."

4 Dhamma Sukha Meditation Center has evolved since its humble beginnings. To learn more, see Appendix A, page 293 or visit www.dhammasukha.org.

5 Also known as "The Foundations of Mindfulness," *Majjhima Nikaya* 10.

6 One of the reasons I at first missed some of the Buddha's basic instructions was because much Theravadan practice today is rooted in the *Visuddhimagga* rather than the suttas. The suttas are the earliest extant records of the Buddha's actual talks. The *Visuddhimagga* was written in the fifth century CE by Buddhaghosa to reconcile some of the schools of Buddhism that had arisen in the ten centuries since the Buddha's time.

Buddhaghosa was a master of the Vedas—the ancient sacred text of Brahmanism (Hinduism)—before becoming a Buddhist monk. He was a scholar more than a meditator. So he drew heavily on his knowledge of the Vedas and Brahman meditation in his writing.

The Buddha was also deeply versed in the Vedas and Brahman meditation. When he mastered those practices, he discovered they didn't work as advertised.

So when he sat down under the Bodhi tree determined to find full enlightenment, he practiced in ways that were significantly different from the Brahman practices. His teaching is more accurately preserved in the suttas than in Buddhaghosa's commentary.

There is much value in the *Visuddhimagga*. But where it is not supported by the suttas, the sutta instructions are more effective.

7 Bhante Vimalramsi, *Breath of Love* (Ehipassiko Foundation of Indonesia, 2011).

8 "Inconceivable Matters," *Anguttra Nikaya* 4.77

9 For example, "Bahudhātuka Sutta: The Many Kinds of Elements," *Majjhima Nikaya* 115, verse 11.

10 See "The Mahāsaccaka Sutta," *Majjhima Nikaya* 36.

11 It is very important to make the distinction between clinical depression and true disenchantment and to not confuse one with the other. Clinical depression can be quite serious and in need of professional help. When in doubt, it is best to consider the possibility of clinical depression and seek help for it.

12 *Saṃyutta Nikāya, The Book of Causation (Nidānavagga)* Section 23 gives this description in the direction of cessation—it starts with "knowledge of destruction of the taints" and traces the proximate causes all the way back to ignorance. Other sections of *The Book of Causation* give other descriptions of Dependent Origination both "downstream" and "upstream."

13 Taṇhā is often contrasted to chanda where "taṇhā" is translated as "unwholesome desire" and "chanda" as "wholesome desire." Examples of chanda include the desire to be happy, generous, or kind or the desire not to be deceitful or violent. Early in spiritual development, wholesome desires are encouraged and unwholesome ones are discouraged.

But as we mature, the distinction is less helpful. Both kinds of desire have tension in them which blocks progress beyond a certain point. The desire to be enlightened is still a desire that may be helpful early on but later must be dissolved. Whether an urge is considered healthy or destructive, it is ultimately treated the same we: we six-R it. We see it, release it, relax, smile, and return to the object of meditation.

In this book I use "taṇhā" in its original meaning—a physical, emotional, or mental tightening. "Desire" refers to a whole complex of feelings, sensations, concepts, and motivations. "Taṇhā" refers to a simple, preverbal, pre-conceptual tightness. This is the root of the root of suffering and dissatisfaction.

14 T. W. Rhys David, *The Questions of King Milinda, Vol. 1 of 2* (Charleston: Forgotten Books, 2007).

15 D. W. Winnicott, *Maturational Processes and the Facilitating Environment.* (New York: International Universities Press, 1965)

16 Thousands of philosophers and psychologists make the same point with different labels.

17 Alexander Lowen, who developed bioenergetic psychotherapy, states it most bluntly: "Self is the body." See Alexander Lowen, *The Betrayal of the Body* (New York: Collier, 1967).

18 Bhikkhu Nanamoli and Bhikkhu Bodhi, *The Middle Length Discourses of the Buddha* (Wisdom Publications, 2005), pp. 1129–1136.

19 A fuller discussion of the seventh jhānas begins on page 219.

20 Ken Wilber has written extensively about these three realms. For example, *Integral Spirituality* (Boston & London: Integral Books, 2007).

21 "Ariyapariyesanā Sutta," *Majjhima Nikaya* 26, verse 25.

22 *Saṃyutta Nikaya* 56.11.

23 "Sona Sutta," *Anguttra Nikaya* 6.55, trans. Thanissaro Bhikkhu, http://www.accesstoinsight.com.

24 Charles Tart, *Waking Up: Overcoming the Obstacles to Human Potential* (Boston: New Science Library, Shambhala, 1987).

25 I'll say a little more about past lives and other-realm experience when talking about the fourth jhāna starting on page 191.

26 These phrases and this practice are slightly adapted from the words and practice I learned from Bhante Vimalaramsi. I'm grateful for his charity in focusing on the essence of forgiveness.

27 There are a number of differences between the techniques I learned in Thailand and the ones I learned from Bhante. One of these is the use of mental labeling. Sometimes I find this helpful when the mind is very scattered. But as it settles further into the jhānas, the effort to label feels coarse and clumsy—just as the mettā phrases can begin to feel clunky. In this case they may impede the mind from settling deeper. Labeling is best dropped at this point.

Another difference is that the practice taught by the Buddha places more emphasis on ease and relaxation at every step along the way. In Chapter 21 (page 269) we'll look in more detail at the efficacy of various techniques. In general I've found the Buddha's meditation as I learned from Bhante much more effective.

28 A sample of these descriptions from "Kandaraka Sutta." *Majjhima Nikaya* 51, is quoted starting on page 202.

29 William Johnson (ed), *The Cloud of Unknowing and The Book of Privy Counseling* (New York: Image Books, 1973).

Glossary

Below are two glossaries. The first includes Pāli terms and sutta names used in this book. Their meaning is given in English. The second glossary includes English terms that have been used to translate Pāli inaccurately. Better translations are given for those English words.

Pāli to English

Pāli is the language of the Buddha's discourses (suttas). Some Pāli words don't translate easily into English.

ājīvaka

A class of naked ascetics. In the suttas they are rarely referred to favorably. An ājīvaka named Upaka was the first person the Buddha spoke to after his full awakening. Upaka recognized something special about the Buddha. But when the Buddha tried to teach him, Upaka didn't get it.

ājīva

Lifestyle, livelihood. Ājīva is the fifth aspect of the Eightfold Path. (Also see "*ariyo aṭṭhaṅgiko maggo,*" the Noble Eightfold Path.)

Ānāpānasati Sutta

The discourse "Mindfulness of Breathing," *Majjhima Nikaya* 118. The Buddha gives an exposition of sixteen steps in mindfulness (sati) of breathing (ānāpāna) and its relationship to the four foundations of mindfulness and the seven awakening factors.

*anattā (*Sanskrit: *anātman)*

Selflessness or not taking anything personally.

anicca

Impermanent. It is one of the "three characteristics" of all things in the conditional world: nothing lasts; nothing stays as it is forever.

Anupada Sutta

The discourse "One by One As They Occurred," *Majjhima Nikaya* 111. The Buddha describes Sāriputta's development in meditation, including a succinct description of the jhānas and how they unfold.

ariyo aṭṭhaṅgiko maggo (Sanskrit: *āryāstāṅgamārga)*

The Noble Eightfold Path. This is one of the major teachings of the Buddha, where he laid out the essence of the path to the cessation of suffering and achieving full awakening.

The Noble Eightfold Path *(Ariyo Aṭṭhaṅgiko Maggo)*		
Pāli	*English*	*Other Translations*
Sammā Diṭṭhi	Harmonious Perspective	Right View
Sammā Sankappa	Harmonious Intention	Right Thought, Aspiration
Sammā Vācā	Harmonious Communication	Right Speech
Sammā Kammanta	Harmonious Conduct	Right Action, Movement
Sammā Ājīva	Harmonious Lifestyle	Right Livelihood
Sammā Vāyāma	Harmonious Practice	Right Effort
Sammā Sati	Harmonious Mindfulness	Right Awareness, Observation
Sammā Samādhi	Harmonious Collectedness	Right Concentration

Ariyapariyesanā Sutta

The discourse "The Noble Search," *Majjhima Nikaya* 26. In describing the difference between the noble and the ignoble truth, the Buddha gives one of the fuller descriptions of his own path to awakening.

arūpa

Without body; "a-" means "without" and "rūpa" means "body." The first three jhānas are considered "rūpa" because of the prominence of sensory sensations. The fourth and higher are considered arūpa because of the attenuation of sensory perceptions.

avijjā (Sanskrit: *avidyā*)

Unawareness, ignorance, delusion about the nature of the mind. Avijjā is commonly translated as "ignorance," though it has less pejorative connotations than in English. As in English, the root is "ignore" and it indicates a tendency to overlook the true nature of things. Avijjā is the beginning of the downstream flow of Dependent Origination. Without it there would be no suffering.

bhava

Habitual tendency or emotional habitual tendency. It is the tenth movement in the flow of Dependent Origination. It is often translated as "becoming" or "existence." But these meanings are confusing. In meditation bhava is experienced as the arising of familiar or habitual patterns of thought and emotion.

bhikkhu

Monk

bodhi tree

A large fig tree in present-day Bodh Gaya, India, under which the Buddha fully awakened. "Bodhi" is usually translated as "enlightenment."

Buddhaghosa

A fifth-century CE Indian Theravadan Buddhist scholar and commentator. He is best known for writing the *Visuddhimagga* or *Path of Purification.* This summary and analysis constitutes the orthodox understanding of Theravada texts since at least the twelfth century CE. There are significant differences between some of Buddhaghosa's understandings of meditation and that found in the earlier recordings of the Buddha's talks. Where differences exist, the earlier texts are a better guide to effective practice. (See "Visuddhimagga.")

brahmavihāra

The four "sublime states" or "divine abodes." They are mettā (kindness or goodwill), karuṇā (compassion), muditā (joy or appreciative joy), and upekkhā (equanimity) .

cattari ariya saccani

The Four Noble Truths. These are the core of the Buddha's teaching. "Noble" refers not to the truths but to the mind that can perceive them. The Four Truths are dukkha (dissatisfaction or suffering), taṇhā (tightness or craving), nirodha (cessation or the release of taṇhā), and the Eightfold Path (ariyo aṭṭhaṅgiko maggo).

chanda

Wholesome desire. Not all desires are all bad. Wanting to be more loving, compassionate, or generous or not wanting to be selfish or stingy are examples of wholesome desires. They can move us in a healthy direction. They can establish a useful intention. However, as the mind becomes more serene and receptive, all tightness must be relaxed and released. Even wholesome desires can block the mind-heart's natural clarity from emerging.

dhamma (Sanskrit: *dharma)*

The law, the way things are, the natural order. The term can also mean a phenomenon in and of itself, a mental quality or a teaching. When capitalized, Dhamma refers to the teachings of the Buddha. To take refuge in the dhamma means to take refuge in how things really are. To take refuge in the Dhamma is to rely on the Buddha's teachings.

dhammachanda

Love of or desire for the dhamma, to live in harmony with all that is.

dhamma vicaya

Investigation or investigation of the dhamma. It is one of the seven factors of awakening *dharma (see dhamma)*

diṭṭhi (Sanskrit: *dṛṣṭi)*

View, perspective, or position. In Buddhism, a view or position is not a simple abstract proposition but a charged interpretation that can shape experience and thought. Right view or harmonious perspective (sammā-diṭṭhi) is the first of the Eightfold Path. It refers not so much to holding a correct view as to having a way of seeing which is clear and holds to no position. (Also see *"ariyo aṭṭhaṅgiko maggo,"* the Noble Eightfold Path.)

dukkha

Dissatisfaction, suffering, stress, discontent. Dukkha is the first Noble Truth, indicating that life has dissatisfaction. The Buddha never said that life *is* suffering, only that nothing in this life can be a reliable base for happiness.

imponderables

Questions which we can never answer. The Buddha tells of four topics that can drive us crazy to try to solve: the powers of an enlightened being, what meditation can ultimately achieve, what karma caused a specific event to occur, and where the universe came from.

jarāmaraṇa

The final "down river" event in the flow of Dependent Origination. "Jarā" literally means "old age." "Marana" literally means "death." "Jarāmaraṇa" refers to the "whole mass of suffering": "sorrow, lamentation, pain, grief, and despair."

jhāna

A stage of meditative knowledge gained by direct experience. In the earliest recordings of the Buddha's talks, jhānas definitely are not absorption states.

kammanta

Action, movement, or conduct. In the Eightfold Path, "sammā kammanta" refers to behaving in ways that are harmonious with life and that encourage awakening. (Also see *"ariyo aṭṭhaṅgiko maggo,"* the Noble Eightfold Path.)

Kandaraka Sutta

The talk the Buddha gave to the mendicant Kandaraka, *Majjhima Nikaya* 51. He describes some of the practices used by accomplished meditators and makes the distinction between people who live in ways that harm or disturb themselves or others, and those who live according to the Dhamma.

kamma (Sanskrit: *karma)*

The effects of our physical, verbal, or mental actions. Everything we do creates the potential for other things to happen. If we are wise, we will act in ways that tend not to create difficulty or unhappiness in the future.

karuṇā

Compassion. It is the second of the four brahmavihāra or sublime states.

kasiṇa (Sanskrit: *kṛtsna)*

One of ten meditation objects. Each of the ten is an element (earth, water, air, fire) or a color. The meditator focuses his attention on the object. The suttas mention kasiṇa meditation; it is likely that these were borrowed from the Brahmin traditions and inserted into the text at a later time.

kāya

Body. "Kāya" refers to the material body alone—what is present in a corpse. "Rūpa" refers to a living body.

khandha (Sanskrit: *skandha*)

Aggregate, heaps. The five khandha (body, feeling tone, perception, concepts and storylines, and consciousness or awareness) refer to the various phenomena people often identify as self. In this context they are often called "aggregates affected by clinging." Bhante Vimalaramsi calls them "aggregates affected by *craving and clinging.*"

kuti

A small hut used for meditation.

magga

Path. "Ariyo aṭṭhaṅgiko maggo" is the Eightfold Path taught by the Buddha.

Majjhima Nikāya

The Middle Length Discourses. The Pāli Canon is a collection of over 10,000 suttas or discourses attributed to the Buddha or his chief disciples. It is divided into three *pitakas* ("baskets"). The second basket, the Sutta Pitaka, is divided into five *nikayas* (collections). The *Majjhima Nikaya* is the second of the five. It contains 152 suttas. They provide a comprehensive body of teaching concerning all aspects of the Buddha's teachings.

mettā

Loving kindness, goodwill, gentle friendship. Mettā is the first of the four sublime states (brahmavihāra) the Buddha recommended for cultivation. These can be very effective objects of meditation.

mudita

Joy, especially but not exclusively the joy that arises from seeing someone's good fortune. Mudita is the third of the four sublime states (brahmavihāra) used as a very effective meditation object.

nāmarūpa

Mind-body. As a phase of Dependent Origination, it refers to a condition before mind or body has arisen as separate phenomena. Mind (nāma) and body (rūpa) are said to co-arise.

*nibbāna (*Sanskrit*: nirvāṇa)*

Extinguished. The word literally means "blow out" as in a candle that is extinguished. In the scientific thinking of the Buddha's time, when a fire goes out, the heat element in the flame does not go away. It simply ceases to cling to the burning object. It disperses. So to those who heard the Buddha use the term, it meant the complete cessation of craving and clinging. Through meditation training, we can relax so deeply that all perception and consciousness cease for a period of time. Coming out of this state, we can see Dependent Origination so clearly that we no longer identify with psychophysical processes. When this is deep and full enough, we wake up.

nibbidā

Disenchantment. Seeing the truth of how the things actually operate, the enchantment or attachment to the world fades. At first it can be quite disturbing. But as it deepens, it moves toward dispassion.

nimitta

A mental sign or vision that can arise during meditation, particularly during the fourth jhāna and beyond. Often it is seen as a white light or a white disk. Some traditions use it as an object of meditation to go into a state of absorption. However, it is wiser to simply know that it is there and Six-R it like anything else. This allows the mind-heart to go even deeper.

nirvāna (see *nibbāna)*

nīvaraṇa

Hindrance. It literally means a covering: it covers something valuable. The Six Rs are the best way to work with hindrances and turn them to our advantage.

nirodha

Cessation, absence, or extinction. Nirodha is the third of the Four Noble Truths, which points to the cessation of all suffering.

Pāli

The language used in writing the suttas and many early texts.

pas'sambaya

Relax, tranquilize as in bring tranquility to.

passaddhi

Calmness, tranquility, serenity. It is the seventh awakening factor and part of the "higher path" in Dependent Origination.

paticcasamuppāda (Sanskrit: *pratītyasamutpāda*)

Dependent Origination. This is the central teaching of the Buddha about how everything arises because of causes and conditions. Seeing this clearly is central to his path to awakening.

phassa (Sanskrit: *sparśa*)

Contact, raw sense impression. It is defined as the coming together of three factors: sensory data (e.g., light), sensory organ (e.g., eye), and consciousness (e.g., eye consciousness). It is the first movement in Dependent Origination that is noticeable by the average person who has no advanced meditation training.

pīti (Sanskrit: *prīti*)

Joy. It is sometimes translated as "rapture," but "pīti" need not be overwhelming. It can range from a huge, overwhelming joy to a peaceful, all-pervasive joy. It is one of the signs of the first jhāna.

rūpa

Body, physical phenomenon, sense information. It has different meanings in different contexts. As the first khandha, it is physical phenomena or sensations picked by sensory organs. In "nāmarūpa" it means physical as opposed to mental phenomena ("nāma").

saddhā (Sanskrit: *śraddhā*)

Confidence, faith. In some contexts it means faith in the Buddha's path. It is part of the "higher path" of Dependent Origination. With stream entry, it becomes unshakable.

samādhi

Collectedness, calm abiding. Often it is translated as concentration or one-pointedness. But it has neither the strain implied by "concentration" nor the blocking out of other phenomena as implied by "one-pointedness." It is a unified and quiet quality of consciousness. Samādhi is one of the awakening factors as well as part of the Eightfold Path. (Also see "*ariyo aṭṭhaṅgiko maggo*," the Noble Eightfold Path.)

sammā

Harmonious, skillful. In the context of the Eightfold Path, it is often translated as "right." But the Pāli term does not carry the sense of right and wrong or good and bad implied in English. The name of the eight aspects of the Eightfold Path starts with "sammā." (Also see "*ariyo aṭṭhaṅgiko maggo*," the Noble Eightfold Path.)

saṃsāra

The world and the suffering found in it. The word literally means "continuous flow" and refers to the continuous flow from birth to life to death to rebirth.

samudaya

Origin, source. It is the second Noble Truth that refers to the origin of dissatisfaction (dukkha).

Saṃyutta Nikaya

The Connected Discourses. The Pāli Canon is a collection of over 10,000 suttas (discourses) attributed to the Buddha or his chief disciples. It is divided into three pitakas ("baskets"). The second basket, the Sutta Pitaka, is divided into five nikayas (collections). The *Saṃyutta Nikaya* is the third of the five. The suttas are grouped into five vaggas (sections), each of which is further divided into *saṃyuttas* (chapters) on related topics.

sankappa

Intention. It has also been translated as "thought" or "aspiration," but "intention" is closer to the original meaning. It is the second aspect of the Eightfold Path as it grows naturally out of wise or harmonious view of life. (Also see "*ariyo aṭṭhaṅgiko maggo*," the Noble Eightfold Path.)

saṅkhāra

That which has been put together or formed; formation; volitional formation. In the passive sense, "saṅkhāra" refers generally to conditioned phenomena or specifically to mental dispositions that have been formed. This is how the term is used as the second movement in Dependent Origination. In this context it is sometimes translated as "potential." In the active sense, it refers to the faculty of the mind-heart that puts formations together (volitional formation). This is how it is used as the fourth khandha.

saññа (Sanskrit: *Saṃjñā*)

Perception, label. It is a subtle but active process whereby we compare an experience to our past experiences and figure out what it is (i.e., what to label it).

Sāriputta (Sanskrit: *Śāriputra*)

One of the Buddha's main disciples who was "renowned in wisdom," meaning he had an exceptionally clear understanding of the Dhamma.

Sarnath

A small town not far from Varanasi. It was here in the Deer Park that the Buddha first taught the Dhamma to five ascetics who had been companions of his before his enlightenment.

sati (Sanskrit: *smṛti*)

Mindfulness, heartfulness, the state of being fully present without habitual reactions. It is a very important quality in Buddhist practice. The Pāli language does not make a distinction between mind and heart, so sati includes both these qualities. It is the balancing factor of the seven awakening factors. It is also the seventh aspect of the Eightfold Path. (See "*ariyo aṭṭhaṅgiko maggo*," the Noble Eightfold Path.)

sukha

Happiness. An important factor in the first two jhānas.

sutta (Sanskrit: *sūtra*)

A talk given by the Buddha. The suttas are part of the canonical text. The term literally means "thread." The implication is that to understand the "whole cloth" of the Dhamma, it's important to know how the suttas are woven together.

taṇhā (Sanskrit: *tṛṣṇā*)

Craving, tightness, holding. Though "taṇhā" is most often translated as craving, it can be very subtle. It is a preverbal tightening as we try to avoid something uncomfortable, hang on to something pleasurable, or space out with something neutral. The Buddha identified it as the "weak link" in Dependent Origination—the easiest place to stop the "down stream" of events by relaxing the tightness. Besides being the eighth phase of Dependent Origination, it is subtly present in all phases as well as being the second of the Four Noble Truths.

tilakkhaṇa (Sanskrit: *trilakṣaṇa*)

The three characteristics of all things in the conditioned world: unsatisfying (dukkha), impermanent (anicca), and selfless or impersonal (anattā).

upādāna

Clinging. It is always experienced as thinking or the beginning of thinking. It is the seventh phase of Dependent Origination. It arises when taṇhā is not relaxed and released.

vāyāma

Practice. It is the sixth aspect of the Eightfold Path and is commonly translated as "effort" or "right effort." But the term should not be confused with pushing or straining. Skillful effort is to remember to relax and release, not to strive. (Also see "*ariyo aṭṭhaṅgiko maggo*," the Noble Eightfold Path.)

Upaka (see *ājīvaka*)

upekkhā

Equanimity. It is the fourth of the sublime states (brahmavihāra) and one of the awakening factors. It is very important, particularly in the higher jhānas.

vācā

Communication, speech. In the Eightfold Path, it is usually translated as "speech" but refers to more than spoken words. It includes written, typed, and any other kind of communication. (Also see "*ariyo aṭṭhaṅgiko maggo*," the Noble Eightfold Path.)

vimutti

Release, liberation, freedom from the constraints of the conditioned mind.

viññāṇa (Sanskrit: *viññāṇa*)

Awareness, consciousness. It is the third phase of Dependent Origination and the last of the five aggregates (khandhas).

vipassanā

Insight into the true nature of reality. Vipassanā is not just perceiving what's around us but also being aware of the mind's response to the perception. The term is often used to refer to the Buddha's meditation practice based on mindfulness.

virāga

Dispassion. It is similar to being unconcerned. However, in virāga, the mind is attentive without being invested in outcomes. It is important for entering the eighth jhāna and for the "higher path" of Dependent Origination.

Visuddhimagga

The Path of Purification. A text composed by Buddhaghosa in about 430 CE. It is probably the most influential text in the Theravadan tradition. Buddhaghosa was attempting to find common ground between the various Buddhist schools at that time. He was not as motivated to discern which aspects coincided best with the Buddha's earliest teachings but gave equal credit to each school's interpretation. Thus the texts differ from some of the Buddha's original teaching in important areas. (See "Buddhaghosa.")

viriya (Sanskrit: Vīrya)

Energy, enthusiasm. This is one of the seven awakening factors.

yana

A knowledge gained in meditation.

zafu

Meditation cushion.

English to English

As noted earlier, many of the later texts and commentaries differ in some significant areas from the earliest recordings of the Buddha's talks. The *Abhidhamma* and *Visuddhimagga* in particular have had a strong influence on some scholars. When these scholars translate the earliest suttas, some of the words they use reflect the later texts more than the earlier suttas themselves.

Below are a few English words often used in Pāli-to-English translations. Each is followed by one or more English words that better represent the Pāli or the original intent of the Buddha. If you find a passage in a sutta confusing, you might try some of these English-to-English translations and see if it makes more sense.

Applied and sustained thought

Thinking and examining thought

Concentration

Collectedness; calm abiding

Contemplate

Observe

Delusion

Personalizing; taking as self something that is not self; lack of objectivity

Eightfold Path

Harmonious path

Pleasure

Happiness

Rapture

Joy

Right

Harmonious. (Also see *"ariyo aṭṭhaṅgiko maggo,"* the Noble Eightfold Path.)

Volition

Formation

Wisdom

Seeing the causal relationships in Dependent Origination. In English, the word "wisdom" has a broad meaning. When the Buddha used the word, he was always referring to seeing the causal relationships. Seeing these is the core of the Dhamma.

Zeal

Enthusiasm

Index

Note: asterisk and bold type are "primary" entries.

About the Author

Doug Kraft began meditating in 1976. He's trained with many Theravadan Buddhists including Larry Rosenberg, Corrado Pensa, Jack Kornfield, Joseph Goldstein, Sharon Salzberg, Christopher Titum, Joanna Macy, and Andy Olendski. He also trained Korean Zen Master Sahn Seung, Tibetan Mingur Rinpoche, Siddha Yoga guru Muktananda, Ram Dass, Sufi Pir Vilat Khan, Emmanuel, and Jean Houston.

Shortly after moving to California in 2000, he became a student of John Travis. He traveled to Thailand to study with the Thai Forest master Ajahn Tong. In 2007 he began training with a jhāna master, Bhante Vimalaraṁsi. In his first few years with Bhante, his practice progressed more quickly than in the previous twenty-five years. This book is a product of those experiences and Bhante's encouragement to teach.

Kraft grew up in a family of five children. His father was an engineer. His mother was an artist and writer. Depression pushed him to explore the depths of human nature while an interest in expanded human potential drew him to explore the heights. Over the years his career moved back and forth between depth psychology and spirituality.

He earned a degree in psychology from the University of Wisconsin and a Masters of Divinity from Starr King School for the ministry in Berkeley, California. He trained intensively in Bioenergetics, a body-oriented psychotherapy.

He served Unitarian Universalist congregations on both the East and the West coasts. He also created and directed a counseling center for street kids. He now works as a private psychotherapist and meditation teacher.

Currently he lives in northern California with his wife of 43 years, one of his two sons, and two cats. For entertainment he bikes, hikes in the high Sierras, plays guitar, studies Dharma, and meditates. He still revels in delving into human nature and mirroring back what he discovers. Inside he doesn't see psychology versus religion versus spirituality: just the ever-changing textures of human experience.

Web site: www.dougkraft.com

Made in the USA
Charleston, SC
18 February 2015